Darkroom

Winner of the

Associated Writing Programs

Award for

Creative Nonfiction

Darkroom

Bowling Green, Ohio
November 11, 2006

A FAMILY EXPOSURE

Jill Christman

For Mike—
Why here?
Why now?
This good. It
feels good to meet a
kindred spirit,
asking the questions
I leave with
with great
admiration
Jill

THE UNIVERSITY OF GEORGIA PRESS

ATHENS AND LONDON

Published by the University of Georgia Press

Athens, Georgia 30602

© 2002 by Jill Christman

All rights reserved

Designed by Erin Kirk New

Set in Minion by Bookcomp, Inc.

Printed and bound by Maple-Vail

The paper in this book meets the guidelines for

permanence and durability of the Committee on

Production Guidelines for Book Longevity of the

Council on Library Resources.

Printed in the United States of America

06   05   04   03   02   C   5   4   3   2   1

Library of Congress Cataloging-in-Publication Data available

ISBN 0-8203-2444-2 (hardcover : alk. paper)

British Library Cataloging-in-Publication Data available

To insure the privacy of people who chose not to be identified by name, as well as some of those who had only a tangential connection to the events in this book, the following names are either abbreviated or fictional: Dr. A, Dr. B, and Dr. O; Mrs. C, Mrs. B, Mrs. F.; Amy, Jake, Jane, Carol, Stan Parker, Jess, Father Anthony, and Brother Dan. All other names, including those appearing in FBI reports or newspaper articles, are either unchanged or obvious pseudonyms. The names of my family members are also unchanged, because my only uncle is my only uncle no matter what I call him, right?

For Colin, Grammy, and Uncle Mark

who watch over me

Not only is the Photograph never, in essence,
a memory . . . but it actually blocks memory, quickly
becomes a counter-memory. . . . The Photograph is
violent: not because it shows violent things, but because
on each occasion *it fills the sight by force*, and because
in it nothing can be refused or transformed (that we
can sometimes call it mild does not contradict its violence:
many say that sugar is mild, but to me sugar is violent,
and I call it so).

Roland Barthes, *Camera Lucida*

Contents

If I thanked everyone who has supported me as a human being in the thirty years of life that it took to create this book, there would be no room for the text itself, so I'll restrict myself to those without whom the book you now hold in your hands would dissolve into nothingness. Gushing opening thanks to Barry Sanders (my "new best friend in California"), the Associated Writing Programs, and the University of Georgia Press (especially Barbara Ras and Sarah McKee). My deep gratitude to Kelly Caudle and Wright Neely, who cleaned up my messes, and to Marianne Merola and Meg Giles for taking care of business. Endless thanks to all the teachers who touched my life and work at the University of Alabama, especially Sandy Huss, John Keeble, Michael Martone, Francesca Kazan, Gay Burke, Elizabeth Meese, and Beverly Lowry, and to the University of Alabama's Graduate School for the gift of time. I am also indebted to design master Ander Monson and to Monza Naff, who inspired me to a life of writing and teaching.

A special thanks to Mike for the title—and for three years of tireless, loving support. My love and gratitude to the dear friends, careful readers, and colorful characters of this book, especially Diane, Jennifer, and Libbie, who served faithfully in all three roles. Affectionate thanks to Sean Lovelace for gritty medical advice and to another Sean—you know who you are—for being my light. To Anna, Daisy, and Melissa—what would I have done for six years in Tuscaloosa without you? And to Tim, of course, for making me feel sane and smilcy.

And most especially, to all of my family—for teaching me to make things, for telling and retelling stories they thought they'd finally left behind, for collaborating in the building of memory, and for loving me always and still. Mom, you're a real trooper. As Ian says, "The good news is my sister's getting a book published. The bad news is it's about us."

To Tango and Walt, for being there no matter what, for enduring long hours of competition with the glowing box, and for love, pure and simple.

And to Mark, for coming out of nowhere when I was least expecting him, and making this book—and my life—so much better than I thought either could ever be.

My father's self-portraits appear with the permission of the artist, Pete Christman—thanks, Dad. "Burned Images" first appeared in the Summer 2001 issue of *River City;* my thanks to the editors. The Indigo Girls' song lyrics appear courtesy of the Hal Leonard Corporation. "Closer to Fine"; words and music by Emily Saliers; © 1989 EMI Virgin Songs, Inc., and Godhap Music; all rights controlled and administered by EMI Virgin Songs, Inc.; all rights reserved; international copyright secured; used by permission. "Blood and Fire"; words and music by Amy Ray; © 1986 EMI Virgin Songs, Inc., and Godhap Music; all rights controlled and administered by EMI Virgin Songs, Inc.; all rights reserved; international copyright secured; used by permission.

⌒ *Burned Images*

On December 7, 1998, I mailed a letter to my father, asking him what happened on the day that my brother was burned.

I didn't think he would reply, but he did.

He wrote back—pages and pages of longhand on paper ripped from a yellow legal pad. And he began with me:

I could come up with all sorts of excuses and justifications for me not being a major part in your life, but the fact of the matter is I have not been a very good father to you primarily because of distance. . . . I feel badly that you were the child I know the least, but as I said it has mostly been the physical distance that has kept us apart, not anything between us directly.

Not anything between us directly; you were the child I know the least, my father tells me in a letter that I have asked for but never really expected to receive, in a letter whose living words I read, again and again, in a rented Tuscaloosa house, more than thirty years after my brother's skin left its indelible print on my father's palms.

I was not yet born.

⌒

My father and I barely know each other. The last time I slept under his roof, I was twenty years old, and for the first time in my life, feeling brave or reckless or grown-up or just too tired to care, I pointed my finger at him. I told him he'd never been much of a father, and he was quick with his reply: *I didn't have a father either. Your mother left me, you know.*

⌒

After that I didn't go back for almost ten years, and he began making gifts of himself. I have a stack of my father's self-portraits in a box somewhere. My father paints and repaints himself in different roles with different faces—a teacher, a man at the bottom of a pool,

Martin Luther, an apple-peel head à la Escher, a man dividing at the belly like an amoeba, a turning man with three eyes or no eyes or the face of a dog—over and over he frames himself. I imagine this stack of fathers tilting upright, escaping the cardboard box one by one, frame by frame, and tottering down the hall, jerking across the hardwood floors on gilded, equilateral feet, and asking me questions: *How was school? Where is your homework? Why can't you understand that I never had a father, either?*

⁓

The story of Ian's burning changes like a hurt and healing body—written, erased, written over with the thick tissue of scars: coordinating palimpsests of words and flesh. Each time memory ignites, details mutate and emotion shifts: she remembers a phone call, he remembers that the diaper was on, they both remember the scream. Elements are scraped away, scribbled in, retracted, and still some pink shows through.

Today my mother breaks in: "I didn't say that—I said that there *might* have been a phone call, and you wrote it down as truth. What does your father say? He was there. I wasn't even there."

"He says he can't remember anything before Ian screamed."

"Well, how do I know, then?"

"Maybe he told you, and then he forgot."

"It was a long time ago."

"About thirty years."

"That's long. I don't even like to think about it."

"I know somebody told me once that his body was blocking the drain, and that's how the water filled up around him. How would I make something like that up?"

"I don't remember that. I never told you that."

"Maybe Ian told me."

"*He* doesn't remember!"

"Well, I don't know how I would make something like that up. I mean, *the baby's body is blocking the drain.*"

~

My brother carries the truth of this story on his body. I don't know how I missed this. For years I wasn't thinking hard enough. Ian has a bald spot on the top of his head, his face is burned, his shoulders are scarred; the top of his back is the worst, and then the rest of his body is unburned. The doctors stripped skin patches from his thighs when they pieced him back together, but his legs were not burned, his buttocks were not burned. There is no way Ian's body was blocking a drain while water filled up around him. His body corroborates my father's written account: *I heard a scream from the bathroom, I ran and found Ian, wearing a diaper, standing in the tub with the shower on. I turned off the water, and didn't realize how hot the water was until I picked him up and his skin came off in my hands.*

~

I don't remember a time when my parents were together, but I am a good listener. A quiet child, in a corner with a book open in her lap, can seem to disappear. She learns from listening, hears many things before she is old enough to understand them. When her mother's friend is fired from her job, and cries, the child knows this firing was a really bad thing and pictures the restaurant where her mother waits tables going up in flames. When she hears about the jungle warfare in Vietnam, she imagines gorillas with guns strapped to their backs and wonders what they had to fight about and where they got the guns.

Sometimes it takes years for her to determine the truth behind the words. She grows into what she hears, forming images when she can, gradually, like a sheet of photographic paper soaking in developer. The pictures fill in piece by piece as she is ready to understand, taking time to color in the dark and the light spaces.

～

I shouldn't even be born yet.

～

If you've ever canned peaches, you probably know that the fuzzy skin can be easily removed from the fleshy fruit by dunking the intact peach in a boiling-water bath. After a minute or so in the boiling water, the peach skin will slide off in your fingers, leaving only a shimmering, slippery globe of fruit flesh. This home-canning technique also works with tomatoes and most other skin-covered, well-fleshed bodies.

On July 22, 1966, one day after my father's twenty-third birthday, his baby boy's skin came off in his fingers like the peel of a dipped peach. This moment is at the core of our family story—some of us talk about it, some of us don't, but it is always there, like a rock at the center of a hurtling snowball.

My mother was at work, serving food to the rich at a restaurant in downtown Providence, Rhode Island—a place where she was required to bone the fish tableside so that her customers could see they were being served and protected. I wonder whether she felt the freedom of some time away from home, enjoyed being out with other people—even at work. Or whether she worried about her baby at home, wished she could be there to give him his bedtime bath, turn the pages of a book, nurse him to sleep.

In this story, my mother is only twenty-one, a young wife, mother, and waitress. She couldn't walk through her art school graduation the previous spring because, at the time, she was nine months pregnant. Her new name is Martha Ingraham Christman. She is pretty in a way that might be called wholesome: dark curly hair, deep-brown eyes, a confident Ingraham nose, breasts that are full and round with milk for her baby. Martha is quick to smile, always ready to comfort, and practiced in the dual roles of caretaker and peacekeeper (in 1966, her father is an alcoholic, her teenage brother is a drug addict, and nobody has started talking about codependency). At only twenty-one years of age, she is a nurturing mother, an attentive waitress, and she is trying to be a wife. Any kind of wife.

She was young when she married my father. "Too young," she tells me again and again. "I didn't want to marry him. I just wanted to live with him for a summer, out on the Vineyard. But Grammy and Grandfather wouldn't let me. They said if I wanted to live with him, I had to marry him. You have to understand, things were different then. I thought I was doing the right thing. I thought I had to marry your father because I slept with him. I even thought I loved him because I had sex with him. I didn't know you could have the one without the other—that's how naïve I was. So I married him. And I'm glad. Because I have you." My mother tells me that my father didn't actually give her the engagement ring. His mother did, because she liked my mother and had decided that she would make a good wife for her son. It was really as simple as that, according to my mother. Or maybe not. My father's letter breaks into the narrative, erases, rewrites: *No woman could ever be good enough for me in my mother's eyes. She didn't approve of Marty until we were separated. Then she was perfect in comparison.* (The story of the ring cannot be corroborated by my father's mother. She has been dead for more than twenty years.)

"Your Grammy Sarah was a difficult mother for your father to have," my mother explains. "She was very controlling. I mean, an amazing woman, and I admit that I might have been more infatuated with Sarah than I was with your father. She threw the best parties on the Vineyard, you know. She'd be wild even now. But definitely a difficult woman to have for a mother."

So, my mother was young, still an undergraduate at the Rhode Island School of Design, when she began a life as wife and mother—a hasty June wedding, nine months of pregnancy spent sprinting from reeking painting studios to the bathroom to throw up, twenty-eight hours of labor, and thirteen short months of healthy baby boy later— and my mother is about to arrive at the instant she will look back on thirty years later as the single most defining moment of her life. It is around 8 P.M., and Martha is pouring Chardonnay, rotating her wrist to stop the flow of wine without a drip, and highlighting the evening's specials for a couple at table number four. Another waitress touches her arm and tells her that she'll take the order. There's a phone call. An emergency. The baby. That is how I see my mother on the night that my brother was burned: content, busy, engaged in normal restaurant bustle, until that tap on the arm. . . . But nothing has happened yet. Her husband is home with baby Ian in this story, and everything is fine.

My father is sitting in the kitchen of their first-floor apartment in Providence, talking on the telephone. I can picture him there, with his bare feet up on the round oak table. Above the table hangs an enormous oil painting, five-by-eight feet at least, of a mass of people in a crowded place, maybe a New York City subway station, and there is an unsmiling woman in a pale pink, formfitting dress. The signature in the lower left-hand corner of the painting is an illegible scrawl. Translated, the artist's name reads: Pete Christman.

(This has not always been my father's name. He was born Adrian Fryers Jr., because that's what his father wanted it to be, but his mother always called him "Pete," after her reckless brother, a Yale graduate who left a good job on the northeastern seaboard and struck out for parts unknown, ending up living a cowboy's life on a ranch in Montana until he died in his thirties of a ruptured appendix. Pete. To my knowledge, my father met his biological father only twice—*I was a product of World War II,* my father tells me in the same long letter. Patrilineally speaking, my name should be Jill Fryers. But then Grammy Sarah went ahead and married—and eventually divorced— a man named Bill Christman. When the man left, the name stayed.)

But this is a story about Pete Christman and his baby, Ian, in 1966. As Pete listens to the voice coming through the receiver, he is probably plucking a hair from the knuckle on his big toe, wetting the root of the hair with the tip of his tongue, and examining it over the top of his glasses. He repeats this ritual—pluck, lick, examination—with hair all over his body: beard hairs, head hairs, mustache hairs.

I don't know who he's on the phone with, but I pretend that it's his mother. She wants to know if his birthday package arrived, how he liked the canned herring, whether the tan corduroys fit, how the baby is doing. When his mother asks about the baby, Pete notices that Ian is no longer in the kitchen with him. Perhaps he's in the bedroom playing with the dog. The corduroys are a bit snug, but the herring is delicious, had it for lunch with bagels and cream cheese. The poor man's lox, my father tells her, laughing; he likes to play the part of the struggling art student even though he attended an exclusive prep school, even though he knows that when his mother dies, she will leave him more than enough to be comfortable.

Where is the baby who is supposed to be in this story?

After the phone call—a detail once provided by my mother, although, of course, the herring and the corduroys and even the line about lox are fictional props in the role of authentic detail—the story gets fuzzy, except for the sound of Ian's scream and the hiss of squirting water. This is where Pete's memory clicks in. The baby isn't in the kitchen. He swings his feet off the table, stands up, and runs down the hall to the bathroom. He hasn't yet turned the corner to the bathroom. For a second or two more he is a husband and father in good standing. The baby is screaming.

For twenty-nine years, until last month's letter from my father, this is the shared family memory, this is what Pete sees when he comes around the corner and into the bathroom: The baby's body is blocking the drain in the bathtub. Steaming water is spurting out of the faucet. Water is rising around the baby. The baby is boiling.

But now we know that it isn't the faucet, it's the shower. And the baby hasn't fallen. He is standing solid on his two small feet. He is standing and screaming. Tilt into my father's version, lean into the past tense of his memory:

I found Ian, wearing a diaper, standing in the tub with the shower on. I turned off the water, and didn't realize how hot the water was until I picked him up and his skin came off in my hands.

This jibes with the shared story. Pete's first instinct is to grab the baby out of the water, and he does this, and that's when Ian's skin slides off into his hands. *I have a mental snapshot of this which I carry with me to this day.* Pete doesn't know yet that the baby has burns on more than 80 percent of his body, but he can see that his son's face is melting away like the wax on a candle. His baby is glowing red—he is a hot coal, a boiled lobster, a peeled peach. This baby boy looks like many things, steaming and unconscious and sticking in his father's arms, but he does not look human.

I have a mental snapshot of this which I carry with me to this day. I knew [he] was seriously hurt, but had no idea of what my then new family was about to face. I grabbed a clean sheet and then a towel, wrapped Ian in it and ran upstairs to the second floor to find someone to drive us to the emergency room.

The thermostat was turned up too high on the water heater in their ground-floor apartment. Maybe my father will read the warning above the dial on the water heater when he returns home from the hospital that night: *Water at or above 125 degrees is scalding, and is extremely dangerous to the very young and the very old.* Then he will curse himself for not reading the warning earlier. And he will curse himself for never even thinking about the temperature of the water coming out of the faucet—didn't he always just add cold? But mostly he will curse himself for not being attentive, for not knowing how carefully a baby needs to be watched. He will curse himself for everything he did that night, any one moment of which, if altered, might have changed the course of events that had brought him to that moment when his son's skin came apart in his fingers. And when he is done cursing, he will begin again. He will curse himself until he has to leave to deaden the sound of his own cursing, and then, a letter written thirty-four years after the burning to a critical daughter who had not been born in time to live through that day, will read like a confession:

I guess the first things to be dealt with are facts to answer your ques-
tions with. Then I will try to remember as accurately as possible what
happened. It is interesting that I can't at this point remember what I
was doing on July 22, 1966, until I heard Ian's scream. You are supposed
to forget the actual event and not what led up to it. That summer I had
just graduated from RISD and was working painting a factory during
the days, and then we would have a change of the guard and I would
take care of Ian while Marty worked as a waitress. Ian was 13 mo. old,
just beginning to walk and into everything. After seeing five children go
through this period of development I know that they must be watched
every second, but at that point I had worked in a hot factory all day and
was I guess more interested in relaxing with a cold beer than watching
Ian the way I should have. . . . I can't remember what was happening
before Ian was hurt. I know I carry a lot of guilt about my part in Ian's
accident, and I have suppressed key details.

There are pieces that will always be missing from the story of my
brother's burning. Ian says he has no memory of that night, and so
he will hold the gaps of the story—how he got into the tub, why he
turned on the water, what that kind of pain feels like—deep in the
grooves of the scars on his body for the rest of his life.

After my brother's skin slides from his body and onto the hands of
his father, the story is less immediate. Time slows down and returns
obediently to the past tense and the frame of my mother's voice. She
says that my father got the upstairs neighbor, although nobody can
remember his name. (But perhaps someone can—*I think his name
was Jim,* my father says now.) Somehow all three of them—the neighbor now known as Jim, the father, and the burned baby—got to the
hospital, and that is when the other waitress touched my mother's
arm: "I'll take it. You have a phone call. An emergency. The baby."

My mother drove to the emergency room in her waitressing uniform and took over the story. She talks still about those months in the
hospital with Ian whenever she wants to make someone understand
that she knows how it feels to grieve and sweat and pray and wait.

The doctors wouldn't allow my parents to see my brother that first
night, so they went home to sleep. My mother says that she didn't

know how bad it was: "My fear was that he would have scarring. Not that he might not live. I had no idea. No idea. Before the doctors let me see him, they told me that I had to realize that Ian's condition was 'grave.' They'd cut in a trach tube, but he still was having trouble breathing. The swelling was terrible. The doctors told us he only had a one-in-ten chance—to live, not to die. One in ten." Here, the stories mesh, in that indelible, corroborated statistic: *At that point we were told that Ian had a 10 percent chance of survival. I think both Marty and I grew up at that moment.*

"When I saw him for the first time, I didn't even know what I was looking at. He was just this little, red, pumping, swollen-up thing on green sheets. He looked like a baby orangutan. He was bright red, but it was the swelling that made him look so strange. An orangutan, or a space creature. But he was my baby, and he was beautiful. Those green sheets *were* ugly. They were special ones that were supposed to reduce the risk of infection—that was the big fear—and not stick to him as much. Everything stuck to him." And, of course, I always want to know if she was mad at my father for being there when it happened. She always says no. "I was more overwhelmed than mad. I was so young, practically a kid myself. We were both young. We were *all* young. And something like that will certainly change your perspective on life."

I think both Marty and I grew up at that moment. Our beautiful child was wrapped in bandages with tubes coming out of the bundle. Everything was hospital clean and clinical.

Ian was in the burn unit for more than four months. My mother slept on a cot in his room. At some point, my father moved to Syracuse, New York, to begin graduate school:

Ian continued to improve. He still looked pretty bad. There were problems of weaning him off of the trach tube in his throat, but this was finally successfully accomplished. He was out of immediate danger. Ian was going to live but would still have to remain in the hospital another two months.

I had been accepted to graduate school scheduled to start in the fall. I was willing to stay in Providence, but we decided that I should move to Syracuse and start working on my M.F.A. I came back to Providence on several occasions with the plan that Marty and Ian would move to Syracuse when he got out of the hospital. As the time approached for the big move, Marty decided that she wasn't going to Syracuse, and we split up.

After my brother's burning, both my parents met other people: a man and a woman who didn't think about the accident every minute of every day, a man and a woman who were both able to take hot showers without smelling the boiled flesh of a baby. The story gets hazy here, but I know there were other loves, and then some talk of reconciliation.

"I went back to him when your brother was three," my mother says. "It was Christmas! Maybe I was in the holiday spirit, maybe it seemed like your brother should be with his father at Christmas. I wanted to have another baby so that Ian would have a little brother or sister. I wanted to have another baby that *matched*."

⁓ Swinging

I am in mid-swing. Look at that bright, toothy smile.
This is a counter-memory.
Countermove. Counterforce. Counterespionage.
Run away. Push back. Stop those spying, prying eyes.

I was born into a family of artists. My parents met as teenagers at the Rhode Island School of Design in the early sixties. Both my mother and father live through the manipulation of images and the creation of objects. I am the only one of my siblings so far who has opted out of art school.

⁓

"Maybe *they* are your art. That's it. Them. You create them."

"But they created me, right? This book is my version—only my version."

"*Version:* from Old French—an act of turning. In medicine, version is the turning of a fetus to bring it into a desirable position for delivery. Your version and then your labor."

"And first, the turning. Since when do psychotherapists concern themselves with etymology?"

"I believe you said that you wanted to talk about beginnings."

"Right. I do. They created me, and now I am creating them. Create. From the Latin *creare:* to bring forth, to cause to grow."

~

My father is a sculptor, a photographer, and a painter. As he would be happy to tell you (to the extent that he is happy about anything), my father creates images of my father. He is, as he would also tell you, his own best model. He will sit still for himself, forever if necessary, and for at least fifty years so far. For Christmas a few years ago I received a familiar, framed gift from my father: my father. The painting had begun as a head-on, squared-up, close-in photograph of his face, but then the face was split vertically, and the one remaining side reflected back upon itself. One side of the face is a mirror image of the other side. The face is distorted and leering, the forehead bulges like a sci-fi alien's—evidence that an actual human face is neither balanced nor symmetrical, and when made so, becomes grotesque. Interesting, then, that psychological studies of physical attractiveness suggest that the most important aspect of perceived beauty is symmetry. Look the most like the composite average of a hundred other faces, right there in the middle, and you're looking *good*.

Sameness begets comfort. Comfort begets sameness—and on and on. That's the lesson we learn as kids: sameness is good, average is good. Strive to be indistinguishable. If the other kids have green alligators marching obediently along white shoelaces and snaking through the shining grommets of immaculate Nikes—never mind that it isn't cool to tie those laces (*nobody* does), never mind that the point of shoelaces is to secure one's shoes to one's feet, never mind that it's all just plain stupid—if you're a kid in Massachusetts in the mid-seventies, you'd better be saving up your lunch money to buy those alligators. And if you qualify for free lunch and therefore you have no lunch money? Well. The beauty of homogeneity is something that my parents never seemed to grasp, so here again is my father, twenty years after I wore the wrong shoes.

He has gone over his split-and-spliced face with oils, and the monstrous result ripples the skin at the back of my neck. Fixating on this grotesque visage, I look at the painting on and off for days before I notice the tree in the background, also cleft down the middle, dividing itself into a frame for an earthenware jug. (Moonshine, my brother will suggest later.) What exactly is my father trying to do with his gift of a re-mapped and re-painted patri-puss foregrounding the splintered family tree? Reinsert himself into my life? Or scare me shitless?

❡

My mother's favorite medium is the collage, one object pasted over another pasted over another. She adores juxtaposition, the functions of light and shadows. If she has a gift, she says, it is her ability to see things.

These collages are also sometimes gifts to me. Above my desk, there is a picture of a barren, red-clay, mountainous landscape—I am reminded of the dry plateaus of Nevada (though I've never been there) or the craggy, pocked surface of the moon (though I've never been there either). A giant, female hand curls its smooth fingers into one of the hard-edged crevices. The hand is joined to a wrist, an elbow, an upper arm, and then, at the top, as if the arm were a vase, a bloom of brilliant yellow gladioli. I know that my mother must have enjoyed placing flesh with rock, bright with dull, living with dead. A cut-out, orange marigold blossom is a sun setting on the horizon, and a couple of black-eyed Susans peek out from behind the shadowed mountains—black-eyed Susans the size of ten-story buildings. The pale arm becomes a vase for the gladioli, and form is function.

❡

When I told my mother that I was writing about Ian's burning in this autobiography, she was surprised: "But, Jill, that's not really *your* life." She's right, of course. I wasn't born yet. But Ian's burning has not only affected me for most of my life—I helped him rub vitamin E oil into his raw flesh when the doctors cut out wedges of muscle tissue so that Ian could grow inside his too-tight skin, I growled at the mean kids, the ones who said, *Gross. Is he like that all over? Bumpy, like he is on his face?* and told them I didn't even notice the scars anymore, and I didn't—beyond that, it has been my understanding all along that both his burning and his survival laid down the foundation for my birth.

"But, Mom," I said, "you've told me a million times that when Ian was in the hospital, you knew that if he didn't make it, you would never have another baby."

The telephone line is silent for a moment. "That's true," she says.

"And I've also heard you say that if Ian hadn't been burned at all, you probably would have taken him and left Dad."

"Yes . . ."

"So, if Ian hadn't been burned, and *then*, if Ian hadn't survived, *I* wouldn't have been born at all."

"But I didn't know you then!"

"Well, if you want to amend your statement, you'd better tell me now. That's just the way I remember it, and I've thought about it that way all my life, whether you really said it or not."

"No, I said it, I'm sure I would have said it. But, I mean, I didn't know that *you* were going to be my next baby!"

"I'm sure you didn't, Mom." Clearly. "My feelings aren't hurt, okay?" Lies. But what story of conception is a pretty one? It's not as simple as they wanted you or they didn't want you. Not as simple as: I want a baby or I don't want a baby. "Mom, this is all I'm saying. I'm just saying, Ian's burning seems important to me."

"Well, Ian's getting burned and Colin's dying were certainly the most horrible times in *my* life. First me and then you. It was almost as hard to see you so sad when there was nothing I could do about it. That's the thing, those times when there's nothing you can do. Unreal almost. You know, if I'd never had kids, I would never have had the most intensely awful experiences of my entire life, but I'd never give you back!"

"Thanks, Mom. Mom?"

"What?"

"I know that."

~

I hadn't seen my father for almost ten years when I made the eight-hour drive from Tuscaloosa to Savannah in the spring of 1998. I was there to attend a triad of ceremonies involving my three half-siblings: the oldest, India, graduated from the Savannah College of Art and Design; the next, Sierra, was liberated from St. Vincent's Academy for Girls; and the youngest, Max, got an award for a third-grade science project. India and Sierra were sharing an apartment at the time, and I stayed with them. Their mother is essentially out of the picture—rattling sabers in her mind, taking up arms against her own body. (*I don't want her in this,* my father says—sternly, as I imagine a father might say something. For the good of his children? To protect his ex-wife? To preserve his own skin? I don't know, but I agree with the imperative: *Keep her out of this.*) Suffice now to say that it was in no small part my stepmother's absence that enabled me to return to Savannah for the first time in nine years, where:

India sat with her back to me, checking her e-mail. I was lying face up on her bed, tracing an arc on the wall with my foot, pointing my bare toes, enjoying the way a human leg extended from the hip can serve as a sort of protractor.

"Dad said something strange today," I said. "Sometimes he worries me."

My sister didn't appear to be really listening. I heard her fingers tapping on the keys.

"We were talking about some people he knows. Or, rather, he was telling me about them, and he said, 'Something, something, blah . . . dumb Turks.' And so, I was like, 'Dad, you don't mean that,' and he repeated it—'Dumb Turks.' Sometimes I think he likes to say things just for the shock value, you know?"

India didn't reply, but her key-tapping had stopped.

"I think he's spent so much time pretending to be a bigot, to be shocking, that he just may have become one."

India jerked her head around to face me. "He's not a monster, Jill. You show up here, and you try to make him out to be some kind of monster. He's not a monster."

"I know he's not a monster. I know he's not. That's what I'm trying to say. I don't think he really is that way, in his heart. I tried to give him the benefit of the doubt. I said, 'Dad, you don't really mean that. You mean that you know *one* person, who happens to be from Turkey, and who you think is not very smart,' but he just said it again: 'Dumb Turks.' And he had this look on his face—this look of obstinate disgust, like a mask. The Intractable Bigotry Face. I think he thought he was being funny."

India got up from her chair and went to stand by the door, as far away from me as she could get and still be in the same room. Her cheeks were lung-blood red, ignited with the fire of full oxygenation: "You're never here. You don't even know. He's not a monster, Jill, and even if he is, *even if he is*, he's the only parent I've got. You've got your mother. You can't just show up here and say he's a monster. He's all I've got left, and *he can't be a monster.*"

"You're right," I said. "I'm never here. I *don't* know."

My father gave me his rearranged face for Christmas two years ago. I don't know what he gives to India.

～

I wasn't a child who wished her parents could live happily under one roof. I had no illusions about a happy, nuclear family. I'd never seen one. I didn't know what I was missing—if I was missing anything at all. (Besides, my mom, my brother, and I lived in Massachusetts in relative proximity to the Seabrook power plant. Nuclear was bad, that much I knew. What connection this badness had to a hundred monkeys, I wasn't yet sure.) It seemed clear to us kids that Mom and Dad were separate entities, living in separate states, and we—their unlikely children—were a floating unit.

We had a thing called "the kid swap." My mother, brother, and I would knock the sand from our sneakers, pile into the old lima bean green Chevy truck, and make the two-and-a-half-hour trip from our house on Plum Island in northern Massachusetts to the Friendly's restaurant in a tourist town right off I-90 called Sturbridge, Massachusetts. My father would meet us there. For an hour or so the four of us must have looked like a family. I always had a grilled-cheese sandwich on white bread, a dill pickle, a side of potato chips, and for dessert, a Friendly's kid cone. Mint chocolate chip. I think my mother liked the Reuben. Both my brother and father had burgers. Most of these "kid swaps" blend into a single memory of pickles and ice cream and the weighted feeling that I was somehow responsible for the time between getting out of my mother's Chevy and getting into my father's Tang-orange Honda Civic for the two-and-a-half-hour trip to New Milford, Connecticut—a time when both my worlds merged awkwardly, like a jigsaw puzzle piece that seems to have all its nubs in the right places and almost fits into the empty space in the picture of the English garden, but not quite, so that you have to bend the edges of the cardboard a bit to cram it in, and you hope nobody will notice so that you can have the satisfaction of getting in one of the green hedge pieces that all look basically the same anyway, but even as you're squeezing the piece into place, pretending that you've found a fit, you know that eventually someone will discover your deception, because for the puzzle to be finished, that piece will have to be moved to its correct position. So there we were—my father, my mother, my brother, and I—looking for all the world as though we fit as a family of four having a happy lunch at a restaurant, filling up our space in the red vinyl booth, but feeling a little pinched around the edges, our picture almost imperceptibly wrinkled, because we all knew that we had two vehicles parked in the lot, and after lunch there would be kisses and hugs, and our faux family would split into two units, one parent with two children and one parent alone, and drive away in opposite directions on I-90. And when the other car had pulled out of the parking lot and driven out of sight, when you could no longer hear the honking or see the other vehicle out the rear window, you opened up your activity book and colored furiously with your magic pen, making words appear where there had been none, hoping that the trip would go quickly, hoping that the parent left behind would neither miss you too much nor be too happy about some time without you. These are the feelings that smear across memory in a homogenous coating, like the beading balls of wax on a page scribbled thick with crayon—overlapping, masking, sometimes sliding away entirely, and only occasionally does a distinct memory presume to form boundaries in the viscous goop:

During one swap, for a change, we went to a different restaurant in this little theme town called Old Sturbridge Village. At Friendly's we always sat at a round booth, and at this place, the booths were rectangular: I sat next to my mother in the square across from my father. The waitress wore a pink gingham, colonial-style dress with a frilly white apron and matching dust cap. My father ordered a ham sandwich with a side of coleslaw. I hate coleslaw. I have always hated coleslaw. To me, mayonnaise is the "white axle grease" my great-grandfather always said that it was, and cabbage gives me gas. Anyway, my father was munching away happily on his nicely mounded slaw, which could have been fresh coconut ice cream, from the scooped, snowy looks of it, except for the occasional orange carrot fleck that was prodded out of the pile by my father's insistent fork.

I watched my father chew. His cheeks bulged with the bulk of a generous forkful of slaw, making the hairs of his thick, closely trimmed beard move like a hedgehog trying to get comfortable. I remember seeing a change come over his face as his munching ground to a slow stop. The corners of his mouth pulled down in an expression of early disgust, and his soft, pink, lower lip emerged from its covering of beard and mustache. He took one more test chew, grimaced, and stuck out his tongue. On the end of his tongue sat a folded Band-Aid.

"Oh, man, gross!" my brother yelled, lifting the bun from his burger and checking under the green disc of pickle for any foreign objects that might have been hidden in his slice of melted American cheese.

"Ewwwww," I squealed.

"Oh, *yuck*," my mother said.

My father made no sound. He removed the Band-Aid from his extended tongue, and using both hands, unfolded it. When he had the non-stick pad exposed, he lowered his chin towards his chest, entirely occluding his neck, and peered over the top of his wire-rimmed glasses at the offending Band-Aid. His lower lip reemerged from its hairy recess and began to tremble. "There's a scab," he said. "There's a Band-Aid with a scab in my coleslaw."

Why do I think that I remember this story so vividly? I was only six or seven. There is no photo of the waitress in the pink dress. No macro-shot of the Band-Aid on my father's tongue. Do I remember because my brother likes to tell this story, too? In other words, do we remember simply because it was so damn *gross* to actually witness our father chewing on the discarded, bescabbed Band-Aid of an unknown prep cook, that we have delighted in the telling and retelling of the Band-Aid in Dad's coleslaw story for the past twenty years? Or, do I remember because of the resolution of the situation and the support it lends to my ruling hypothesis concerning my father: He has no backbone.

This is the end of the story: After finding a Band-Aid in his coleslaw, my father paid the bill—including the price of the infected slaw. Of course, this story could be used as evidence to support a variety of other hypotheses as well, couldn't it? Perhaps if my father had got upset and demanded restitution for the chewed Band-Aid on the end of his tongue, as I suggest he should have, maybe then I would have used this story as an illustration of my father's reckless temper. I could be writing the story of how I survived my father's rage, and this would be a piece of evidence. But he didn't yell. The Betsy Ross waitress apologized to my father and brought my brother and me free ice cream cones. Maybe my father, having been separated from his children for months, was happy enough to see us eating free ice cream. This should be a sweet thing. Maybe my father is not spineless at all, but gentle. Maybe he is spineless *and* gentle. (*He's not a monster, Jill. . . . You can't just show up here and say he's a monster.*)

~

In art my mother does all the things my father does. He would say: "I am a photographer. I am a painter. I am a sculptor." She would say: "I like to make pictures." This is the difference between the two people who created me. My father puts himself in the picture, but my mother? My mother acquiesces to the image and moves behind it, claiming there is no artist in the final construction—the negative capability of scissors and glue.

None of us is to be trusted.

⁓ Baby in the Bubble

I have always been obsessed with family photographs. When I was a kid, say between the ages of six and twelve, say, in fact, during those same six years that I was hoarding bad secrets that nobody could know about, we would visit my mother's parents in Fishkill, New York. One of my favorite things to do in Fishkill was to go up into the attic closet—an act of courage, given that my brother had told me many times that this was the closet wherein lurked the evil closet elves, who, if they touched any part of you, except your face (my brother needed to leave us airholes for sleeping at night), would inflict wracking pain and a horrible death. So there was risk. But in this closet there was a giant cardboard box filled with photo albums: picturebooks. I would start at the beginning, with my grandmother as a baby, the pictures bound in brown leather, and work my way up to my brother and me on our last vacation, the pictures of which were bound much less gloriously in blue vinyl three-ring binders. This careful review of our family pictorial history often took the entire four or five days of our vacation.

The more recent, blue-bound picturebooks at my grandmother's house had three-inch spines labeled with wide numbers in indelible black marker. Picturebook Number One began with photos of my grandmother standing on her "kissing stool" to gain access to my grandfather's lips. After this kiss Number One documents intermittent microseconds of the beginning of their lives together: my mother's birth, my grandfather's return from Korea, my uncle's birth, the purchase of a gray house with a red door on a hill with a neat row of green hedges. By the time my grandparents bought the family home in Fishkill, color film was widely available to the amateur photographer, and the progress of the American Dream was tinted with colors that didn't quite match the world they were supposed to portray. But they were pretty.

~

My grandmother had been a high school librarian, working with agile fingers in the solid days of card catalogs, and I appreciated her post-retirement determination to keep a photographic inventory of a family that was going off the page in ways that no one would have planned: a waitress/sailor daughter with two fatherless children, a drunk husband and a drunker son (is that possible?), a father dead and a mother dying in a Poughkeepsie nursing home (she wanted to keep her at home, but with the chemo and the long drives. . . .), and so many hours to herself now that not even trips downtown to the Grand Union and the hairdresser, the long marinating of rump roasts, and daily visits to the nursing home could ever keep her busy. But with the photo albums she had an ongoing project. No family is a picturebook family, but my grandmother was a professional, and in her picturebooks, on her pages, she could construct a family history that made sense—even to a child, especially to a child, who craved the diligent alignment that her grandmother produced with her card-worn fingertips between every New York visit.

I imagine my now-dead grandmother in '76 or '77 working in her place at the kitchen table, where she always sat: photos fanned across the smooth, faded, lemon-yellow linoleum, a Benson & Hedges burning down to the filter in the square black plastic ashtray, a Schlitz beer sweating helpfully at her calloused elbow, and a six-inch black-and-white television sporting a mid-career Johnny Carson so small that he could have stepped out of the box and into the album and have been just about the right size.

During that period of at least six years, those picturebooks attached me on one end. Like a wooden swing secured to a stout oak by braided ropes, I was bound to a grandmother, a family, a life, and a little girl beneath the plastic who could have been me.

~

I was born *after* the memory that shaped my family, after Ian's burning, but there are no photographs of the time to serve as evidence. I cannot glue the players on the rough pages of the album because there are no pictures of the swollen red monkey baby on the treated green hospital sheets. (Yet my mother has painted this picture of Ian as an orangutan in my mind so often—*Oh, Jill, the swelling, you wouldn't believe that a baby could be that swollen*—that I see it in that year-long gap where there are no album pictures. In fact, perhaps I see the Year of the Monkey Baby more vividly than all the other years combined.)

Then the pictures in the album begin again—Ian is alive and scooting around my grandmother's driveway in a three-foot, red Chevrolet convertible, propelled Flintstones-style by small, whole, unburned feet that run along the bottom of the frame.

Ian is back and I am born. I am born *because* Ian is back.

But we won't stay together long. I will be only two when our family splits apart as smoothly as a baby's skin in the hands of a father who has arrived too late to help. And now I can't help wondering whether my father wanted that burned, firstborn son to be the final thing he couldn't hold.

~

I could try to start at the beginning with the story of my own birth. I could record the date and tell a simple story that starts out like this.

I was born in the dog-breath heat of a Miami summer, three years after my brother almost died, exactly one month after Neil Armstrong walked on the moon, and right about the time Janis Joplin was belting out "Piece of My Heart" on a rain-soaked stage in Woodstock, New York. On that day, August 16, 1969, I was born at the Miami Baby Hospital—100 percent babies—to a mother deep in twilight sleep. *That's the way they did it,* my mother tells me. *Back then, it was radical to breast-feed. They wanted me to feed you from a bottle. But my greatest regret is that I wasn't awake to see you kids being born.*

So while I was getting my toe tagged—remember, *all babies,* they couldn't be too careful—my father and my scarred-but-breathing brother were at the Miami Serpentarium watching Cookie the Giant Croc snap up live chickens for her lunch. *This was no sit-down affair,* my father would tell me later. Imagine such a flurry, such a pandemonium of flying white feathers, bright gnashing teeth, and red, red chicken blood that Cookie, who was once the longest crocodile in captivity, would bite off five feet of her own tail, and thus truncated, surrender her dubious distinction.

But I can't start with this bloody beginning and move cleanly to the now, the year 2000, a new millennium, if you believe we don't have to wait another year to be official, where I live in a rented house in Tuscaloosa, Alabama, and sit at a chunky wooden desk that looks out over the lawn I mowed last weekend—a ragged, weed-choked lawn that is already accumulating this week's piles of dog shit. Strangely, the great orange butterflies that I'm watching, today in Tuscaloosa, are as drawn to the piles of crap as they are to the bright Mexican sunflowers that I have cultivated along the fence. The butterflies battle the common houseflies for a sit on the shit.

I don't like it. I don't want to see these fantastic creatures, these ethereal insects with their glowing, gossamer wings fluttering in the morning sun, quivering like the uncertain lips of a new lover. . . . Oh, shit. I just don't like to see pretty things on shit. I mean, this shit has been soaking in the morning dew, and now it is being roasted in the Alabama sun—this shit is *steaming.* These butterflies are wallowing in shit steam. Disgusting. My butterfly expectations are dashed. It has come to this with me and butterflies, and this cannot be the beginning of my story.

My greatest regret, my mother says. *My greatest regret is that I wasn't awake to see you kids being born.*

Crocodiles close their eyes when they attack. Appetite is not about vision—it is about instinct and teeth and passion and flesh and that delicious moment when all these ingredients collide between bone-crushing jaws.

～

Conception

I did not know a French word which might account for this kind of human interest, but I believe this word exists in Latin: it is *studium,* which doesn't mean, at least not immediately, "study," but application to a thing, taste for someone, a kind of general, enthusiastic commitment, of course, but without special acuity. . . . This second element which will disturb the studium I shall therefore call *punctum;* for *punctum* is also: sting, speck, cut, little hole—and also a cast of the dice. A photograph's *punctum* is that accident which pricks me (but also bruises me, is poignant to me). (Roland Barthes, *Camera Lucida*)

~

In Picturebook Number Three there is a black-and-white photograph of my mother, huge in a billowing, striped tent of a dress. The dress is sleeveless, and I recognize my mother by a flap of skin above the dimple in the elbow of her arm. (I rely on the flap because her face is occluded by something, but we're not there yet.) The much-loved arm, with its dimple and flap, is reaching down into something that I cannot see. Her fingers are curled in, gripping, but the knuckles hit the photo's bottom frame here, so I can only guess that she is dipping a wand into a soap solution. Her left hand grips the edge of a picnic table. Her body, her belly, is big, and she needs support. The figure of my brother in the lower right of the frame is poorly focused, but even this blurry outline signals his comeback to the family album after years of burning and recovery. He is four. He is in profile, facing my mother, and I can see a light, smooth place—a reflection—on the left side of his head and recognize this as his bald spot. The hair will never grow back. His right hand is visible behind his body. Just his hand, curled like my mother's, the one that is bumping the frame, and I imagine that he imagines a wand in his own hand. The tent dress, the bald spot—these things interest me, place the photograph on the Christman timeline after my brother was burned and before I was born, but this is not, to use Barthes's term, the *punctum.* Rather, the prick for me, the poke through time, is the giant soap bubble that dominates the shot. Twenty-nine years ago my mother dipped her wand in a solution of dishwashing soap, water, and a little glycerin, if she had some, and waved this wand through the Florida air. A huge soap bubble formed, and someone caught this bubble midframe and made it matter. In a fraction of a second the story of my birth was captured on film. Later, made into a print. Later, chosen for the photo album. Still later, I had long since been born, and sat in my mother's lap, pointing to the picture with the giant soap bubble to hear her say (always): "Here *you* come!" (She knew this was my favorite part. On the next plastic page, after one more flip, the expected photo from the Miami Baby Hospital: banded wrists, Alfalfa hair, half-open eyes.)

For years I thought I was born from that bubble. I studied this photograph more intently than any other. I wanted to see *inside* this bubble that commands at least a third of the photo. The bubble is perfectly round, not newly cast—it has settled into its spherical shape, and there is no wind—it maintains its form. My mother's face is behind the bubble: she isn't smiling. She appears to be looking into the bubble, looking for something, not looking through the bubble and at the photographer. The lower right curve of the bubble seems barely to touch the top of my brother's head. So, while I know that I am influenced by the flattening effect of this particular shot, the foreshortening of a family world, I let myself be fooled by the illusion that the bubble is resting on my brother's head, and is therefore more solid, sturdier, than I know a soap bubble to be.

I am getting closer.

What *wounds* me is the bubble itself, both sides of a world reflected, up and down from the center. My expectation for the view in the bubble is not for a baby me, a suspended fetus in a giant bubble womb, but rather one of my father, face hidden by a camera, body striped by the spindly legs of his tripod. Holding steady. A whole family portrait, missing father and all. But there's nobody there.

The composition allows no room for a father. The principle of thirds precludes him: My mother's body strains at the left third, my small brother shares the right third with the textured trunk of a

Florida palm, and the center third is fat with my birth bubble. My father taught me about thirds himself when I was a student in his class: Introduction to Photography. These are the basics, but what tricks of the trade did he use to evade the bubble's insistent reflection? My father is a consummate craftsperson, and you won't find a glimmer of him in that bubble.

To Jill: Happy Birthday

My father sent me himself in a bubble for my twenty-eighth birthday: *Happy Birthday and the 20th Anniversary of Elvis' Death. I have finally stepped into the realm of Post Modernism. This image is my tribute to Escher's Self Portrait in his studio. This is an impossible photograph, but with a little help from my computer possible.*

I look and look. Only palm trees. Palm trees growing up and leaning in, like feather dusters reaching for the bright spot of the sun. Palm trees heading down, more like toilet brushes now, pointing down at another luminous stain. In the bubble there are two of everything, but there is no photographer. No father. No baby. "Here *you* come!" my mother would say.

There are no unselfish reasons to have a baby. So what? This is not a bad thing. Name for me an unselfish act. We always want something, every one of us—maybe it isn't something we're told it's bad to want, like money, sex, power, attention—but it's always something: credit, love, that feeling of selflessness that might be the most selfish thing of all. This should not be a bad thing. Should I not have a baby simply because I can't think of a selfless reason *to* have one? And if I could think of that reason—and I've tried, I've researched, I don't think it's possible—if I could find that reason, would I simply tell people: *This*, people, this is the purely unselfish reason that I want to bring a helpless little person into the world. Probably, yes. Selfish. Do I want a baby because I know I would be good at being its mother and I'd have this omnipresent feeling of being good at one thing? Or because I narcissistically want a little me? Or because I want to raise a child as I might have raised myself?

∼ The Ingraham Family, 1970–1980

For most of his life my mother's only brother was either in prison or way out in the woods without any phone. Isolation made him quite the letter-writer. Typically, Mark's letters are two pages long—front and back of a single piece of paper. When he reached the bottom of the back page, the letter would simply end. Because of this space constraint, he usually ran his words flush to the right edge of the page and often divided words with hyphens at their syllables to pack them in more efficiently—like a well-stacked woodpile.

Uncle Mark Writes: From a Woodland, California, Jail in 1970

Postmark: Woodland, CA P.M. Jan 23 1970
The red U.S. Air Mail stamp cost ten cents, and the stamp above it reads: PRAY FOR PEACE. Stuffed into the envelope along with the letter is a diagram that Mark drew of the cell he inhabited with nine other men. The page is divided in half, and on one side he has drawn and labeled five sets of bunk beds, a john, and a sink (*In here from 6 P.M. to 6 A.M.*), and on the other side he has sketched one long table, a shower, a john, and a sink (*In here from 6 A.M. to 6 P.M.*).

Dear Martha, Pete, Ian and Jill,
Received your checkerboard letter. Glad to hear everybody is in livable shape. My release date has now been set for Feb 14, Valentine's Day. My heart will really be in this one. They didn't give me any good time, and in the end I am serving about 75 days. 105 days all together. Egads! At least with a date marked off on the calendar things appear to be under control. Nothing can stop me February 14 from reaching fresh air. . . .
Got some Christmas pictures from mother and everyone looks pretty much on the top of things. Jill is looking more like a baby I'm glad to see. It was beautiful but sad finishing *The Hobbit*.

Tolkien really has an amazing mind. I wish I had some pepeweed in here right about now. . . .

Love and peace, Mark.

⌒

On all his letters from the Woodland jail, Mark signs off with a peace sign. I wonder if Woodland is where he got the black peace sign tattooed on his wrist.

⌒

Wednesday
Dear Martha Pete Ian and Jill,

Your letter was by far about the brightest I have seen and warmed my heart thoroughly. Now that I think about it, colors are things I have been almost completely cut off from. Looking around—all I see is a light green, gray, and white lights. Colors are really beautiful. They don't allow magazines so the only other color would be found on paperback books (and then, as you know, only the covers). I have been pretty well. February 14 seems quite a ways away but I know it isn't and have decided that after all, I may make it yet. I finished the trilogy and Gollum is in the shape of a very crisp lizard. . . .

Peace, Mark

Uncle Mark Writes: From a Cabin in the Middle of Nowhere in 1972

"12/72"—My mother's handwritten date is printed on the first page of Mark's three-page document of yellow, lined legal-sized paper lettered alternately with brown marker, pencil, and finally, blue ballpoint. The blue was probably written inside the post office in Selma, Oregon, where Mark wouldn't have to worry about the ink freezing in the tip. This is Mark's first letter from Oregon. He had found the home of his soul—the deep wilderness, the mountains, the rushing waters—a place called the Carrot Claim.

Dear Martha,

What I knew for sure was what I'd heard from friends. There was a bunch of my good friends, who grew up in Berkeley living in the woods in Oregon on a patch of land they called the Carrot Claim. They had found this place, an old mining claim, and had bought the rights from the previous owner. The instructions were—go to Selma, Ore. and take the Illinois River Road 30 miles to the end, and expect to walk as it's a dirt road and not frequently traveled. . . . I left the fuming Bay area and pointed my thumb towards the North. . . . The road twisted like a Christmas ribbon in and out of the most fantastic redwood forest. Trees as tall as mountains and as big around as whole houses. They had me gasping, these ancient giants found only in a few locations on the West coast. The only traffic on the road that far north are a few cars aimed maybe nowhere and logging trucks. The largest trucks made are loaded every one with these slaughtered redwoods. . . . I arrived in Selma, guitar in hand and pack on back, feeling that I had just seen and passed some of the nicest country there is. . . . I found the Illinois River Rd. and was happy to start hiking up towards some very large mountains. The road was paved and there were a few houses and a good sized cattle farm. Once past the farm, the road turned to dirt and started to thrust upwards out of the valley and into the seemingly endless range of peaks. Then I saw it, the Illinois River, a dark turquoise thread winding through the valley. Sometimes spreading and turning white as it rushed over a collection of boulders and small rocks then back to an even deeper blue as it was channeled through passages of sheer rock cliffs and then widening again to run with sand beaches on both sides. Every drop unspoiled and drinkable and crystal clear. The road was all up and down finding its way somehow along ridges always hanging over the river. . . . The beauty took my breath away as did the hills and I was speechless (having no one to talk to). After about a good 15 mile jaunt which took me past countless streams, creeks, and brooks, all transparent and shimmery, . . . I came upon a little shack, built out of cedar shakes and paper. Out of it came an old friend of mine, Tim. His little place is really beautiful—cook stove, heat stove, water that never shuts off, dirt floor, plastic sky lights. This was a part of the Carrot Claim. The big house was about 20 minutes from there down a small path. After winding this way and that, staying right along the edge of Soldier Creek, I came to a large clearing with a fairly large cabin sitting up on the hill. This is like an old house cabin with wood floors, kitchen, loft, porch, outhouse, garden, chickens, goats, etc. . . . Throughout this National Forest there are maybe 10 little couples or families living about 1–5 miles from their nearest neighbors who also live in tar paper shacks. The cabin I am living in this winter is one that is called the Hidden Cabin and believe me, it's hidden. . . . It's a small cedar cabin, one room, that needs a lot of sealing. It has a small cook stove, a heater stove (wood burners) natch, a lot of tools, some nice, 1 RAT, 2 bunks with primitive springs, blankets and really a lot of other old semi precious stuff. There is a beautiful waterfall right behind it and the stream flows right by the cabin and empties into Briggs Creek which rushes along right in front of the cabin about 30 ft. It is truly euphoric. Never, even up in the White Mts. have I ever lived in such wilderness. Every day I have to cut enough wood, sometimes hauling it ½ mile because the supply is short, to keep warm and cook. If I ever cut myself with the axe or got attacked by a black bear no one would ever know. Not even my friends will visit here this winter, it's much too treacherous getting here and there's already a foot of snow on those slides. With $32 a month food stamps I eat a mere shadow of what I put away out there. It's really very exciting knowing that you have yourself and yourself alone to keep you alive. . . . Most anyone who can runs hoses from the nearest stream to their house and lets it run constantly so it doesn't freeze. The stream is so close to the door here I can always just step outside and refill. Bathing is almost a forgotten luxury.

The letter ends with the blue ballpoint closing:

Just called you got Ian and Baby sitter, sorry Collect NO TIME
Love, Mark

~

Later that same year, Mark's in New York, and we both look sad,
as if we know something we're not telling.

Looking through the picturebooks, I come across another photo
of myself at age two—a color print. I am wearing a purple dress with
three white stars sewn on the front, looking like a young Star-Bellied
Sneetch who wandered out of the pages of her Dr. Seuss book and
into an unfamiliar world. I look lost and utterly alone, but I know
that this is not possible—somebody must have taken the picture.

In the picture I am surrounded by roses, familiar roses—but I do
not remember the star dress. *I remember,* my mother says. *That's
what I remember—the feel of the fabric. That star dress, the couch in
Grammy's living room, the little white hat you used to wear. Not the way
things looked so much as the way they felt.* Any memory I have of that
dress is one that I have fabricated from studying the picturebooks and
seeing myself in that dress at least a thousand times—flip, flip, flip,
there I am in the star dress in Grammy's garden, but why do I look so

alone?—no, I don't remember the dress, but I do remember that rose garden at the bottom of my grandmother's yard, so my brain tips this photo forward in time—the girl grows from two to seven, and all the rose memories compress into one story, one Fishkill visit, one family history—as if I could know everything at once.

A grandmother and her granddaughter are getting ready to tend a rose garden. The year is 1976, and the granddaughter, Jill, is proud that she was chosen to represent her class as a pioneer woman in her school's bicentennial celebration. Wearing a dust cap and a brown calico dress made by her mother, Jill had been in charge of exhibiting the quilt stitched by Mrs. B's second-grade class. Her job was to stand in front of the quilt and point randomly at the crude, fabric-penned squares depicting happy, feasting Indians, pioneer girls posing in pretty dresses, pioneer boys chopping, hunting, or hammering, and the occasional representation of a bountiful harvest: a pumpkin or a butternut squash.

In all the photographs of the big event, Jill smiles brightly, but her eyes glow a sinister red, because in the year of the bicentennial, point-and-shoot cameras were still called "instamatics," and they didn't feature red-eye reduction.

Nonetheless, the grandmother in this story enjoyed getting the pictures—she will put them in an album, of course. Everyone is very proud.

Now Jill waits by the backdoor of her grandparents' house in Fishkill, New York. Not in a photograph, her eyes are blue with yellow specks around the pupil. She is a chubby girl with round cheeks and a generous spill of freckles, and for this morning's project she is wearing a canvas gardening apron into which she has tucked a small shovel ("A spade," the grandmother tells her) and a powdered raspberry-jelly doughnut. She licks her finger, runs it over the top of the doughnut, leaving a slippery trail, and licks her finger again.

"Grammy!" she shouts, much too loudly, because her grandmother is crouching right there in the kitchen, loading up a plastic bucket with jars from beneath the sink. "I'm ready!"

"Go on ahead, " the grandmother says, lifting a jug of kerosene and pouring some into the wide mouth of a clean mayonnaise jar. "Grandfather's out there."

The acrid smell of the kerosene cutting into the greasy bacon odor is disgusting to the granddaughter, and she careens out the back, slamming the screen door behind her. The backyard is lovely—a long, sloping, impeccably manicured and brilliantly green yard that assures the grandfather's place as Respectable Male Head of Household here on the hill in upstate New York in 1976. This particular lawn is at least half as big as a football field, and the grandfather has his work cut out for him, but it is also shielded on all sides by tall shrubs, so this buys him a little extra time each week. Fortunately, no one here is questioning the effects of run-off from toxic chemical fertilizers. In fact, the grandfather applies a liberal treatment of DDT to his lawn twice per season to discourage insects. A creek bubbles joyfully across the bottom of the yard, and the smooth line of the lawn is interrupted by just one tree—an oak—the branches of which hold an old tire swing that contributes a whimsical effect to the overall look of the yard. The granddaughter never swings on the tire because it perpetually contains a few inches of stagnant water and rotting leaves, and she is too short to dump it out.

Enjoying the fruits of his early morning labors, the grandfather has set up a cot in the middle of the lawn and covered it with a green army blanket—he was a captain in World War II and in the Korean War, and he still likes to use his army-issued blanket for sunning. It is Sunday, and he is wearing yellow trunks that reveal long limbs of bare skin, browned to a tough leather and oiled slick with Johnson & Johnson's. The clear bottle with the pink snap top sits by the metal leg of his cot beside an insulated mug that the granddaughter assumes contains ice water. (She is mistaken. The cup contains wine—thick, sweet muscatel. It is 10:30 A.M.) The grandfather is propped up on his elbows, filling in the squares of the *New York Times* crossword with a well-sharpened pencil. He is absolutely glistening.

"Hi, Grandfather!" Jill yells, and he lifts his dark glasses to squint up at her. Then he smiles, and both his teeth and his hair glow a snowy white against his dark, dark skin.

"There was a little girl, she had a little curl," he begins.

"Right in the middle of her forehead!" she says.

"And when she was good, . . ." he continues.

"She was very, very good."

"And when she was bad?"

"She was horrid!"

"Who?" the grandfather asks. The granddaughter knows that each day of the visit they will have this conversation at least three times, and she should pay close attention. She does not yet know—as she is not yet aware of the contents of the insulated mug—that her grandfather is laying the groundwork for her future career in literature. She is seven, and she is thinking about the doughnut in her apron pocket.

"William Wordsworth Longfellow," she says obediently, licking her finger and tracing it over the top of the doughnut again.

"Henry WADSworth Longfellow," he corrects, and sighs dramatically, filling in more squares on the puzzle. "Poor Jill, the grass is on her grave. . . ."

"Has forty years been growing," the granddaughter responds.

"What?"

"The Spelling Bee."

"All I want is peace and quiet, . . ." the grandfather continues.

This is the grandfather's sign to the little girl—he knows it, she knows it.

"And a chance to grow your hollyhocks!" Before he can ask the final question in this round, the granddaughter skips down toward the rose garden at the bottom of the yard. She can't remember who said that, and the sun is too hot for thinking. There are no hollyhocks growing anywhere in the yard. This is just the way the grandfather talks. In college, after the war, he studied literature. He went on to become a high school principal who believed in poetry, corporal punishment, and dress codes. Once, he paddled a boy for wearing outrageous purple sneakers to school—an unpleasant task that interrupted the putting practice that he'd hitherto been enjoying in his ordered and well-lighted office. Ben Ingraham enjoyed his time at his post, and he particularly enjoyed his clear view of the clean, green span of lawn that stretched out beneath it—so much so, in fact, that he'd had a sign posted: STOP! DO NOT WALK ON THE GRASS.

Mr. Ingraham's own children had been pupils at his high school—very different pupils. His daughter, the elder child and now the freckled girl's mother, had joined all the school's social clubs and was the darling of the establishment ("Disgusting, really," she would say of her school spirit in later years. "Embarrassing—what a goody two-shoes!"). While the daughter was selling muffins at the marching band's bake sale, the little girl's uncle, considerably less "goody" and not one to wear any shoes at all, stole a Mustang from the garage where he worked and drove it through a store window during a high-speed pursuit by the sheriff. His father, the then-principal and the now-grandfather in this story, kicked the little girl's uncle out of his school and sent him to a military academy. Jill has seen pictures of her uncle in his blue uniform with the shiny, gold buttons: He is standing in front of a neat row of hedges at the Fishkill house, and he is holding a black snake by the throat.

When the grandmother arrives down at the rose garden, hauling her bucket of jars and a squat kitchen stool, Jill is waiting for her. "Look, Gram," she says, extending a leaf for the grandmother's inspection. The leaf is a coppery green color, and it has been gnawed so diligently by some insect that what remains of the leaf, held together by a slender stem, looks like delicate lacework.

"Oh, shhh . . . ugar!" the grandmother hisses, by way of a curse. "That's what I was afraid of." She sets her bucket and stool down on the grass with a grunt. "You know what that is, Jill? Beetles. Japanese beetles."

"Japs?" the granddaughter questions, not quite understanding. She has heard about Japs from the grandfather—something about being sneaky and dangerous, something about a war. She supposes that her grandmother is upset because these are sneaky, dangerous beetles.

"No," the grandmother says, casting a frown in the direction of the leathery man on the cot and then turning her critical eye back to the rose bushes. "Look! There's one." She bends uncomfortably and pulls the mayonnaise jar with the kerosene from her basket. Quietly unscrewing the dark blue lid, she approaches one of the rose plants and uses the lid as a scoop to push something into the amber liquid. She holds it up for inspection, "See?" Looking into the jar, the granddaughter sees something flailing, its black legs treading the liquid more and more slowly. The beetle is magnified by the thick glass of the mayonnaise jar.

"Ohh. Look, though. It's kind of pretty. Don't you think it's kind of pretty, Grammy? See how shiny it is?" The beetle has stopped struggling now, and its metallic body bobs passively in the kerosene like a charm on a bracelet.

"Pretty," the grandmother agrees. "And dead. Look what it did to my roses!"

"Look, Gram, there's another one," says the little girl, becoming an accomplice to the extermination. The beetles are slow and dimwitted—they're no match for the grandmother and her killing jar. To the granddaughter the grandmother is a rose garden unto herself— dressed in a cotton housedress pulled taut on the globe of her body, sprinkled recklessly with a floral pattern of peach, green, and yellow: a garden in a garden.

Standing at the center of all of these flowers, Jill cannot wait. She pulls the melting doughnut from her pocket and takes a hungry bite—the raspberry jelly is so red and so sweet that her cheeks suck inward, and she thinks, in surprise: This is so good it hurts.

Ben Ingraham Writes: A Birthday Letter for His Daughter in 1980

7 January 1980

Dear Martha,

Happy Natal Anniversary! I have a little time while I'm sitting under the dryer, so I thought I'd cheer you up.

Your mother was arrested for welfare fraud this morning and broke her arm while punching out a deputy sheriff. I fell out of a tree where I was hiding and suffered a severe concussion. I'd forgotten that there were no leaves on the tree.

If this news doesn't cheer you up, at least it will provide a belly laugh from Ian if you can interrupt him from his gleeful task of pulling the toenails of the squirming field mouse Tigger brought home just now.

Jill, of course, is reading *Black Beauty* by the fireplace, and is weeping her little heart out (some day it will swell up to the size of a pea) because the mailman who has Black Beauty hitched to his wagon had his whip break while he was lashing the poor animal.

Mark, I assume, is playing a tardy Santa Claus to the ragged urchins of Plum Island, passing out presents of packets of marijuana gaily packaged in holiday wrappings.

It is a scene that brings tears to my eyes. It's an old-fashioned family portrait right out of Norman Rockwell. It was a similar picture recalled from my last visit to Plum Island. You were all huddled around the television set. The set wasn't on. You just liked to huddle around the television set. *That's* togetherness!

I hope that Ian doesn't take exception to my remark about him. He is well-liked—except by the people who have met him.

Oh, well. As Samuel Butler said a couple of hundred years ago, "Parents are the last people on earth who ought to have children." Martha, these new laws are confusing, but I think that you'll find that the government will pay you *not* to raise Ian and Jill.

Your mother is in the kitchen opening the last of a six-pack. (I must get her a can-opener. She'll ruin her teeth.) So now she starts to insult and berate me. You've never heard her at her best.

This morning I said, "Oh! Higher interest rates. That means that the market will go down." She said, "I didn't think you knew anything about the stock market. . . . In fact, I didn't think you knew anything."

I said, "If I do the dishes, will you be nice to me?" She snarled, "Forget about the dishes!"

Beatrice, uncapping another Schlitz, said, "I could make a jerk out of you—but why should I improve your status?"

But she can't buffalo me. Anyone who takes me for a fool makes no mistake.

Thinking to put your mother off guard, I said, "Mark is coming back here. Why don't you straighten up the house?" She replied, "Why, is it crooked?"

Well, it's time for breakfast. Your mother doesn't serve me instant oatmeal anymore. She lost the recipe.

Even though our darling daughter isn't named Clementine, I wish I could be with her on her 23rd birthday.

I enclose my birthday gift—$3 in worn bills. You may distribute them as you see fit. I've saved them up without your mother's knowing! She says that she sent you more.

Love to Ian, Jill, Mark and much love and happy birthday to you.

Daddy

P.S. I found another $5 in my pillowcase.

I thought that I was born from a bubble—like Glenda the Good Witch in *The Wizard of Oz*. But Glenda's bubble glowed, reflected no palm trees, and Glenda burst forth fully grown, in a gown, with all her Good Witch intentions and a wand of her own. When did I first see *The Wizard of Oz*? Did I bring this image of Glenda to the "Here *you* come" photo? I don't remember that I did. Looking at photographs is like reading books—each year a different picture. My reaction to that photograph, the idea of being born from a bubble, must have changed after my mom brought home the facts-of-life guide—*Where Did I Come From?*—with its pen-and-ink drawings of the rounded man and the rounder woman getting as close as they could because they loved each other very, very much. After that book I must have become aware that my mother's bulk in that giant striped dress had more to do with my birth than that shimmering bubble ever did.

But wait.

There's a new hole punched into the time bubble of the photograph: by age six I myself had already been penetrated with a blunt object like the one that was drawn between the legs of the round man. By the time I turned pages to learn the story of the two pen-and-ink people who posed naked (to display their obvious differences), then climbed into bed and got as close to each other as two people could be because, always with the *because*, they loved each other very, very much, and for no other reason, I should have known exactly what they were doing. Maybe I already knew that an orgasm could be compared to the sneeze that comes at the end of a nose-tickling session with a downy feather—the book explained that the rubbing of the two people who love each other very, very much ends in a long shiver for both of them. (With the retrospective knowledge of twelve years of adult sexual participation, I realize that the implication was simultaneous orgasm every time—nice for the pen-and-ink people, I guess, but what a thing to teach children to expect!)

When my mom brought home this book, I was seven or eight: had I known the feeling of that downy feather? Vagina rhymes with Carolina. Pee-NUS. Say it like *peanuts* without the *t*. The man puts his pee-NUS inside her Carolina because he loves her very, very much, and *this,* children, *this* is as close as two people can be.

I'm sure that I was confused by the book's insistence on smoothness and roundness and love, but this is what must have been revelatory: the condition of pregnancy. I was not born from a bubble. I was, in fact, born of woman: a mother, not a bubble.

~

Even if, some day, the *remembering* can be proven, how will scientists ever prove the forgetting? *Okay, I'm forgetting now, come study me, I'm forgetting, and some day I might remember.* When does the forgetting *start*? At six, how cognizant was I about what happened in the back of my neighbor's garage? When did I get the language? Or did not having the language contribute to not having the memory? Now that I remember, I know that I was schooled in blowjobs and handjobs. I got nailed or screwed. In the back of that garage, there wasn't any fellatio or cunnilingus, or even sex. We didn't *make love* like the round people in the book. From age six to twelve I was humped, balled, or banged. I had a cunt, a clam, or a pussy. He spit on it to make it wet, and then he stuck it with his prick, dick, or one-eyed mackerel.

I was scared and broken and often bleeding, but back then it wasn't *abuse.* It's not abuse until somebody tells you that it's abuse. I wasn't *sexually abused* until I was nineteen and sitting in a therapist's office. Now I'm a *sexual abuse survivor,* but then I was just a kid in the back of a garage getting fucked, and I cannot remember that I ever felt too young.

If I didn't "remember" until I was nineteen, what did I have before then? The space of my memory couldn't have been all black; otherwise, I wouldn't have remembered how to tie my shoes or write my name in cursive with all the slanted letters coming up to the proper lines on the Rhinehart handwriting chart. Uppercase to the top and lowercase to the center, except the little *t* at the end of *Christ* and before *man*. The little *t* should touch the broken line of the three-quarters mark.

When I was eleven, I connected the dots between *Where Did I Come From?* and the back of ***'s garage. It had taken me that long to figure it out, four or five years at least, and I wish I had an isolated moment of epiphany to report—an event—but it wasn't like that. I put the pieces together gradually. I *studied*. I studied my stepmother's nursing books and *What's Happening to Me?*, the sequel to *Where Did I Come From?*, and then I figured out this horrifying possibility: I cannot become pregnant until I get my first period, *unless* that first falling egg from my first ovulation before my first period is fertilized by one of ***'s swimming sperm (which, thanks to the book, I pictured with a black top hat and a single red rose).

From that point on I knew that I could become pregnant, and we would be found out, exposed. I began the resistance.

~

"Will we ever hear ***'s name? Or is he as nameless as I am?"

"Call him Triple Asterisks, if you like. There were three letters in his name. I need to call him something, right? I can't just use a blank space on the page."

"Like you did in your brain?"

"Right. I need to reference him somehow, but I don't want to say his name."

"You are protecting him?"

"No. Not at all. I hope he's dead. I am always hoping that he's dead. The word, his name, is abhorrent. The name alone palpates the back of my neck with its grimy fingers—a word so repugnant that it is accompanied by an unpleasant odor . . . smoke and the closed-in, rotting smell of underwear worn too tightly and too long without changing or air. I am sickened."

"So, right then, with this revelation of first ovulation and pregnancy, you began the resistance. . . ."

"Yes."

When I was twelve I got my first period.

I spent the summer before the blood came with my father in Connecticut, and for two months I was numb with the fear that I was pregnant. My breasts had begun to swell, to grow tender nipples that were softer than the nose of a rabbit, and I became convinced that they were filling with milk for the baby. I poked and prodded them, to squeeze out a drop of milk, to extract evidence from my body, but of course the pinching only made them sore.

My fear was not rooted in the unborn baby itself, but in pregnancy, in cells multiplying against my will: my body's betrayal. My chest rising into breasts I'd never asked for, giving us away, nipples swollen like spoiled berries. Forced excretion, cream—this would have been evidence of my badness, and I knew I would be punished. I continued my painstaking study of one of my stepmother's nursing books, which I hid under my mattress like dirty magazines, determining over and over again that the pregnancy I so feared was indeed impossible before the first period *unless* the egg has been fertilized during the very first ovulation. This was the worst-case scenario, I reasoned, and my period had never even had a chance.

I prayed for a period. Before that, I'd never made bargains with God, and I didn't feel as though I deserved any consideration, having been to church only twice during Christmas to see the live nativity scene, but I hoped my prayers would somehow be sanctioned by my mother's earlier precautions. "I had you baptized just in case it was really true," she had told me, and I'd verified this in the picturebooks: my mother is holding an infant me way up on her full hip, but my long white gown reaches all the way down to kiss the ground.

"If you take this pregnancy away from me, God," I prayed, "I will never, never, never, never do anything dirty with *** again, ever, ever, ever." I refused to go to Animal Camp that summer. I also shunned Indian Camp, Horse Camp, and Mime Camp. I hid my body under big T-shirts, read books, and waited for the baby to begin kicking. I told no one.

And when I got home again, it came. "Mom! It came!" I had wiped and come up with blood. I wasn't scared. I was jubilant, unburdened by this sludgy smear of dark-red-beautiful-I'm-not-pregnant blood. Thank you, God.

My mother came into the bathroom with a pack of pads and showed me how to peel off the paper and fasten the stickum to my underwear, because she thought that I was still too young for tampons. And we went out to a place in town called Steak and Stein to eat red meat and celebrate my new womanhood.

At twelve I had escaped pregnancy the way the field mouse evades the hawk.

~

Go away. His hands grope for my body underneath the blankets. On my bunk bed, it's too easy for him to reach me. Get away, I say again, Go away. We can't anymore. He kisses me. Stale tobacco beer tongue. Gross. I bite him. You little bitch, he hisses, do you think that you can tease me all day and then not give me anything? Come on. Come on. Just one little kiss. One kiss? Then you'll go? Yeah, just one. Okay. Go ahead. Just one. Only kissing. I close my eyes, and his tongue presses past my swears to God. Pushes down into my throat. I gag on it. It wasn't always this bad. Don't fight, Jill. Come on. Just one kiss. Just one little kiss. He pins my head to my pillow, clamping my lips with his sharp teeth. I am something stuck. Pinned. But I am not a butterfly. Under the blankets, his rough nails jab into me, hard and quick. No! My brother and some of his other friends are in the next bedroom, smoking dope and playing electric guitars. It's a party. I can't let them hear. You have to, you little prick-tease. When you make a guy's dick hard you have to let him fuck you. That's the way it works. Move over. No, please. We can't. Move over. I can't. I could have a baby. I lift up the covers and pretend that I am going to let him into the bed, but while he's trying to climb up, I jump off the end of the bed, run to my mother's room and lock the door. His heavy feet come after me, but they are drunk and slow. Open that door. No. Leave me alone. If you don't leave, I'll call my mother at work and tell her about everything. They'll put you in jail. You said they could put you in jail. Bitch, he hissed. Get out here right now. If you tell, I'll kill you. Now. Open the door, you little slut. I crumple down in the corner, hugging the phone to my chest. I think about the ways that he could kill me. He makes weapons in his garage—in the front, I mean, not in the back where the bed is. Throwing stars to stab into walls, slingshots to shoot birds off high wires, air guns with needle darts to kill rabbits, wire things with sand bags on the ends that wrap around her ankles and trip her when she is trying to run away, wind around and around until she is tied to herself, as if she's a calf in a rodeo, brought down to the sand, hard, without air, numb from the impact.

~

How can something that feels so soft between bare toes be so unyielding? Except, she figures, that sand is rock. Crushed, but still rock.

~

If I hadn't myself recovered memories, I might not believe that it could happen. (*Recover:* v. To get back, regain. *Re-cover:* tr. v. To cover anew.) There's just too much that doesn't make any sense. So, let's break it down. If I was six years old, in second grade, and that's the day I threw up in the water fountain outside the classroom, and I remember, have always remembered, the image of my second-grade teacher, Mrs. C, picking the kernels of partially digested corn out of the drain, how then could I forget that when I returned home that afternoon, I was in a dark room with a guy who told me to rub harder, like this, harder, and now that I do remember, I remember it in real time, as if it's happening again, and I can feel the calluses on his palm scratching the back of my curled hand as he grips me, holds me, shows me how. How? I'm telling you, if I didn't have to believe in order to feel sane, I might not believe.

I've figured it out from photographs and from events, and I was six when—the proper thing to say is "when the abuse started," but that's not really accurate, given that I didn't even know "abuse" then, and what is "abuse"? "Rape" is not the right word either, because while he did sometimes force me to have sex ("sex"?) when I didn't want to, didn't know what I wanted, that's not the name for the pattern, the thing that we did, he and I, for the six years between my ages of six and twelve, and his ages of thirteen and nineteen. What we're really talking about is our relationship. I don't think that he ever told me he loved me. I don't think he ever told me I was beautiful (I wasn't). I'm sure I never told him these things either. I was wretched (I thought). And so was he (I still think this, and I'm sure he does also, if he's still alive to think at all). We were two contemptible beach urchins, one big and one small, and we did sneaky, dirty things together in the backs of garages and wide American cars. Wherever we were, it smelled like engine oil, and the fabrics beneath our naked skins were sticky with grease and cum.

*** was practical: he told me never to tell because he could be arrested for "statuary rape." I remember this. Maybe he said "statutory," maybe he got it right, but I heard "statuary." Or, rather, I remember hearing "statuary" and knowing that if this was "statuary rape," then I was the statue, and if he could be arrested for it, then I could be arrested for it, too. *Statutory rape:* Sexual relations with a person who has not reached the statutory [enacted, regulated, or authorized by statute] age of consent. *Statuary:* n. pl. 1. Statues collectively 2. The art of making statues 3. A sculptor; adj. Of or relating or suitable for a statue [a three-dimensional form or likeness sculpted, modeled, carved, or cast in material such as stone, clay, wood, or bronze]. Both words from *sta-* To stand; with derivatives meaning "place or thing that is standing." He didn't have to threaten me. I never told. I would never have told. Sex that stands still in a world that is standing. Nobody was going to arrest him. Nobody would arrest him now.

To begin again, my most visceral memories emerge from that year I was six, the year I started—what?—the year I started going back into ***'s garage: There was the upchucked canned cafeteria corn in the water fountain drain. Yellow on chrome on white forefronted by Mrs. C's probing, fleshy finger. The classroom was on the second floor of a small wooden schoolhouse that contained only the first and second grades. There was a round table in the corner where our reading group met every morning, and through the window we could see the huge swing set where a kid had once pumped his legs too hard, swung too high, flipped over the top bar, lost contact with the swing, plummeted to the packed dirt, and broken his back. I don't know whether this was urban myth spread by teachers on recess duty, but I remember the reverence we held for that swing set. Between the swings and the school was the shabby lawn where the boys smashed one another with inflated rubber balls in a game they called "Smear the Queer," while the girls sang out, "Red rover, red rover, send Mary Beth over." Closer still, on the steps going up to the front doors, I sat out recesses with my new Snoopy notepad. The pages were rectangular, not Snoopy-shaped, and they were layered pastel colors—more yellow, then pink, blue, and green. I sat and wrote notes to a boy named Sam, who I thought might like me. In kindergarten Sam had refused to sit next to any girl in morning circle but me, even though I had not won the right to play Gretel to his Hansel in our kindergarten play. (I was too big. Instead, I crawled across the carpet with white cardboard feathers tied to my shoulders and Sam's Gretel on my back. I was just the right size to be the sturdy swan ferrying the delicate Gretel across the lake.) But Sam was a redhead, and he was not concerned with size. He liked my freckles, he said. "Do you like me? Circle one Yes No." I remember the wooden staircase up to our second-story classroom and the meaty, steamy smell that soaked into the wood from the Styrofoam lunches stacked hot on the long table in the downstairs hall. I was a free-lunch kid, and I could have double lunch any time I wanted for free, and when there were tater tots, I wanted to, but I never did because double lunch was like a sign: "I'm a free-lunch kid, and my mother doesn't feed me at home so I have to stuff my fat face here." Or something to that effect. My mother fed me at home. She just didn't feed me tater tots.

Here, I wish I could order the memories, but I can't. I don't know why I sat at my wooden desk, put my feet up on the rack of the desk in front of me, and peed. But I did. I peed and peed and peed. In this memory, I can't remember an individual face in the whole room, but I remember the screaming: "Jill peed her pants! Jill peed her pants!" Logic would say that I froze, stared down at my desk, wished to be somewhere else. But I can see the flow of the pee as it made a straight line down the wooden floor beneath the lifted, twitching feet of my classmates. Not a fast line, but a rolling line, soft, rounded at the tip, yellow, yellow, yellow. I twisted around in my seat to see where my pee would stop. Humiliation doesn't catch up with my memory until the desks are pushed out of the way and the orange, pine-smelling sawdust is sprinkled down the length of my river of pee. Passive voice because I have no memory of who sprinkled the sawdust, only that it was there for the rest of the afternoon, and I was wearing bright green sweatpants that were too tight for me: "Jill, you have to *tell* me when you need to go to the bathroom." I didn't find out until I was much older—college-age—how aberrant, how *bad*, it is to pee your pants in the second grade. I remember that my pee stream was rounded at its tip, and yellow.

∽

I have always been obsessed with photographs. Now I am obsessed with memory. They are not obsessions that belong in the same category, except that they tend to negate each other. Marguerite Duras: *Photographs promote forgetting.* I built a childhood out of the photographs in my grandmother's picturebooks. This childhood did not match my life, but I chose it as my episodic memory.

> Shareability theory suggests that memory for never-discussed events is likely to be qualitatively different from memory for events that have been discussed. This difference will be greater when the sensory, continuous memories for the events were not recoded internally in the anticipation of verbal sharing. Thus, if an event is experienced but never recoded into shareable formats, it is more likely to be stored in codes that are continuous, sensory, and dynamic. (Jennifer Freyd, *Betrayal Trauma: The Logic of Forgetting*)

∽

Unlike Mark, I thought that I wanted the life that my grandmother recorded in the picturebooks—a life with patterns to depend on and rules to follow. There were six o'clock meat-and-potato meals eaten after perfunctory blessings. Gravy was served from a real gravy boat with a matching ladle. There was a rose garden in the backyard and a cherry tree in the front. There was a lawn to be mowed, garbage to be taken out, and a daily newspaper to be taken in. These were normal things that people did. My grandparents did not lead extravagant lives, but they were—I thought—what my mother, my brother and I were not: normal.

In my grandmother's picturebooks, we were all part of that ordered world, and thus, the albums created the family.

⌒

Two School Pictures

The first is my second-grade school picture. My hair is long, chestnut-colored, shiny, and straight as the ruler that sits on the calendar desk pad in the picture. The picture is posed. My hair is parted in the middle, and two long, pencil-thin braids trace down either side of my face, holding my hair out of my eyes. There is a highly polished Red Delicious apple on the corner of the wooden desk, but I don't touch it. My hands are folded neatly just as the photographer instructed. I am smiling, and the flash makes my eyes sparkle.

The other picture is labeled on the back in my mother's writing: *Grade 3*. If I didn't know that it was me, I'd think the chubby, sad-faced girl in this picture was somebody else. In the picture, the girl's hair is chopped in a bowl shape ending just below her earlobes. Someone, I can't believe it was my mother, it must have been me, chose the reflection prints, so there are two of that gloomy stranger. One looks dully toward the camera. The other, ghostlike and faded, watches the corner of the photograph as if she will be able to catch someone creeping into the frame and fix him with her flat stare.

⌒

Foolishly, I sent one of the sections about *** to my mother. I wanted to ask her about some things, and she'd been asking to see what I was working on, so I sent it to her. To me, it was a text—my life, but on the page, a text. I sent it to her, vaguely thinking, *Oh shit, my poor mother,* but figuring she could handle it—she knew about everything anyway, mostly, so I sent it off and then, conveniently, typically, forgot about it.

Then the phone rang. I was sitting at my kitchen table in Tuscaloosa, drinking a latte, grading some freshman essays, and the phone rang. "Hello?"

When my mother heard my voice, she started to cry, "Oh, sweetie, I want to go back and get that little girl and keep it all from happening."

"What?"

"You. It makes me so sad. I just want to go back and get you."

The book. "I'm okay, Mom. I'm all right."

"I know, but I wish it didn't have to happen."

I have never held my mother responsible for what happened in the back of ***'s garage, though it has been suggested to me that I should. *It was her responsibility to protect you. You were only a child. She is partially to blame.* Perhaps. But she was doing her best. She had to work at the restaurant or on the boat. There was no money for a babysitter. She was doing her best, and she loved us. Always. She always loved us. *How come Mom gets off so easy? How could she not notice what was going on? When you peed your pants in second grade, didn't she see that as a sign?* It was different then. There wasn't this climate of awareness. Nobody was thinking about warning signs in 1976. And what am I supposed to do? Blame her and then forgive her? Is that the way it's supposed to go? Are those the appropriate stages?

I don't blame her. I never have.

Where's the rage, Jill?

"I wish I could go back and get that little girl," my mother said.

"I know, Mom. I know that you were doing the best you could."

∽

My father's mother, Grammy Sarah, was dying of cancer by the time that I remember knowing her. *She was a hard mother to have,* my mother says. Her indulgences, for herself and for her grandchildren, were otherworldly. When we spent the night at her house for Christmas, but had forgotten our knitted stockings to hang by the chimney with care, she presented a large pair of pantyhose, cut cleanly through the cotton crotch, and nailed a leg for each of us to the wall. In the morning, when we made our way down the creaky wooden stairs in the predawn, we saw that our legs had grown beyond proportion, stretched, bulging, dragging down onto, and across, the floor. Inside, no trinkets, but big things. Useful things. Hammers, threepenny nails, screws, a hand drill for my brother, boxes of sugarcubes (for building miniature igloos, Sarah explained), oranges, apples, hunks of wood on which to use our new set of tools, and corncob pipes for smoking dried-out corn silk. She wanted us to learn to make things, and enjoy ourselves while we were at it. Drill a hole, hammer a nail, pause for a smoke. When we turned her whole house into a blanket fort and instituted an entire day of Can't Touch the Floor, she told her son, our father, not to touch the floor. We adored her. *She was a difficult mother to have.*

If I were to employ the characterization technique of describing Grammy Sarah as a food, there would be no question of my choice: Yorkshire pudding. Puffed to an elaborate perfection, melting on the tongue, bathed in fatty juices. Can't you just picture a Yorkshire pudding lighting up a cigarette for a satisfying drag after a large and decadent meal? That was Sarah. Fuck health. If I were a food, I could never be so succulent.

~

My father's mother died when I was six. The cancer spread everywhere at the end, my father told us, and I have never got over the image of cancer as a group of maggots—crawling around on the inside and gnawing en masse on stomachs and lungs and brains—leaving chewed-up, empty places.

Grammy Sarah's was the first funeral I ever attended, and I remember two things about the event: (1) the very thought that this was my first funeral, and that there would be many more, but this would always be the first one, and (2) the hollow sound of that first shovel of dirt hitting the lid of the coffin, and the desperate feeling that we were doing the wrong thing, that we had to pull her out of there—we couldn't just *bury* her. How would she breathe?

~

Your Grammy Sarah, my mother says, *was a hard mother to have.* And then India chimes in. *He's not a monster, Jill. You can't just come here and say he's a monster.*

~ Care and Feeding

When I was six or so, my mother received a copy of *Diet for a Small Planet* as a gift, and the world of food and nutrition as we had once known it was forever altered. "I didn't know!" she says, laughing. "I just didn't know." Things changed fast. Ian and I no longer accompanied her to the IGA to choose among all of the brightly colored packages: Froot Loops or Cap'n Crunch with Crunch Berries? Chocolate or Peanut Butter Instant Breakfast Bars? Tang or Juicy Juice? Bologna or ham? Ring Dings or Twinkies? "Hard to believe, isn't it?" my mother says. "I thought Tang was good for you kids. Vitamin C!"

Our food world was subverted, and soon the oranges and purples of commercial food labeling morphed into the dull browns and greens of food "grown in Mother Earth." Instead of bouncing through the grocery-store aisles and picking up double bonus points in the cookie section, like a pinball in an IGA game, I sat with my mother on the cornmeal-covered floor at the co-op in the library basement, measuring cups of bulgur wheat into paper bags. Our new foods were hard to pronounce, never mind swallow: tabbouleh, falafel, garbanzos, tofu, tempeh. Nothing came in pretty packages anymore.

And my mother didn't just buy the food, she swallowed the whole lifestyle—sort of the way you can't just buy a pitchfork from Smith & Hawkens or a little black dress from the J. Peterman catalog. Appliances were banished. Microwaves nuke food. Food processors scare food. Nuked, scared food makes nuked, scared people. We were fair with our food. Carrots were chopped cleanly and quickly with a well-sharpened knife. Coffee grounds were splashed with a thoughtful dribble of boiling water, to wake them up, before drowning.

These were the days when my mother sprouted seeds and cultured yogurt at home by day, and served beer, chili, and chicken wings in a downtown bar by night. But the eating was not all bad. There was the year that my mother's fisherman boyfriend decorated the Christmas tree with live, squirming lobsters, and we untied the twine and plunged them headfirst into a steaming pot. In her newly enlightened state, my mother considered the method of death carefully: "See, Jill, you need to hold them like this, right behind the ears, and plunge their little heads into the boiling water. Fast. They never know what hit them." She assured me that the whistling noise the lobsters made as their little heads were plunged was just the steam trapped beneath their shells, not screaming. "Lobsters can't scream," she said. To me, it sounded like screaming, but soaked in lemon butter, their meaty tails were ambrosia.

We did some strange things back then: sat cross-legged in well-packed groups of hippies, ate mushroom-bulgur pie, sipped wheatgrass smoothies, and chanted at a gold-framed photo of a short, round guy that the glassy-eyed grownups called Maharishi. These were not moments we shared with the other kids at recess. There were many things we did not share.

We saw our father, stepmother, and new siblings in the summers and during school vacations, and life moved along at a child's pace, but then the fisherman boyfriend took a trip out West to visit Uncle Mark. On the way there or on the way back, I'm not sure, the fisherman smoked too much peyote, received a colorful vision, and realized that he was some sort of messiah—not far from Jesus Christ and somehow linked to Black Elk and the Lakota Sioux in South Dakota—so he sold the 90-foot boat that he'd christened with the name of my mother, bought an old yellow school bus, cut a hole in the roof for the stovepipe, stocked it with food jars stuffed with dried fruit and nuts (earth food, you know), and made ready to leave New England for good and strike out for the West and certain spiritual fame.

My mother knew that her fisherman was planning to leave on a bus. He was the love of her life, she says, and that's saying something. She knew also that she could go along, but she didn't. "He asked me to go with him, but I couldn't *go with him!* I had you kids. You had school. I couldn't just *go with him.*"

And then he was gone. But our respite was short-lived, and when I was thirteen, my brother left for art school, and my mother carried me off to a mountain in northeastern Washington where the major cash crop sure wasn't soybeans and where the closest school had only one room and no electricity. I got the horse that I'd always wanted— a chestnut quarter horse, named Moona—so that I could haul water and ride her to school.

But here's where the shit really starts to fly into the 9-volt-battery-operated plastic fan. In the three-month transition from the island to the mountain, I had become a hardcore bulimic. Try that without indoor plumbing and on a grazing ground you share with the common black bear. I trust that one of my very few genuine claims to fame is this: I was a teenage bulimic without a flush toilet. Puking in the outhouse was out of the question, of course—bulimics are many things but being glaringly conspicuous usually isn't one of them. I had to walk far, dig deep, and cover my tracks as best I could—mostly, I tried not to eat.

⌇

"Do you remember the very first time?"

"That I had sex?"

"No, that you threw up. The first time that you made yourself throw up."

"Isn't that funny? Usually, that phrase—'the first time'—usually that's used for sex. Your first time. I don't even remember 'the first time' with my high school boyfriend."

"Was it bad?"

"No, I don't think so. I was fifteen, I was drunk, and he was seven years older than me. I was already on the Pill, just in case. So I must have been planning it, right? But the actual night, I'd apparently had one wine cooler too many, and I blacked out. He said that he was sleeping on the couch *like a gentleman,* and that I'd been sleeping on his waterbed until I came out to the living room, wearing only this tiny string bikini with hearts and a bow, and pulled him into the bedroom. Sounds like a male fantasy, I know, but I remember the valentine underwear best of all. Just as my mother says about looking at pictures—in my mind's eye, or fingers, I guess, I can *feel* the fabric of those stupid heart panties—a really soft cotton. Other than the panties, I vaguely remember the waves we made in the bed, my hand jammed between the wooden frame and the mattress, and the feel of the rubber sticking to my shoulders as the sheet pulled away from the bed. He thought I was a virgin. He thought he was *taking* the virginity of some hot, drunk girl."

"Did you feel bad? That you didn't remember?"

"No, not really. I mean, at that point, I thought I'd been a virgin, too."

"What about the other first time? With the throwing up?"

～

The first time I made myself throw up by sticking my finger down my throat, I was flying, unaccompanied, to Savannah, Georgia, where I was to spend the summer with my father in 99 percent humidity. I was twelve—too old for the coloring book and the cardboard captain's hat, but still young enough to sit in the first row of coach and get extra bags of peanuts from an attentive stewardess named Carol.

～

"You don't really remember the flight attendant's name, do you?"

"No, but it was something like that. I remember her. Someone like her. And back then they were still called stewardesses. What I remember best are the peanuts, although I can't be sure they were honey-roasted. I remember my own panic."

～

I realize now that Carol was probably a freak, but back then I was sure that the tiny, sculpted, golden wings on her lapel pin were verification that she was an angel. She smiled at us—the front row of kids—each time she passed, and her broad, flat teeth were so unnaturally white I imagined sparks shooting out, just like in the Gleem toothpaste commercial.

Carol was a model of control. She preserved a hypnotically gentle voice that I had to lean closer to hear, even when she was telling the eight-year-old kid next to me, *Please sweetie, try to stay with your bottom in the seat and your seatbelt on, won't you?* The kid was wearing his cardboard captain's hat, coating the pages of his coloring book with waxy red globules, and then folding the ripped-out pages into simple V-shaped planes. Turning onto his knees and using the seatback as a blockade, he chucked them at the passengers, yelling, "Die, Yankee, die!" *Come on, sweetie, bottom in the seat.* Then Carol would toss the little rebel another bag of peanuts, and one to me, too, since I was sitting between him and the plastic porthole.

~

"Did the kid really say that?"

"No, I think I'm making that part up, but there was a boy sitting next to me—and he was a little shit. I wanted to clobber him, but she stayed so calm."

~

Tearing open the peanut bag with my teeth, I wondered if the clouds were as soft as they looked, if they would support my weight, take me into a billowing embrace. I popped a peanut into my mouth and sucked on the rough honey coating until the peanut felt smooth against my tongue. More likely, I thought, the clouds were in fact the atmospheric vapor that my science book said they were, and if I jumped out the emergency exit, the deceptive fluff would dissolve beneath my feet, sending me tumbling through empty space, my body in search of the solid ground.

I turned sideways in my seat, jamming the base of my ponytail against the window and creating an intentional pressure at the back of my skull. Carol stood in the aisle and scooped ice cubes. Holding a cocktail napkin to the bottom of a clear plastic cup with her pinkie, she smiled at me, teeth flashing, and when the rebel kid threw a plane at her, it glanced off her creased blue uniform as if off the blade of a knife. She leaned over him, still smiling, and asked me, *More 7-Up, sweetie?* I nodded, wishing I had the willpower to be so unflappable and crisp-edged thin. A flying angel.

I sipped my 7-Up, putting my nose close enough to feel the bubbles fizzing in my nostrils, and breathing the carbonated vapor. I drank ice-cold 7-Up and crunched peanuts until my stomach felt bloated. I ate faster. We were too high up to see the clouds anymore—just blue, blue, blue. The roof of my mouth was raw from sucking the honey-coating from the peanuts. I tasted a trace of blood.

I pulled up on the seatbelt buckle, just like in the preflight demonstration, and loosened the strap. My stomach gurgled and expanded into the new space. I ripped open another peanut bag with my teeth, imagining what a plane crash would be like and trying to decide whether I would like that better than landing, if I should maybe wish for mechanical failure and try to make it happen. I stepped over the little rebel and out into the aisle. Carol slid easily between seat rows to let me pass down the aisle, smiling a smile that felt to me like her blessing.

Staggering a bit as I moved down the aisle, I groped at the seatbacks for balance, embarrassed, and wanting to make it look easier than it was. The sign showing through the rectangular window on the bathroom door read: VACANT. I stepped inside, turned the handle to the right until OCCUPIED appeared in the cutout, and stared at my face in the mirror. I stared and stared, but I couldn't focus on my own face. My bloated-looking features, slick with peanut oil, blurred and became someone else. I knew I had to get this other girl out.

〜

"Do you remember that specific time in the mirror?"

"I think so, but who's to say? After that, it happened so many times. What's weird is the timing. The first time I threw up I was on a plane flying away from six years of sexual abuse. We moved that year, and I knew I'd never see him again. This is my theory: my body was stuck in a pattern. It was never the food that I craved—not really. It was the throwing up that I really wanted. I needed the feeling of getting rid of something; I wanted to feel the food leaving my body. After vomiting the food, I'd usually drink a glass of water or cup my hands under the faucet and drink from the bathroom sink, and then throw up again. I liked to rinse out my body, wash away anything that might be sticking to the edges. With bulimia there's never any nausea, and you never know hunger. It's a ritual and a drug. I've read that the euphoric feeling that a bulimic gets after she vomits is similar to the feeling after sex, or a long run, or a lot of chocolate."

Crazy, I know, and I wish—at thirteen—I could have told my mother, asked her for help, discovered what this thing I did *was:* Who pukes like this? Crazy. But when I think about what I was getting away from, and what was rushing up to meet me, it all makes more sense than it should.

During that first winter on the mountain, we lived with my mother's new boyfriend—a Vietnam vet who was smart, mean, loving, funny, and crazy—the most sensible, highly principled, and wildly irascible hippie I have ever known. Soon after we arrived, he asked, "Can you pull yourself out of a hole?"

"I don't know. Probably."

"Can you do a pull-up?"

"No."

"Then you can't pull yourself out of a hole."

And so, on his good suggestion, I spent many hours pumping iron in a shed that was sometimes used as a weight room with the initial goal of achieving the upper-body strength necessary to pull myself out of a deep hole—should such a stunt ever become necessary to save my own life.

Although we never worked out together, I always felt close to him when I was in the weight room. Somehow it made me feel as if I were surviving something, too. I remember that time as a perpetual winter, so when I lay back on the bench and wrapped my fingers around the frigid metal bar in the rack above my head, the steel hazed over with vapor from the heat of my palms, and my hands fixed to the bar. I tried to imagine what it might have been like in the jungle. My mother had told me that he had been the only one in his platoon to survive—so he must have known how to hide or run or shoot—or maybe he was just the luckiest goddamned motherfuckin' hippie (his words) ever to make it back to the woods of Washington State and build a cabin.

He never talked to me about Vietnam. Never. But pressing the heavy bar up from my chest, as heavy as I could lift, I would imagine things I'd seen in movies, and I'd put him in the middle of my cinematic memory—the crazy, wet heat, the sucking mud and the long grasses, the hungry mosquitoes and leeches. Bullets from nowhere shooting everywhere at all things real and imaginary—snakes and snipers and mines to blow your legs off. Raining and raining and raining. Everyone else dead. I strained to lift the bar, which grew heavier with each pump. Only three more reps, but what if stopping meant dying? Pretend to stop is to die—and then push. A whole platoon dead: Every. Single. One. Letting the bar slam down into the metal cradle above my head, I sometimes wondered how many Vietcong he had killed. Maybe ten. Or twenty. Maybe more. Or none at all. I lifted the bar again. Blood pounded in my brain. He had told me it was okay if it hurt. It was supposed to hurt some.

I became addicted to growing stronger, and in the second phase of my imaginings I believed this: if I got strong enough, I could make him proud of me. I would not be a girly wimp. I would be strong—but I couldn't seem to help being a fool, and I can suspect only now that I had already lost any memory of ***'s garage.

In this cabin in the woods there were many rules to live by, but the most important was this: when approaching the cabin or the shed, I was supposed to whistle—one short, one long, one short, one long—to let him know I was there, that I was on his side. One March afternoon I got home from school, put Moona away in her corral, and decided to go straight to the shed to work out. The snow was starting to melt in patches, but it was still a cold day. I ran down the path and burst through the door without thinking. He was in there, silent, and his shotgun was leveled at my head. I pantomimed trying to whistle, but I couldn't—the shock of the gun's barrel had clogged up my whistle like a mouthful of crackers.

He lowered the gun, and I started to laugh and cry. "I'm sorry! I forgot! Oh my God. You were going to shoot me!" He didn't laugh, or say a word; he just walked out of the shed. It was the only time I really felt afraid of him, and even at that, mostly I just felt stupid. Of course he wouldn't have shot me. You don't survive Vietnam and then shoot your girlfriend's daughter accidentally. No game is all luck.

My mother denies it, and I'm sure she had a thousand and one reasons for what she did and when she did it, but I've always thought that something must have snapped in her head when I told her about forgetting to whistle, because soon after—that night or the next—from the lookout of my upstairs bedroom, I watched the light from the kerosene lamp on the kitchen table flicker up through the cracks in the floor, drawing shaky lines on the sloping attic ceiling, and I heard my mother's low voice telling him about the land she was going to buy. We were leaving, and I'm sure she knew I was listening.

~

When we had first arrived on the mountain, my mother had thought she'd like to learn how to hunt—just little things she'd feel okay about shooting. She started with grouse, because grouse are both dumb and ubiquitous. Soon after she'd made up her mind to give tracking and hunting a try, she came home with a dead grouse. She hadn't liked shooting it, and she didn't think she'd do it again. Besides, it seemed like a lot of effort for such a little bird—all that soaking and plucking and gutting—but of course, we were committed to eating this one she'd already killed. It was winter, and the bird must have been feeding on tamarack needles for months, because chewing the tough flesh of this bird was like gnawing on pine bark in turpentine gravy. Yuck. After her first and only kill, my mother understood that it was not the self-sufficiency or the meat that she wanted, but the part before the killing—the part where she could walk deep into the woods, silent and part of something.

~

You will know yourself better. This is another kind of survival knowledge. The more intimate we become with other lives, the more aware we are of how those lives connect with and affect our own. There may be only a few obvious connections at first—two animals in the same woods, hearing the same sounds, smelling the same smells—but as we track the animal farther, we find that its trail is our own trail. As it moves, it affects its surroundings. What changes the animal changes its environment, and thus changes us. In a sense, we are tracking ourselves. (Paul Rezendes, *Tracking and the Art of Seeing*)

~

On March 17, 1983, my mother and I moved out of her boyfriend's cabin and onto our own twenty acres on the mountain. There was still snow on the ground, and for the first week or so we lived in a three-person tent while we built a structure framed by tipi poles cut from saplings and walled by green tarps and clear sheets of visquine. Our "Plastic Fantastic" was heated by a tiny $50 woodstove called a "Tin Wonder." The names alone were enough to crack me up, appease me a bit.

During this time, my mother, who had become my partner in life, tried to comfort me: "It's okay, Jill, this builds character. It's an adventure! This is *real*."

"Yeah," I'd mutter in reply. "This is real all right. Real fucking cold." Forgive me. I was a teenager. I was prone to small acts of more visible rebellion. And it *was* cold—it had been so cold that first winter that the snow packed into Moona's hooves, even though we took her shoes off, where it would freeze into solid balls of ice as we picked our way down the path to the schoolhouse—have you ever skied downhill on a fifteen-hundred-pound animal? It's something else. It would have taken my breath away—if my breath had been in gas form. Yeah, it was real cold. "Character building, my block-ice ass," I'd grumble.

And my mother would say, "But look, Jill. Look at the snow. It's a winter wonderland! Give it a try."

~

When we were living in the Plastic Fantastic, we had some problems with the native wildlife. The most immediate threat came in the form of furry, well-toothed, sharp-clawed, and undoubtedly diseased rodents—mice and chipmunks, primarily. When you live in a house that has only thin wooden poles for a foundation, and beneath that, light, loamy earth, easily dug, you haven't a prayer at keeping out the smaller creatures of the forest. At first we tried to live in harmony with them, but they scampered through our food boxes, shit on everything in sight, and ate the laces out of our shoes; and then, one night, I rolled over in my sleep, disturbed a mouse on the pillow, and was actually bitten on the cheek by the little beast. I was sure they were diseased.

We took defensive action. At first we tried Have-a-Heart traps, but honestly, with such an endless rodent population, what good are those? And then what do you *do* with the hoard you catch every night? The farther you walk with them, the longer it takes them to get back to the house—but they will get back, or at least, their friends will.

"We have to kill them," my mother decided one morning, as we sat on our sleeping pads drinking coffee and listening to the night's capture scrabble at the edges of their aluminum prison.

"What do you propose?" I asked.

"Drowning?"

"Ugh. That seems mean."

"What else can we do?"

"Burn them?"

"No. . . . Oh, I know! You can get ready with a hammer, and then I'll pull up the door, and as they run out, you can hammer their little heads!"

"Gross! Why do I have to do the hammering?"

It was impossible. We couldn't kill them once we had them, so the next time my mother drove into town, she came back with about twenty snap traps. The racket on that first night was awful. Clean, neck-breaking snaps were rare—instead, a single mouse leg would get caught beneath the steel lever, and the suffering mouse, very much alive and more desperate than ever, would run in circles with the trap like a kid on a scooter with a broken wheel. Even louder were the chipmunks, two or three times bigger than the mice, who, catching just the tip of a nose or tail, seemed able to drag a jangling trap around for hours. Sometimes they screamed. It was like sleeping in the Chamber of Rodent Torture, Dismemberment, and Death in a cosmetics company lab somewhere.

Of course, we got used to it—you can get used to just about anything—and my mother made a certain peace with the animal world. In the morning, while the coffee water was heating in the kettle on the Tin Wonder, she would gather up all the traps from the night's kill and climb the mound beside our little house. There, she would pull back the levers, extract the broken bodies, and lay them in the top of a bush—hanging them by their tails like sacrificial ornaments. When she was finished, she came down the hill and washed her hands. As we sipped our morning coffee, we'd watch the ravens swoop down from the pines and scoop up the prepared morsels for breakfast.

My mother was happy. "There," she said. "This works."

⁓

Compared with the rodents, the black bears seemed a lesser, but potentially more serious, pest control problem. On the matter of bears my mother was intrepid—to the point of foolishness, I thought. She told me, "You can't let them think that you're afraid. What is there to be afraid of, anyway? They're not like real bears. They're like dump bears. Big shaggy dogs."

Dump bears, I gathered, are like seagulls that congregate at the dump. They're not *real* gulls if they're not in the appropriate environment: on the shore, catching fish, not eating rotting garbage scraps. Those scavenging gulls are *flying rats*. But the bears my mother chased from our plastic house were in the *woods*—as were we. Don't bears *belong* in the woods? As in the classic rhetorical: does a bear shit in the woods?

During the spring that we lived in the Plastic Fantastic, we had a bear. Almost nightly, as a sort of bold counterpoint to the death throes of the trapped mice, we would hear a clumsy snuffling around the perimeter of the house or an awkward crashing about in the brush, and my mother would leap from her sleeping pallet, push through the hanging wool blanket that formed our door, bang two boards together, and yell, *Go away, bad bear!* Her banging sounded like the staccato hoof-clopping of an enthusiastic kindergarten class playing wood blocks, and not at all like the rapid gunfire she intended, but the bear always went away for the evening. This midnight music lesson became a ritual between my mother and the bear. Perhaps the very fact that this bear participated so complicitly—like a man who always calls when he says he will—caused my mother to lose her respect, dub our bear a Dump Bear. If you're going to be wild, be wild.

I only *saw* our bear once while she was still alive. Late in the Plastic Fantastic spring, I was riding up the path through the aspen grove on my way home from a game of horseshoes with Uncle Mark, who was still living only about a mile away across the draw. As we were about to come around the last bend before the paddock, Moona got skittish and wild-eyed, and I almost lost my seat when she sprang into a jolting, backward dance. I looked down. No rattlesnake. I didn't see anything for her to be afraid of. "C'mon, Moona." I clucked my tongue. She continued to dance. I planted my heels into her ribs and squeezed: "C'mon." Moona, forced, took diagonal steps, tracing around a wide berth, and reluctantly rounded the final stand of trees. The bear was standing in front of the paddock gate, looking surprised but unmiffed. I didn't know who was staring down whom: me and the bear or Moona and the bear. We were still. The bear wasn't as big as I'd imagined a bear would be. She was a black bear, not brown or cinnamon, and about the size of a Newfoundland dog—I was thinking in dog similes because my mother had said, *Like a dog, a dump bear*—but a short Newfoundland, fatter, with sawed-off legs and a patched and mangy coat. All around, an unimpressive beast, but deserving of my respect in a Charlie-Brown-Christmas-tree kind of way, and thinking this, with no conscious feeling of fear for the little bear with the dark nose, dark eyes, I became aware that my heart was beating fast. I looked at the bear, the bear looked at me. I felt the skin over Moona's ribs ripple beneath my legs, although I wasn't squeezing her now—my legs were resting gently on her sides.

We might have stayed this way forever, but the bear snapped the long hypotenuse of our triangle, reeling on her hind legs and running, faster than I knew a bear could move, her rear legs moving up past her round ears as one leg, a wishbone lever attached to the fulcrum of her hairy hips. She tumbled fast down the hill in this bear-adapted leapfrog and was gone.

"Mom," I called toward the plastic house. "Mom! The bear!" Moona exhaled hard, blowing a trumpet of air through her nostrils, and snatched a bite of grass, tearing it from the ground with a jerk of her head, the bear seconds gone and she no longer afraid. "Mom!"

By the end of that week, the bear was dead, shot through the heart by my mom's mountain man, who took aim and fired a clean shot without even standing up from his bed. Bear meat tastes like pork. Not chicken.

⁓

The question, for those of us who have the luxury, is how to negotiate our lives in relation to those of our parents. In my case, how am I supposed to behave—or *not* behave—as the child of an absent father and a free-spirited, countercultural, if-I-had-an-inside-toilet-I-might-miss-the-phases-of-the-moon mother? Do I follow in her footsteps and fix up the cabin on the other side of her property? The cabin that was featured in *Mother Earth News* back in the seventies because it is made entirely out of recycled mill ends? Do I bake bread, soak beans, drink red wine, haul wood for the winter, smoke dope, drain the water hose so it doesn't freeze, and stay away from the rest of the world—the real world, the on-the-grid world—as much as possible? Do I do that—live there and do whatever else I might do—or do I, to use a term that became a part of my vocabulary when I was a teenager living on the mountain, get the hell out of Dodge? Either way, what will live with me always? And what choices do I make concerning my own children—if, indeed, I have them at all? What do I rebel against when there have never been any rules to follow in the first place?

That's not true. There were rules: *Be honest and nice. Don't be wasteful or wimpy or snobby.* Rules for living, but nothing in the way of a plan—no "get into medical school" or "start your own business" or "get married and have babies." *Do what makes you happy.*

In the end, all I could figure to do was go off to school—go to a university, work at a university, go back to another university for another degree, where I am now—and all the time I'm getting farther and farther away from the mountain, and after a point, I can't tell whether I'm still making anybody proud or whether my ascent of the ivory tower has crippled my mountain-going legs.

"Maybe you should try to get a C," my mother told me once. "It'd probably be good for you." This is a good thing and a bad thing.

~

When I was fourteen, Uncle Mark decided I was ready to be his partner at the end-of-the-year horseshoe-tossing competition. He bought me my own set of "competition" horseshoes, dug some pits out behind the house, and told me to practice every day. At first, I was terrible.

The object of horseshoes, of course, is to throw the horseshoe onto the stake at the other side—for which feat, your team receives three points. Counting down from here: two points for a "leaner," and one point for a shoe that is within or closer than a horseshoe length away. (Thus, the saying, Close only counts in horseshoes and hand grenades.)

To this day, I am aware of few sounds more satisfying than the multiple clang of a shoe catching on the stake and spinning around a few times before coming to rest with a happy thud in the pit. The problem was, I tended to throw a vertically aligned shoe, so that when the shoe came down, it caught an edge and rolled away from the pit. Bystanders had to watch their toes. There were still three months until the competition, but things were looking grim for the Uncle Mark/Niecey team. Mark watched me, shook his head, and explained The Flip.

He held his shoe at an angle, a quarter-turn away from the exact bottom of the curve, and when he threw, his shoe flipped through the air in The Arc, rotating smoothly, sticking to the ground when it hit, square-on. Top bottom top bottom top bottom thunk—and when the dust from the loamy earth settled, we could see Mark's shoe embracing the stake like a protective parent.

When I threw, things went badly. I clenched my shoe at the very bottom of the curve, and when I released it, it skidded through the air haphazardly. I lacked form and finesse, and I don't know why he picked me as his apprentice, except that I was a girl, and it was a mixed doubles competition.

But there I was, bathed in Deep Woods Off, trying for The Flip. "It's not a bowling ball, Jill," Mark said. "It's a horseshoe."

Mark held his hands over mine, demonstrated the throw, and we practiced until it was too dark to see the stake at the other end.

I got better—much—and when the tournament finally rolled around, we made it to the championship round and ended up in second place. The winners got a trophy and a bottle of Jack Daniel's, and I got Mark's approval. In his eyes I'd dug my heels into the loose dirt and finally learned how to *do* something. It seemed as though the things that I could do well—school, for example—he'd never cared to do at all. But after that summer, we had horseshoes.

～

Mark was an alcoholic. I know now that he must have been drunk during those late afternoon practice sessions at the horseshoe pits, but he never seemed drunk. He always just seemed like Mark.

～

My mother called me today to let me know that she'll be hosting a party next week—a memorial party for Mark, down by the river, with a barbeque and music and a giant give-away of Mark's belongings. To my mother so much of this dying business has to do with *stuff*. Stuff goes into boxes, and then gets sorted through and moved to other boxes, and maybe along the way somebody says, "Hey, I'd like that particular chunk of stuff," and my mother is relieved and hands the stuff over to that person saying, yes, "Gladly. Oh, *perfect.*" As if matching up the right people with the right stuff will put Mark at peace. Of course, she wants her own peace—if she can clear the stuff out of her house, she won't have to fumble around through Mark's stuff every time she goes into her sewing closet to find a particular length of ribbon for a doll she's making.

The metaphor is too simple, and I've tried to write my way away from it, but there it is: my mother's internal space, the place where she grieves for her brother, is cluttered with stuff to be boxed and sorted and reboxed and bagged and given to someone who will put it to good use. There is that stuff that cannot be given away, even to someone who would treasure it, and there is also that stuff that must be hoarded and held on to and cried over and kept in a box forever and ever amen. My mother hangs on to one of Mark's old camouflage jackets: "I don't care about the newer, fancier shirts. I'll give those away at the river. It's the camo stuff. That's what I think of when I think of Mark." And my mother must know that in sorting through the stuff, she is actually getting the chance to reshape who Mark was: she gives away the "fancier shirts." Those were the shirts that Mark bought and wore once or twice and then put down and forgot about because he was too damn drunk and high to keep track of the little things. Besides, there was money for more shirt-buying, and that's what he did, bought more, and so my mother's Hefty sacks are piled with linen and cotton and silk in bright colors that boast of fat bags of cocaine and plenty more where that came from. "Good riddance," I hear my mother grumble. She will box and sell and give away until she is left with those things that represent the essence of who she wanted her brother Mark to be: an old camo shirt, a mobile of colorful wooden Mexican fish, a musical saw in a beaded leather case.

And, of course, more than two thousand miles away from the mountain, sitting at a desk in Alabama, I will do the same thing: sort, shuffle, and shape until I come up with something that I know I can keep.

~ *Sentencing*

Uncle Mark Writes from Prison: A Ten-Year Sentence in 1992

Three thousand six hundred and fifty days on the wall,
three thousand six hundred and fifty days,
Take one off, weep, go to sleep,
three thousand six hundred and forty nine days on the wall.

~

Jill Writes: A Six-Year Sentence in 1982

The summer that I turned thirteen and we moved away from Plum
Island and followed the westward path that my Uncle Mark had laid
down ten years earlier, I didn't strike out with the lightness and hope
of a pioneer spirit. Before I reached the mountaintop in Washington State where Mark, my mother, and my mother's mountain-man
boyfriend were all waiting, a black curtain fell over my memory, and
I pulled the heavy door shut behind me—I was a bad girl, I was a sick
girl—and I heard the clang of metal falling into metal and making a
fit. Beginning at the age of thirteen, I served a six-year sentence in
the prison of my own body—framed by flesh and desperate to forget
what I had done.

It worked. I forgot the fucking, but it didn't forget me.

~

A Prison Visit

Go north on the interstate for at least two hours, take the exit that
your inmate indicated in his letter (the one in which he told you
that you'd checked out with the FBI, you were on the list), turn left,
and go back under the highway. Now drive. Keep driving. Prisons are

built way out in the boondocks, far away from healthy populations of decent citizens, often near tiny towns whose residents are largely employed by the feds. Do they fear escapees? Do they chuckle at an occasional visitor's projection of such a fear? In any case, this is a typical prison location: the backwater, the boonies, the sticks. Nowhereville.

(I did this when I was thirteen: I took myself far away from those good citizens who didn't want me in their neighborhoods.)

After driving for quite a while, eight miles or more, you'll see the first sign—Federal Correctional Institution—and you'll follow it. Maybe there will be a gas station, some cows, an ill-kept cemetery with tilting stones, and when, finally, it's time to turn in, you'll read a more intimidating sign with bold red lettering that will tell you to stop at the booth. The sign will threaten you. You will, of course, stop at the booth—a booth that looks as unassuming as a common tollbooth on the Massachusetts turnpike. You will see no person inside, you are tired from driving, and although the coffee in the bottom of your travel mug has been reduced to cold and grainy dregs, a thick sweetness—disgusting, really, and no help at all to the dismal state of your mental acuity—you will drink it anyway, in one determined gulp, and still be quite certain that there is no one inside the booth. A sign instructs you to push a red button: *Should I push it? Is this what we do? Do we have to push it?* This is your first time, and you don't yet know all the rules. You don't yet know that, in fact, if you're feeling bold, you can blaze right past the booth, because it doesn't really matter. They can see you whether you stop or not, but this is your first time, so you will have to push the red button. When you do push the button *(can fingers sweat on their very tips?)*, a voice will tell you to list the names of all passengers and give the inmate's number. And beyond—no—and *above* the distinct sensation that you are being watched (of course you are) will be the visual image of long rifles pointed in the direction of your powder-blue Subaru station wagon, taking aim, drawing a bead on your head, and on your mother's head. It is like a movie. You see your head from the outside, the base of your skull where spine meets brain, and superimposed over this image of your own skull: a red, blinking crosshair. The last image, of course, is all in your head. *On your head.*

After the command to drive forward, you do, and you wind past the work camp, where there are men outside pumping huge iron barbells, shooting hoops, walking briskly around a track—it doesn't matter what they're doing, they're going to turn and look at you as you drive past, and some of them will wave, and you will smile and wave back. Of course you will.

You will have the urge to drive badly as you enter the parking lot—smash down the accelerator and squeal into a dramatic doughnut, or at the very least, bump a fender on a guard's car, scream, *What the fuck do you think bumpers are for?* and jam it into reverse, but you don't. You drive like somebody's grandmother (not your own), turning the wheel gently in your fingers as if you are fluting the edge of a pie crust, and you turn into a wide, empty spot, putting the Subaru into the big space with the same delicacy that you would employ to ease that filled pie onto the center rack of the oven. You will slide into your space with no squealing, no crunching, and no cursing. After all, this is not a demolition derby; this is the parking lot of a federal prison. The demolition happens somewhere else. Not here.

(And back to my brain's sentence not to remember, here we are again. In those teen years, after the abuse and before the remembering, I thought I was so much bolder than I really was. I wanted to feel somehow that I was racy and daring and dangerous, when in reality I was scared shitless, and my only blisters of danger emerged in what psychologists call "intrusive thoughts"—for me these thoughts were sort of a Tourette's-like beastliness couched by the *What-if-I?* clause of a terrified teenage girl who would never really act on anything. For example: *What if I smashed my car into that federal guard's car? What if I spit in the face of the guard when he came out to determine how it had come to pass that I'd smashed my car into his car? What if I screamed at him you-mother-fucking-bribe-taking-dick-sucking. . . .* Etcetera, etcetera. Except that I was young, Mark was not yet in prison, and I'd never seen a prison guard. In place of "guard," substitute "old woman with a cane on the street" or "bearded manager at the Italian restaurant on campus." In my mind, no one was safe and nothing was sacred. These were fantasies I didn't ask for and never acted on, but they required constant vigilance and management. What if someday I *did* kick the old woman in the knee or expose my breasts to the restaurant manager when he asked me if I needed more bread? I was not to be trusted. My body had to sit on its hands and keep my restless brain in check—or was it the other way around?)

Securely parked, you and your mother gather up the things that you will need inside—Ziploc bags full of quarters and a driver's license each. That is all. You apply lipstick, and your mother brushes her hair—violently, it seems to you, but this is no time to proffer advice regarding split ends.

You enter through the double doors of the guardhouse. From here you can see the long spans of chain-link fences with their coils of razor wire. The fences are double, and there is a space in between— in that space, you expect a pack of dogs, snarling, drooling even, salivating for the taste of flesh that has been tenderized by an initial pass over the wire, dripping in juices. The dogs you imagine sport fed-issued spiked leather collars with shiny American flag tags. But there are no dogs. Just grass. There is even a sign in front of the guardhouse—KEEP OFF THE GRASS. Green, green, government-fertilized grass. What there is, however, in lieu of Killer and Bruno and the gargantuan Doberman whose name would surely be Jugular—in lieu of these imagined beasts—there are double coils of razor wire at the top of each span of fence; even without the dogs, the place has plenty of gleaming teeth, and before you can stop the thought, you're imagining struggling up over these fences, taking the first one, coiled razor wire be damned, going for it, because you don't really care if you are slashed. Hell, you can hardly feel it. You don't care if you're slashed, sliced, slit to bits, just as long as you get out. And maybe, finally, after years of nothing, you'll feel something. Maybe you'll get out and survive. But then there's the second fence to consider. And, oh yes, the guards in the tower, the red, pulsing crosshair blinking at the base of your skull—they are still there, too.

(During my own sentence, self-imposed though it may have been, I did not know how to leave, nor did I know if the perimeter of my body—my skin?—held the danger on the outside, or whether Killer and Bruno were already on my side of the freckles and fine hairs. I didn't know what was real and what was imagined, and I was paralyzed by this inability to discern.)

Finally, you're inside, and you and your mother each fill out a visitor's form—it's not like being at a doctor's office, where you get the handy clipboard with the pen attached on the slinky ball-link chain. No. You stand at a high counter along the wall where the regulations are posted and carefully fill in your name and his number. Then you select a paperclip from the cup of government-supplied paperclips, attach your driver's license to the front of the form, place your form in the wire basket on the guard's counter, and wait. This is the first in a long series of waits: You will wait for your name to be called; you will wait to make your pass through the hypersensitive metal detector; you will wait in the holding pen beyond the metal detector until there are enough of you to warrant a guarded escort through the central courtyard; you will wait in the second holding pen while everyone runs a stamped hand under a desk-sized black light; you will wait on the other side of the courtyard to do this hand check one more time—but this time the waiting is better, this time you can peek through the glass doors of the visiting room, the place where you've been heading for almost four hours now; you can peek in and see if *your* inmate is there, waiting for *you*, but he never is, since they don't give him the call that you've arrived until after they process your form at the front desk, and then of course, there's waiting to be done on his end as well, proper channels to be navigated— and so you and your mother are finally passed through the visiting-room doors to choose your adjoining plastic orange seats, preferably in a corner, where you can be a little farther away from the cameras, and then you sit and wait for your inmate to come in, thinking, not my *inmate,* no, not number #07157-085, but my *uncle,* my mother's *brother.* Today, he's having to wait a long time to get in. You watch the door, and every time it opens, you hope to see him, hope he'll not look too different from the way he looked the last time you saw him, hope he'll look as though he's been eating, bathing, resting. You could stand up, step behind the red line and into the vending machine area, and begin your wait for the sandwich machine, but now you are too anxious. He could step through that door at any moment, and when he does, scanning the crowded visiting room for you, you want to be right there, watching, ready to catch his eye and move toward him. You do not want to waste all that waiting time by missing that moment. There will be plenty of time for sandwiches.

~

The word *penitentiary* comes from a concept that the Pennsylvania Quakers had in mind when they built prisons where criminals would at once be segregated from law-abiding society and have plenty of time and space to engage in a conscious act of "penitent reflection." This reflection would, it was hoped, lead to personal change. With two million inmates and growing in this country, our concept of reform seems to have adapted to keep up with the changing times (and Draconian sentencing laws for drug offenses): lock 'em up, lock 'em *all* up, and keep 'em there.

Mark had two primary complaints about prison: it is never dark and it is never quiet. Intense, glaring light, and a ceaseless cacophony of discord: metal on metal, man on man. Prisons are loud because they are hard—there is nothing to absorb the sound, except, perhaps, the bodies of the men inside. Mark wore an eye mask to darken his world and earplugs to muffle the sounds of so many men confined to such a small space, but for me this is the point: Mark was always struggling against something. He could never have simply nothing, and you don't get to live in a world that you need to block out.

This is how my own sentence began *after* I was out of physical danger—I must not see, I must not hear, I must not let anything into my body, and above all, I must not remember. I must not know. Not remembering is not a passive exercise. Not remembering is the fastidious application of eye masks and earplugs. Not remembering requires an active refusal to participate in the sensory functioning of your body. This is hard work. This is all-consuming labor. This is at once the most gorgeously adaptive, self-preservative function of the brain that I know, as well as the most destructive. For those six years I lived—but not really. For almost six years, Mark did the same. And worse, I know, much worse.

⌇

I lost many of my childhood memories, and at age eighteen, as a freshman at the University of Oregon, I believed fervently in the construction of empty spaces.

I was skinny, but never skinny enough; one of my greatest pleasures was running my finger between the elastic of my panties and the deep groove beside the jut of my hipbone. I loved that the elastic didn't touch my skin. Yet, despite these delicious hollows in my body, I would hear Roy Orbison's "Pretty Woman" and think how I could never be such a woman because, *walking down the street,* my thighs would rub together, and any man who saw me would turn away in disgust.

I was wrong.

I was promiscuous, but not to the point of penetration—I was, they told me, boy after boy, a prick-tease, a heartbreaker, a bitch.

I hadn't learned, at eighteen, that it was possible to go out drinking and remember. I was accustomed to nothingness, and I didn't know that my black spaces were unusual.

But I was trying to hold my life together. Sometimes, after partying on a weekday night until two in the morning, I'd sneak down to the unfinished basement of my dorm where there was a small laundry area, a giant television, and a stationary bicycle. Lit by the surreal glow of the fluorescent strips above the coin-operated washing machines, I would pedal for an hour, reading Homer or Shakespeare or Beckett—a pathetic, sweaty, teenage girl, alone in a basement, squeezing a bicycle seat between her legs, pedaling hard for the burn in her thighs, going nowhere, thinking to herself: *If I read, if I study, if I get all A's, if I don't eat, if I don't get fat, if I don't pick at my face—if I do all of these things, and I survive, and someday I find happiness, then I will be ready to be happy.*

To me, perfection and happiness were the same—and equally elusive.

~

When my brother was a year old, his skin fell off in my father's hands. When I was twelve, I learned that if I touched the back of my throat, top and center, I could empty out my body, become a frame of flesh for nothing. Sometimes, without eating a bite, I drank a glass of water so that I could rinse myself out. Throwing up, I expelled the shreds that clung to my stomach wall, hung tight to my esophagus. I was sickened by the thought of my own organs, wet and full—large intestine, small intestine, liver, kidneys, stomach, pancreas, ovaries, womb. I wanted to be dry and hollow, and thus my bulimia was a dream for mummification. I wanted to be nothing more than what people could see of me from the outside. I wanted to be so light that I could crumble, blow away in the wind like ash from a cremation fire. The fleshy weight of my human body was unbearable. At sixteen, I scheduled a secret trip to the dentist and had a protective coating put on my teeth to shield them from the acids of my body. At eighteen, my periods ceased and I learned a new word: *amenorrhea.* Without-Month-Flow. For this, I sought no remedy. Drying out, drying up— my bulimia was working.

~

Sometimes when I first tell a story, I make it a fiction. Perhaps after shaping the narrative, I never get back to what really happened. *What really happened?* In the spring of my freshman year, I was invited to California for a weekend houseboat trip hosted by a group of fraternities. My date was five years older, drove a Porsche, snorted coke, sported large biceps and a fake tan, and believed at the center of his puny heart that the world was for sale.

In this story all the facts are true, but the voice is not really mine because I am not this tough. I would like to be that tough.

Okay, I don't really like to tell this story. It's embarrassing. I don't mean to be victim-blaming. I know that's not cool, and I'm not saying that the rape was my fault. I'm not, really. I hate the guy. I do. I truly believe in my heart of hearts, as my mother would say, that if I were actually to run into this guy on the street, you know, I would say right to his face, because I've never had the chance, I would say simply, "You raped me, you asshole." And I would feel a lot better, or I think I would anyway, but even with that, I don't know. . . . I know he wouldn't admit it. He wouldn't. And that would be his reality, I guess. He's had ten years now to chalk up that experience on a houseboat anchored down on the banks of Lake Shasta as good sex, right? Maybe really good sex.

Just as I've had ten years to make my version sound like date rape. Fair enough, I guess. But if I'm the one telling the story, I guess you'll have to be subject to my version. I don't believe in objectivity. I'll just be up front about that.

When I go to talk to high school kids about date rape, and go over the same old rap about true consent, I exaggerate a little. I have to. I'm try-ing to make a point to seventy or so sixteen-year-olds who covet driver's licenses still hot off the laminator and think it's sexy to put your tongue all the way into someone's ear canal. Give me a break.

Believe it or not, the girls are the hardest to deal with. They hate me. So you're saying that if I go to a party in a really short skirt, and I'm flirting all over the place—if I get raped, it's not my fault? *And I tell them that's just what I'm saying. Most of them don't believe me. They want me to tell them it's their fault, because then they'd have something to believe in, rules to follow, reasons the other girls get raped and they don't: Short skirt equals rape. Too much beer equals rape. Unlocked door equals rape. The part they don't understand is that those equations don't stay put. They can expand to take over your whole life until you're sitting in a locked steel box breathing through an air hole and wondering,* Now am I safe?

Before I even open my mouth, these kids think they've got me all fig-ured out. Because I work for an agency run by women, primarily for women, they think that I'm a lesbian. I don't tell them whether I am. It's none of their business, right? But it's a question that comes up a lot:

So are you guys all dykes or what? *Well, I answer, I'd say, statistically speaking, we have the same percentage of lesbians working in our organization as, say, the Department of Motor Vehicles or your yearbook staff—about 8 to 10 percent.*

But the public speaking gigs come later. The thing that still really gets me about this guy who raped me is that the morning after, when the boat docked, he walked up into town and came back with a paper bag of Dunkin' Donuts: cream-filled, jelly-filled, powdered, plain. At least two dozen doughnuts, and he said to me, "Here, Jill. You get first choice." So, eight hours before, he's got a pillow stuffed in my mouth and he's riding me into the berth on this fucking houseboat in the middle of a lake, and then he's got the nerve to give me first choice on doughnuts for breakfast.

The actual rape doesn't stick in my mind. It sticks to my body but not to my mind. I do remember that I didn't fight hard enough—I didn't bite off his earlobe and spit it in his face, I didn't jam my bony knee into his testicles with all the force of my eighteen-year-old body, I didn't leap to my feet and ram a well-placed heel into his knee cap. I pleaded, then cried, and finally I screamed for help, but I didn't hurt him back—and that's what I regret.

The last thing I remember is the pillow in my face, and when there wasn't air enough left for my screaming, thinking breathe, breathe, breathe.

~

Fork You: Real-Life Therapist #4

WINTER 1995

I've had only one male therapist in my life, and he loved to hear about my dreams. I suspect now that he got off on them somehow, because he was always asking about them.

Last night, I dreamed that I was walking across the university track field, taking a shortcut to my car. This man grabbed me. Actually, I know who it was. It was the guy who owns the frozen yogurt shop down on 13th

Street—it was him, it looked like him, but it wasn't him, you know? Somehow I knew that he was going to rape me and then kill me. He didn't say anything in the dream. I just knew. I had a fork in my backpack that I'd used to eat my lunch, so I slid my hand around, undid the zipper, and pulled out this stainless-steel fork. So, he's attacking me, and he won't stop, even though I keep stabbing him and stabbing him with this fork. That was the most vivid part. I can still see it in my head when I close my eyes. I was stabbing him in the bare chest, and I really had to thrust the fork in hard to make it go through the skin and into the flesh. Occasionally, the fork got stuck, and I had to wiggle it back and forth to pull it out so that I could stab him again. The fork made small puncture wounds in his chest, but he didn't bleed. I don't even remember hearing any kind of hissing or sucking sound through the holes. Wouldn't you think that there would be a sucking sound at least? And no blood. It was weird and awful. It takes a lot of conviction to stab somebody with a fork, you know. And he just wouldn't stop. All I wanted was for him to stop, to run away. . . .

"No, you didn't."

"Yes, I did. I'm telling you."

"You wanted to kill him."

"No, I didn't. I just wanted him to leave me alone. He was going to kill me."

"You were going to kill him."

"It was self-defense!"

"You dreamed that man attacking you, so that you *could* kill him. You're like a volcano getting ready to erupt. Deep down, you're simmering. This is the rage you feel for all men. You need to recognize your rage. Let it come out. Explode. You wanted to kill the man in your dream."

"That's not true. I'm telling you, it was self-defense. It's my dream, and I'm telling you."

"Women do bad things, too, you know."

"Yeah, I know. Do you have any other insights to offer today?"

"You know what?"

"What?"

"I've never had to tell a client to fuck off before."

"Is that what you're telling me?"

~

Things Overheard on the Inside: An Excerpt from Mark's "Jail Talk" Journal

I hate kissing. Just sit there kissin' a chick and don't get no piece of ass. Drive me nuts.

~

Take 2: Real-Life Therapist #4

SPRING 1995

"You need to admit that you're sexually attracted to me," he said.

"Why are you always trying to get me to admit things?"

"Because you're in denial. The most important relationship in your life right now is the one you're having right here in this room. Until you recognize that, you're not going to get anywhere."

"I'm not sexually attracted to you. Not at all."

"You see? That's just it. You are, but you don't know it. You can't see the little ways that you try to seduce me."

"What the hell are you talking about?"

"You use your sexuality, *right here in this room,* to get what you want from me."

"What do you think I want from you?"

He didn't answer me. Instead, he wrote something on his legal pad, moving his hand in large, dramatic strokes. He tossed the pad down onto the rug between us: SEX IS IN THIS ROOM.

"For you, maybe," I said.

"For you, too," he said. "When a man and a woman sit alone together in a room, there is always sex. I'd like to hang this sign on the wall in here, but I can't."

"No kidding."

"But I want you to remember this sign every time you come into this room. You don't need to feel guilty about your sexuality. You just need to recognize it. It's not your fault, but it is your responsibility."

~

There's more to the rape on the waters of Lake Shasta than I fit into the doughnut narrative. I was not so good. Before the rape I'd eaten some mushrooms—not too many, but enough—and when they began to kick in, I snuck away from the hordes of drunken Greeks, climbed over the rocks bordering the thin beach, scraped up through the thick brush of the hillside, and finally found shelter next to what seemed at the time to be a fantastically magnanimous scrub pine. From my elevated perspective I could see a few bonfires burning red on the bank of the lake, and the twelve or so houseboats moored in the cove bobbed menacingly like a flotilla of dark crocodiles.

The night was hungry, but I was well hidden. I watched my "date," the man who I knew even then would rape me that night. I watched him as he moved from boat to boat to boat, up and down the bank, looking for me, screaming my name, yelling, *Where is she? Where the fuck is she? Who's she with? Who'd you see her with?*

I was with nobody, alone on top of the hill, but I knew that when I came down, I would be caught, so I stayed under the tree: two o'clock, three o'clock, four o'clock. The mushrooms wore off, and I was tired, so tired and so cold. When I didn't see him anymore, I crept back down to the boat. This was my thought: if I am in bed, if I am in bed and sleeping when he finds me, maybe he will let me sleep. I will sleep until tomorrow when this boat will return to the dock and I will be safe. But when he found me, I was not safe. They will wake you up to rape you.

The fraternity brothers on the boat where I was raped had assigned me a nickname for the weekend. *Carcass.* How could they have known me that well—those stupid, drunk boys on the boat? *Carcass.* This had been the goal of my bulimia, and I should have been happy in my bare bones. I crawled inside ribcage arches and wrapped my fingers around the bars. Clang-clang-clanged my empty tin cup.

Rattled the cage of my own body. I was eighteen. Before Colin, before Prozac, before the memories came to flesh my bones. There are no pictures.

In Fishkill, New York, in my grandmother's attic, I went through the picturebooks, nibbled raspberry jelly doughnuts swaddled in powdered sugar, and tried not to smear the plastic pages with my gooey fingers. In the beginning I loved doughnuts, and the white doughnuts that surprised me with their sticky-sweet fillings were my favorite.

I have learned not to love those deep red surprises.

A 1988 Excerpt from Jill's Journal

Memoirs of a Bulimic
    a verbal collage of its tastiest moments
    *just emerged from a frenzy peaceful again look in the mirror
pull up the shirt is it flat? suck it in more is it flat? hollow? good
wipe off the toilet you're still a mess vomit on the rim wipe it off
on the floor clean it up throw it all in the bowl flush oh, yes all
gone hidden gone in a whirl of water I love that whirl of water why
can't I have something that would do that for my life uh oh does
it smell? will anyone be able to tell? brush your teeth twice rinse
well drink water spit now your face look at it God, when will you
stop? you're pathetic swollen eyes puffy everything vomit on your
chin did you pop any blood vessels? that happens, you know did you
know? look at your right hand still slimy lines of saliva, and vomit,
running from fingers to wrist lines drawn by the ridges of your
teeth? are the scars worse? one little white line on the back of your
hand, only ¼ of an inch long glows livid with the fever of the binge
a permanent record beside it, a smaller scar more of a puncture
wound don't forget the spoon next time use the spoon who knows
what it does to the back of your throat stainless steel sometimes you
bleed your urgency but at least it won't scar at least it won't give
you away wash your face again cold water it feels good you're clean
again all rinsed out you look at your face still in a trance it seemed*

like a dream at least it's done for a while walking home from the
restaurant you needed it so bad you hoped that nobody would see
you you knew that they would know what you had done people
would know you had eaten eaten too much eaten fat in public,
your eating habits are usually flawless you can replenish your body
during moments of sanity friends, friends help, the ones that know
anyway today didn't help and she knows too you joke about it she
thinks you're controlling it because you're not afraid to talk about
it French onion soup, bread not hungry to begin with chocolate
mousse, coffee with cream might as well at this point can't keep all
that greasy cheesiness down anyway might as well make it worth it
besides, coffee will make it easier and more water, too all that bread
is going to be tricky want to get it over with go on with your life

~

A little girl named Martha, six years old, walks into the bathroom
just as her mother is flushing a nest of baby mice down the toilet.
"Mother! What are you doing?!" The baby mice writhe in the toilet
water like lively pink slugs. The mother presses the shiny, metal handle down on the toilet. The water in the toilet spirals gently, spinning
the mice around the perimeter of the bowl, lining them up like ducks
in a row, and slowly, too slowly, sucking them down the drain. The
little girl is horrified. "Mother!" She starts to cry. Cries for a week.
Won't talk to her mother, who asks practically, "What? They were
under the refrigerator. What did you want me to do? Bottle-feed the
little worms until their little necks were big enough for me to catch
them in a snap trap? No, thank you." My grandmother, the mother
in this one, loved to tell this story.

From my grandmother's picturebooks.
Jill at age one.

I was nineteen when I met Colin, and with him, for the first time
in my life, I grew hungry for memory to light my dark places and
appetite to flesh my bones. But the day we met wasn't spiritual, and
it wasn't love at first sight. I like to tell myself that our bodies were
processing faster than our minds.

It was the day before Thanksgiving 1988, and I'd gone to San Fran-
cisco with my new friend Dyan (who is now my closest friend and
has had the good sense to revert back to the original spelling of her
name, Diane), and her little girls, Courtney and Haley, to visit her
parents and various holiday-attending siblings. We spent the eight-
hour drive from Eugene speeding along in a red Toyota Camry named
Portia, singing Indigo Girls songs—*I'm trying to tell you something
about my life / Maybe give me insight between black and white*—eating
Teddy Grahams (which at that time came in only one flavor—and of
course, I was *counting* each bear), and playing random road games.
"I went to the Albertson's, and I bought apples, bread, candy. What
comes after candy? Don't tell her! Shut up, Court-neeeeeeee! I can't
remember! Dog food. Dog food, eggs. . . ." Haley was only four, so
we had to keep the games simple and the stereo cranked. *The best
thing you've ever done for me / Is to help me take my life less seriously,
it's only life after all.* . . . "Haley-bo-baley. . . ." *Well, darkness has a
hunger that's insatiable.* . . . "Banana-fo-fana. . . ." *And lightness has
a call that's hard to hear.* . . . "Fee fi mo maley. . . ." *I wrap my fear
around me like a blanket.* . . . "Haley!"

Traveling in this manner, we didn't reach the house dug into the
side of the hill in San Rafael until after midnight, and everyone was
already in bed. I knew as we tiptoed around the downstairs bed-
rooms that Dyan had brothers, but I didn't know, well, that Dyan
had *brothers.*

On Thanksgiving morning I dragged myself up the spiral staircase. I was wearing cut-offs and a T-shirt, and my hair was twisted on top of my head and skewered into place with a pencil. When I rounded the final curve of the climb, I saw Colin, who was wearing faded Levi's—and nothing else. Naked from the waist up, he was holding Haley and a mug of coffee almost as big as she was. Our eyes locked in a moment of fireball candy lust that I wish I could reconstruct here as love. I gripped the railing. The room buzzed. I got wet. Colin seemed to lose his grip on the coffee and Haley at the same time. There was some awkward juggling, but he regained hold and Haley squealed, "Jillian!"

Colin and I raised our eyebrows at each other wordlessly: *Damn, you look good. Thanksgiving, indeed.* Then came the bad dialogue.

"Hi," I said, smirking, intentionally breathless.

"Hi," he answered, bending his knees and bringing Haley's little feet down to solid ground without unlocking the grip of his eyes.

"I'm Jill," I said. Haley's swinging feet gained purchase and she trotted down the hall, toward kitchen noises. We were alone at the top of the stairs.

"I figured. I'm Colin."

"Yeah. I figured. Dyan told me about you. Sort of."

"Yeah. Me, too. I mean, she did, too. Told me about you." He paused. "Sort of. Umm. Coffee?"

"Yes. Please. Coffee. Coffee would be great."

It was only 8:30 A.M., and I was already feeling grateful—except that the day was much, much too long. Colin and I danced around each other all morning: a short hike with the girls, a drive to the gas station, a game of cribbage on a board carved from the tusk of a walrus. In the afternoon, he brought me an endless chain of vodka cocktails as we lounged around in the study—I pretended to read a book and he fiddled around on his acoustic guitar—to demonstrate the reach and sensitivity of his long fingers, no doubt. It worked like a charm. Dyan would later report gleefully that she had heard a ruckus from her bed around midnight, a ruckus of such range and magnitude that she had thought somebody was spinning an unbalanced load in the washer. It wasn't love at first sight—it was lust, it was sex, and I swear I'd never done that before, not on the first night like that, but it was just fine.

I sailed my ship of safety till I sank it, I'm crawling on your shore. . . .

And then, despite our lascivious beginnings, it wasn't long before we were talking three or four times a day on the phone (he was living in San Diego, and I was in Eugene), swearing our love for each other, wishing in that first love way that we could forgo the laws of physiology and inhabit the same body, settling instead for long, earthly visiting weekends of perpetual lovemaking. But now, up against this other person, up so close, my crazies really began to show. I was still puking all the time. I couldn't stop. I'd always thought that I would stop when I wanted: when I was skinny enough or smart enough or happy enough.

> *There's more than one answer to these questions pointing me*
> *in crooked line*
> *The less I seek my source for some definitive*
> *The closer I am to fine.*

Colin wanted me to get some help, any kind of help, he didn't know what to do for me, and because I wanted to be someone he could love, I agreed.

∼

So, on a wet, early spring, Eugene day, I locked my bike to the rack and went in for my first appointment in the University of Oregon's Student Counseling Center. I marched into the softly pastel office, sat down in the spot nearest the Kleenex decorator box, and got right down to it: I was depressed, all-the-time tired, I couldn't stop puking, and I didn't understand it. I was in love, after all. Wasn't I supposed to be happy?

There should be a photo of this: *Jill's first time on the couch, March 1989.*

The psychiatrist met this first question with a professional gaze that was at once bemused, concerned, and utterly disinterested. She was fortyish and tailored—smartly accessorized with a gold-plated pen and a shiny black clipboard. (Since she was my first, I'll call her Dr. A.) As I babbled on about food and sex and the gray, gray Oregon skies, Dr. A scratched the shining pen across her pad and made noises in her throat. I was, as yet, unacquainted with the therapeutic animal and her habits. I could only do what I'd seen other nutcases on television do—talk. I felt strangely comfortable, as if I were acting out the part of a troubled teen in an after-school special. Eating disorders, I was learning, were a taboo that you could talk about. Wrong, but racy. *I know I should keep some food down, but it feels gross. I eat cereal in the morning and do okay. No fat. 100% Bran with skim milk. I can't do lunch. Usually I have a frozen yogurt cone on campus because it's pretty slippery and easy to throw up. Tortilla chips are the worst. Have you ever thrown up tortilla chips? They scratch your throat. At least five times a day. Not including drinking water and throwing up. Sometimes I just want to feel rinsed out. Like washing your face, but inside your body. I feel best when there's nothing in my body. Washed out. I can see it: clean and pink.*

I didn't like the way this doctor gripped her golden pen, so I didn't tell her all I knew about the girl I had become. I didn't tell her how, when the girl showered, she would marvel at the streams of water as they ran down the hollow places in her body: tracing the relief of her ribs, dribbling over the bowls of her hips, finally sliding down the straight lines of her thighs. She saw these bones, felt their sharpness like a lover, and still she felt too big. When she washed her hair, it fell out into her fingers in clumps. When she looked in the mirror, she stared for hours at the strange girl with the swollen eyes—eyes webbed with fine, red lines, vessels burst by the unnatural pressure of blood rushing to the head.

I didn't tell the sharply dressed woman all this, but I did admit that I was tired—very, very tired.

At the end of the session, Dr. A tapped the thin barrel of her gold-plated pen in a staccato rhythm against her clipboard, and scribbled something onto her pad, saying, "This is a prescription for Prozac. It's relatively new. They're just starting to use it to treat eating disorders. I'm giving you two weeks' worth. Let's see what happens." She warned me that I probably wouldn't begin to notice the effects of the Prozac for at least a week.

~

In the mirror the next night, I stared into pupils that had melted and spread into warm, inky pools, reflecting dual images of a stoned-out nineteen-year-old in their glossy finish. I couldn't feel my feet on the bathroom tiles. Reaching out with my hand I pressed my warm fingertips to the glassy cheek and thought she was beautiful. I hadn't remembered her so beautiful and whole.

Distracted by the mirror, she forgot she'd gone into the bathroom to vomit. She brought her hand away from the mirror and concentrated on her feet, trying to find them, reground for walking. Ricocheting from skin wall to skin wall, inside a body quivering with sensory perception, she step-by-stepped back to her room and wrote this:

March 3

Day two of my new life—an unnatural life fueled by Happy Pills—but a good life, a more productive life, a thinner life, a brighter life, a life of acute perception—sights, smells, sounds, all are clear again. I love the way I feel—the calm feeling, never in a frenzy to purge, in control of my eating and my feelings, stronger during workouts—but I'm suspicious, and wary. I didn't bring on this happiness through my own strength. My psychiatrist (doesn't that sound yuppified?) gave me a prescription for a new anti-depressant that increases the body's natural production of serotonin, which allows messages in the brain to bop across the synapses smoothly—equivalent to the endorphins released after a workout. It feels like starting every day with a mini-dose of Ecstasy—not a bad prospect, admittedly, actually it's quite fun, but a little worrisome and unnatural. We'll see what happens—I sure do feel good. I

like people again, I can concentrate, I haven't binged/purged, on
and on, but *my pupils are dilated and I feel a little too giddy—in*
the first couple of hours, I'm downright euphoric—*it's amazing*
that happiness can emerge through the adjustment of a chemical
imbalance in one's system—amazing—hmmmm. . . . Looking to a
previous page: My life is now satisfying. I can't really explain it to
Colin. It's nothing I've done. *But how long can this last? I feel out*
of touch.

~

"Well, that's not exactly accurate, Jill. Prozac doesn't increase the
production of serotonin. It inhibits reabsorption."

"Yeah, I know that now."

"Is that what she told you?"

"I can't remember exactly, but I think so. I remember thinking that
my brain was just pumping out this happy serotonin stuff. I pictured
it like strawberry syrup—all this pink, happy goo, lubricating my dry,
gray brain. I think I'd remember if I'd pictured it like a traffic cop,
blocking the little serotonins from reentry."

"Your metaphor seems off to me. Not syrup. Not sticky like that.
Prozac is a *clean drug.* That's what's so great about it. You should have
just felt better, not drugged."

"I felt drugged."

~

Things Overheard on the Inside: An Excerpt from Mark's "Jail
Talk" Journal

Dude's name is Poison 'cause of the shit he deals. It killed a couple
of guys. That was funny. But I swear, that shit's worse than the
sauerkraut they give you here.

~

Prozac had been approved by the FDA only a few months before I
started taking it, but even so, I knew at least five other women in the

Honors College at Oregon who had also picked up prescriptions for happiness at the student counseling center. We kept extra green-on-white capsules in our lockers side by side with the heavy, red *Riverside Shakespeare*, Aphra Behn's *Oroonoko*, plastic spoons from the yogurt shop, Tylenol, tampons, and toothbrushes. We were smart and crazy, but I wasn't throwing up. Not anymore. Not two weeks into it.

Dr. A was thrilled—as thrilled as a woman with an affect as flat as Kansas can be—that is to say, her gold pen scurried across her pad like a mouse on the trail of a hunk of extra sharp cheddar. As a case study, I was golden. Actually, everything was golden—the sun, the spring leaves, the glint off passing bicycle spokes. In my first month on Prozac I could spend an hour studying the perfect concavity of a spoon, or I could jam out a five-page "A" paper. For as high as I felt, I was an academic machine.

I began to believe that maybe there really was something to Dr. A's theory of chemical imbalance. By my second therapy session I had gone for days and days without puking. I definitely felt better—or, if not *better*, certainly *different*. I'd lost that sharp edge, and sometimes I even felt weirdly giddy. I thought: I can do this. Just keep those happy pills coming, and I can *do this*. Continued therapy wouldn't be necessary—just the script, please.

During my second session I learned that Dr. A was of a like mind. I was probably smiling, grinning ear to ear, when, in an effort to keep up my side of the therapeutic dialogue, I told Dr. A that when I was able to get to sleep—which wasn't often, but it didn't seem to matter, I didn't need that much sleep in any case, not with the pills, but when I did get to sleep, it wasn't for long, because I was having these wake-up-sweating nightmares about this man trying to get me. Maybe to rape me, I couldn't really tell, but he was definitely *after* me. Typical dream stuff: my feet are leaden, and the floor looks like the rug I had in my room when I was little, the gray one with the pink roses, but my feet sink into it, up to my ankles, as if it isn't really the rug, but quicksand, and I'm trying to run, to get away, but I'm so heavy, I can't move, I'm sinking and my thighs are aching from the effort to unstick myself, so I try to hide instead, to roll under the bed, but no matter how I tuck and pull, part of me pokes out—a finger, a foot, my hair. I can't get small enough, so he always, always finds me, no matter where I try to hide, he can always see me, and I'm sinking again, and even though he can see me, I'm being covered up by my own looped rose rug, and I'm suffocating, I can't get a breath. . . . and sometimes, I told Dr. A, sometimes when I wake up I'm screaming, and my nightgown is so drenched in sweat that I have to change it.

The golden pen slapped twice against the clipboard—providing punctuation, this time, not rhythm. Then Dr. A took a deep breath of her own before speaking.

"Have you ever been sexually abused?"

⌒

Binding and Grinding

A description of the process called "rat synaptosome," or "binding and grinding"—a technique that was used in the development of the antidepressant Prozac:

> The synaptosome promised to be immensely useful in neuro-biological research. You might, for example, pretreat a rat with imipramine, allowing the drug time to bind to nerve endings. Then you could kill the rat, grind up its brain, centrifuge and separate out the nerve endings, and produce an extract that was still active—still worked like the terminals of living nerve cells. You could then expose this extract (the imipramine-treated synaptosomes) to a neurotransmitter, such as norepinephrine or serotonin, and see how much of the neurotransmitter was taken up. This procedure almost defied belief—you could more or less blenderize a brain and then divide out a portion that worked the way live nerve endings work. (Peter D. Kramer, *Listening to Prozac*)

⌒

"Have you ever been sexually abused?" Dr. A repeated loudly, as if sheer volume would help me to understand.

"What? What do you mean?" This wasn't my shocked denial speaking. This—as hard as it is for me to believe now—was a genuine question: *What is sexual abuse?* It was only 1989. People weren't talking about sexual abuse, at least not in my world.

I guess she must have told me. I can't remember what she said, but she told me. More questions, I think. Did your father ever touch you in a way that made you feel uncomfortable? Did any member of your family ever. . . ? Of course not, of course not.

And I said, "No. No. This is just a dream I'm having. It's just a dream."

She scribbled something down with her golden pen, and I noticed how the light from the overhead reflected off the sleek barrel, so pretty, as if Dr. A could write with pure light. When the pen stopped dancing, she was still for a miraculous moment, studying me, and then, for reasons I understand even less now than I did then, she decided to share with me her fiscal-based theory on the role of psychotherapy in an undergraduate population: "In most cases, Jill, I would stop this line of questioning about sexual abuse right here. First and foremost, I am an employee of this university. As such, my primary responsibility is to the university. My job is to keep students functioning well enough to stay in school. If a student can't handle dealing with the issue of sexual abuse in her life, I am not benefiting that student or the university if I dredge up memories that will only incapacitate her further. In most cases I would simply treat the symptoms and let the cause wait until after graduation."

But I must have been a special case, because after her explanation, Dr. A continued matter-of-factly to brief me on what a *history of sexual abuse* could do for me in my life—apparently, childhood molestation would explain it all: fear of intimacy, binge drinking, low self-esteem, and of course, the bulimia. She suggested that perhaps the guilty culprit was my father. She didn't use any magic truth serums, nor did she suggest hypnotherapy, but barring this, she personified the greatest enemy of the False Memory Syndrome Foundation—an evil planter of false memories.

"No," I said again. "No. That's not possible."

Satisfied, Dr. A refilled my Prozac prescription.

~

Not far into April, the childhood that my grandmother had ordered so precisely in the picturebooks began to break apart—it was as if my brain had taken up a pair of scissors and started hacking away at the plastic pages. Pictures were flying everywhere, floating down through the air like drying leaves, collecting in messy piles on the floor of my apartment, especially in the hallways, the places of transit, the places where no real living is done. I tripped over them on my way to the bathroom to puke.

Only a few weeks into my Prozac reprieve, I was back to my old tricks, only now I wasn't sleeping, trying not to sleep, oh my God the dreams—and more sweat than I knew my body had moisture. Where was all that pink, juicy Prozac? I was drying up, drying up, falling off myself. This is just a dream. This is just a dream.

Soon, the dreams didn't care whether I was sleeping or awake. They came anyway. In between the page where I stood high on the green ladder beside my grandmother's tree to pick cherries so red they were almost black, and the page where I unwrapped an Uncle Sam coin bank, a gift from the old Binghamton aunts, I was in a dark room. It was too dark to see his face.

And here, I disappoint: there is no epiphany to report, no single rush of crystalline memory. It was a confusing time. I remember shaking my head a lot. Hard—as if I could break something loose from the edges, or rattle it all away. I knew it couldn't have been my father. *He's not a monster, Jill.*

One day I knew that the dark room was ***'s garage. A neighbor. My brother's friend. Everybody's friend. A young man who apprenticed at a blacksmith's shop in town. A young man who once came to our rescue during a bathroom flood by drilling a hole in the floor and letting all the water drain down into the dry sand beneath the house. A young man, my mother had said, who was clever and good with his hands.

I was six when it started—and almost thirteen when we moved away.

And then this: I was not the only one in the dark room. Not always. Sometimes there was a boy there, too—two years older than I was. I knew him still. I knew him well. He was twenty-one and living not far from our childhood home.

Colin was the first to suggest that I write to him.

And I thought, yes, I will write and ask: Do you remember? I'm going crazy, Jake, and I need to know: Do you remember? Am I making this up? I wrote a letter, a letter that was more of a list, beginning, *These are the things I remember.* Strip poker. Peppermint schnapps. Double handjobs. Double blowjobs.

Dr. A said, "No. Don't send it. It's fine that you wrote it, but don't send it. He won't answer you. Either he won't answer you or he'll say that you're lying. Don't send it."

"Why," I asked Colin on the phone that night, "why would he lie to me?"

"Will he?" Colin asked.

"No," I said. "He won't. If he remembers, he'll tell me."

I sent the letter. Jake's reply came within two weeks. He told me that he had never forgotten any of it.

﹏

"Jill. You're in a dark room. You need to touch everything in the room, but there is no light. When will you know that you're finished? When will you know that you've touched everything?"

"I won't."

"Why don't you turn on a light?"

﹏

Three months later, Colin and I had moved together to Seattle, and my new therapist—Dr. B—scolded me for going off my meds and told me that I quit because I wasn't getting enough. On only twenty milligrams per day, I'd dropped below the frame of my "therapy window." Double that to forty milligrams per day, and I would be a girl framed by her own therapy window: talking, making progress, staying on my medication. "What if the frame falls down again?" I asked.

"We'll up the dosage," she said, matter-of-factly. "We'll keep you in that window. We'll bring you up to meet it."

I was nineteen. I was young. I didn't know any better. Before Prozac, I had never entertained a suicidal thought.

⁓

"Oh, come on, Jill. Who did know better? Prozac was just out on the market."

"So, you're saying, even if I had known better, I would have got the same thing?"

"What would you have done if you had known better? Refuse all drugs? Are you saying that what you got from the doctor at student health and from the psychiatrist in Seattle was bad therapy, just because they prescribed drugs?"

"Bad for me. I don't remember any therapy, only the drugs."

"Standard practice, I'd say. Prozac was making life easier for everyone."

"Yeah, right. Including the psychiatrists, right? Everybody thought she was hap, hap, happy again. Nobody was calling up the emergency line in the middle of the night, I'll bet. We just sat home smiling at ourselves in mirrors, and trotted in for our regularly scheduled appointments to get refills. That's the way to make a living, eh?"

"I thought you were miserable."

"I guess it didn't work on me. I kept falling out of my 'frame.' I was the kind of crazy girl who hid meds under her tongue and pretended to swallow. I was prone to the cold turkey method of getting off drugs. But I have never placed an emergency call to a therapist."

"Well, here you are, ten years later, so apparently Dr. B in Seattle did something right."

"Thank you very much. Excellent point. Do you think that the second voice in Sarraute's *Childhood* was a voice inside her head, a kind of inner critic, or someone more like you?"

～

—Don't be angry, but don't you think that there, with that cooing, that chirruping, you haven't been able to resist introducing something a little bit prefabricated . . . it's so tempting, you've inserted a pretty little piece . . . completely in keeping . . .
—Yes, I may perhaps have let myself go a little . . .
—Naturally, how can one resist so much charm . . . those pretty sonorities . . . cooing . . . chirruping . . .
—Yes, you're right . . . but so far as the little bells are concerned, no, not there, I can hear them . . . and also the rattling sounds, the rasping sound of the red, pink, mauve celluloid sails of the toy windmills, revolving in the wind. (Nathalie Sarraute's autobiography, *Childhood*)

～

The therapeutic relationship can act as a frame. Once you get comfortable in it, secure around the edges, you're stuck there. You're jelly without it. I don't want to live in the Smucker's jar. I don't want to pay someone to hold my edges together—the very financial arrangement cracks the glass, and I'm oozing my strawberry red.

∾ Picture This

Memories can boil you alive. In the summer of 1989, Colin and I got our first apartment together—a Cracker Jack box in a complex near the Seattle airport that boasted "all the amenities": a pool, a Stairmaster, the audio-enhancement of low-flying jets, and a little deck with a view of a hundred other little decks. We were the first people ever to live in the apartment. It had no history or memory of its own.

Colin was on the crew of Virgin Lightships, a British blimp company, working out of Sea-Tac, but I was too medicated and unstable to work. I never knew when the next memory would come in for a landing.

The best simile I can think of involves LSD. The final time that I dropped acid, I had a bad trip. I was at a festival, in a big crowd, and it seemed as if everyone there was reaching for me, tunneling toward me, trying to touch me. I started to cry. I knew this not because I could feel myself crying, but because, when I held my hands to my face, it was wet. I couldn't stop. My mother was there, and she tried to comfort me. Everyone felt responsible, and I listened to them talk all around me: *How many drops did you give her? I don't know. Two, three, tops. I can't even feel it. Jess didn't even know I dropped.* I could access the part of my brain that processed what they were saying, and I wanted to tell them that I was okay, because I *knew* that I was having a bad trip, but there was no way out. I could think, but I couldn't control the sensory input. No matter how many times I blinked to clear the tears, and my vision, the decorative sparkles on my mother's face were still pocked excavations, the fried chicken in my friend's hands still crawling with maggots. *Sparkles, fried chicken,* I told myself, but I still saw holes in my mother's face and a geyser of maggots. Then my mother touched my arm. I screamed, and when she pulled back her hand, chunks of my flesh hung from her fingertips. I moaned, and she touched me again. My flesh fell from my bones like forked meat from an overcooked pork roast. I couldn't be touched.

This is what recovering memories can be like, with one crucial difference. On acid, I still inhabited a corner of my brain. I could say to my mother: "Don't touch me. When you do, it looks to me like you're pulling my skin away." I knew my flesh was still intact. When the memories came, I wasn't sure. I didn't know.

At night, in our brand-new apartment, Colin and I often slept with all the lights on, and the white, unsmudged walls were four blank movie screens.

    ~

I may be losing my skin again. Might I, like my brother has done, grow it all back someday? Rough, but thick? In the thirty-five years since the burning, Ian's skin has thickened, formed hills and hollows, bridges of taut flesh from his shoulder blades—his back is a topography of the thoroughly healed and unconcerned. My brother's scars don't bother him. They are part of him. Why am I the one tempted to pick at my scars? Bring the blood to the surface? Peel back everything and look underneath?

You are in a dark room. You have to touch everything. How will you know when you are done?

I won't.

Why don't you turn on a light?

    ~

I was alone a lot, because Colin was either working or sleeping. For the first time in my life I had nothing to do, and it was driving me crazy. But here was the catch: I was too crazy to do anything. I tried to do temp work, but after my first day typing envelopes and invoices at the plant—I can't even remember what they were making there, car parts or office equipment—I cried and cried and cried. I was terrified to go back, and Colin convinced me to call and quit. It wasn't worth it. We could live without the money. So I decided that my job was to get better, to stop being so crazy. I spent days by the pool, even though the sun never seemed to shine that summer, and in the clubhouse, climbing furiously on the Stairmaster for as long as my legs would move.

The Stairmaster was in this funny little glass closet, crammed in with a weight bench and an exercise bicycle, and I would have felt self-conscious, but I remember thinking that no one could really see me in there. I was invisible.

So I sweated, and I slept and cried, and that was that. I tried to be a decent homemaker-type, but that just made matters worse. Cookies! I'd think. I'll bake some Tollhouse cookies, and wrap them up, still warm, for Colin to take for his midnight snack. It's the least I can do, and I'll just save a few for me, for a treat, and of course, ten minutes after Colin had shut the door, I was on my knees by the toilet, thinking about softening up the butter for a whole new batch.

～

Somehow, through all the memories and the drugs and the puking, I was the girl that Colin loved. To sleep with her, he had to adjust to sleeping with the lights on, or he would wake up to screaming: in the dark, the girl would forget he was there, and the innocent flopping of his big arm in the night would become an attack. In the dark he would change skins with the bad guy—like the chair with a laundry-pile head, a whiffle-bat tail, and teddy-bear eyes that was still a monster in the corner of her childhood room, no matter how violently she shook her head, blinked hard, chanted: *No monster. No monster. No monster.* Colin darkened his eyes in the crook of his elbow, learned to sleep with the lights on. He loved her. He wanted to marry her. Crazy girl with the bright blue eyes and the dark places in her brain. Here was someone who needed him. *Shhhhh. Shhhhh. It's me. Just me. You're okay. I'm here. Shhhhh.* When memories would come, he encircled her with pillows, removed sharp objects, and waited with her for the memory to pass through her body like a seizure.

～

No photos here. Forty milligrams of Prozac didn't pin me in my frame. I was throwing up again. While we were living in Seattle, Colin didn't let me go into the bathroom and close the door. *How terrible!* you say, *what a control freak.* But you know, it actually helped. I couldn't do it when he was watching. The less I did it, the less I needed to do it. Like smoking.

~

Colin moored the blimp with his body. Rope around waist. In the photo he looks bored and too cool. A blimp is soft sided, a malleable form born aloft by helium gases. Lighter than air, it floats away if nobody hangs on to it. Pressure is important to a blimp—too little and the blimp will sag, too much, and the material is stressed. Pumped full beyond its expanding capacity, the blimp could burst, bright advertising colors flying everywhere, scraps of a birthday balloon stuck with a pin. When we lived in Seattle, Colin sometimes spent nights at the airport, babysitting for the blimp. Hourly, he checked her pressure. She was lighter than air. In between checks he sat in a trailer full of gauges and logs and played his guitar.

She was a little girl. Six, seven, eight, up to twelve, who *screwed* regularly with a neighbor guy young enough for her to pretend he was her boyfriend—thirteen, fourteen, at almost twenty he was pushing it, and so was she. She played house, and she must have felt okay about it, although she knew that she could never tell, and although he did, once or twice, mention that he could kill her, not that he necessarily would, or even wanted to, of course he wouldn't want to, but that he could if it ever came down to that, or if he were to change his mind. He cut weapons at the metal shop where he worked—throwing stars and knives mostly—and at home, in the garage where he liked to take her, he mixed up powders and stuffed them into casings. Explosives were his hobby.

As a prank, he and her brother fed an M-80 to her Baby Alive, a doll who didn't know the difference between chicken-colored powdered food mix and a small bomb, and so she chewed obediently—she had been built to chew and to shit, that was all—and when they lit the wick as it disappeared down her throat, she didn't know to stop chewing. When the M-80 detonated, her head was blown off, and the rubbery plastic skin that had stretched across her hard plastic skeleton blew apart also, splitting into ribbons of doll flesh and rolling back upon itself like a latex glove snapped off a surgeon's hand.

The brother says that the sister is wrong, that she is exaggerating on this point: there was no peeling of skin. Her head was not blown off because the explosive in question was smaller than an M-80: *We didn't even have a plan to blow her up. We put one of those ladyfinger firecrackers in her mouth because we thought it was funny that she would eat it. But when she kept chewing, and the wick was left hanging out of her mouth, we lit it, and she kept chewing. There was this muffled thump and a puff of smoke came out of her mouth.*

She never ate again, but her head wasn't blown off. She was just a little black around the mouth.

～

"The next year I asked for a new Baby Alive doll for Christmas. I can't remember exactly how old I was. Around ten. But my mother said she thought that it was silly to get another plastic doll. Why couldn't I ask for something practical, she wanted to know—like a baseball bat? Something I could use. She said that I was too old for a Baby Alive. Too old. I was ten! Now I'm almost thirty."

"Did she know what happened to the first doll?"

"No. I don't know. I don't think so, no. Nobody likes a tattletale."

⁓

Things My Mother Says

Jill, nobody likes a tattletale.

If you pick up as you go along, maybe you'll find what you're looking for. It's like a reward.

Look, it's fun. It's like a puzzle. (A tidbit of overseer sagacity applied to a multiplicity of tasks: loading the car for a trip, fitting broccoli into a small vegetable steamer, packing the groceries into the cooler, etc.)

It's good for you, Jill. It builds character.

One year. Just give it a chance for one year, and if you can't stand it, we'll try something new.

Beginnings are never easy, except in love.

The key is low overhead. If you have a low overhead, then you don't need to make a lot of money.

You can't let them know that you're afraid. What is there to be afraid of, anyway? They're not like real *bears. They're like dump bears. Big shaggy dogs.*

My criteria for a man are that he be adventurous and skillful.

⁓

Sometimes memories are stored raw, like undeveloped film. The input data are there, light and dark through the flash of an aperture, but nobody has processed the pictures. When I was nineteen, eating Prozac for breakfast, and keeping my head out of the toilet, the rolls started to develop. My brain traffic had thinned out enough for me to make it to the neural photo lab with those exposed rolls that I'd been hiding in the underwear drawer of my brain. The prints that came back had been missing from the picturebooks for all these years, and I had no narratives to accompany them.

> Van der Kolk suggests that one reason why traumatic memories may be difficult to consciously recall in a narrative, episodic form is that they were never stored in such a form in the first place. Further, he suggests that in some ways traumatic memories may be more accurate than nontraumatic memories, because of the nature of the memory stores for the two different sorts of memories. Traumatic memories, according to this viewpoint, are not reconstructed narratives as are most memories, but the reactivation of undistorted sensory and affective traces. (Jennifer Freyd, *Betrayal Trauma: The Logic of Forgetting*)

So perhaps my gesture is fitting, but the metaphor is inaccurate. Unprocessed memory is not a still photo. When it comes back it's more like raw film footage. Uncut. Uncoded. Not filed in a labeled canister. In playback, nothing is rated to protect a young audience. There are no subtitles for a lost language. Moreover, you get to be the star, but you don't even know that it's you. Roll film.

The smoke is thick and flavored like spice, and it's not totally dark because when the little girl isn't squeezing shut her eyes, she can see the bottom of a wooden shelf where there's a sticker that says in block letters—ARE YOU STONED OR STUPID?—and she never answers that question because something comes between her eyes and the sticker, blocking her view, but here the camera angle is strange and tricky; at once it's the top of his head, dirty blond, shaggy, and greasy, and then the side and a hand removing a pair of thick-rimmed plastic glasses and thrusting them away, toward the lens, and then from the bottom up, where his face is close to her face, no head now, and this shot comes with sounds (heavy breath) and smells (smoky, heavy breath), as stale and solid as his words. *Doesn't it feel good? Do you want it harder? Can you take it harder?*

Jake was there, too. He never forgot. I stopped searching the black space. Jake held the memories for both of us. For this I love him so much I no longer know how to talk to him. I don't know what to do with him or the things that only the two of us will ever know, no matter how many ways I write it down.

When we were still children, I saw the patterns he made on his forearms with the tip of a razor. Two years ago he was arrested on a beach in California for possession of heroin, and everyone except me was surprised when his ten-year addiction was revealed: What did they expect him to do with what he remembered?

I have enjoyed the protection of my own dark spaces.

～

"What if Jake is lying?"

"What? Why? Why would he lie about that?"

"Why not? He's your hero now, isn't he? A bit of a savior? Everybody likes to be a hero. *Oh yeah, that happened. What you said.*"

"What's wrong with you? Why are you saying that?"

"Because you think he's some kind of knight in shining armor who came in on his great white steed, swept you out of confusion and recovery, and deposited you on the righteous, secure side of healing. No questions asked. You gotta ask questions, Jill."

"Of course he's not lying. He's not lying. He couldn't be lying because he knows things that he wouldn't know if he hadn't been there."

"And who's corroborating his story?"

"I am!"

"If you are, then why can't you just do it on your own?"

～

It is hard for her to believe in the truth of a memory in which she sees her wrists tied to the bedposts with tube socks. In the memory— a memory so fragile that she can crush it into dust with the grinding of her mind—she stares through the mingling smoke of incense, candles, and pot, at that sign she will read a thousand times and never answer: ARE YOU STONED OR STUPID?

She is old enough to read, but not old enough to know why he likes to lick her toes, lick her thighs, lick her belly button. In her mouth his tongue is dry and thick and smoky, like a piece of charred meat that she could bite clear through. But she can't make her teeth come together, and she doesn't have any words to push him away, so she spreads lips and legs wider, while her memory snaps shut like a trap on a rat.

Over time, the rat's flesh rots. Patches of coarse, gray hair fall away, and the flesh loosens and dissolves. The smoke—from the pot, the incense, and the candles—cannot cover the stink. In the end, the toothpick rodent bones are brittle and easy to break.

~

In Seattle I lived mostly in my head. Sometimes, at dinnertime, Colin would sit me up on the counter with a drink and hand me little jobs to do: peel the garlic, squish the hamburger into round patties, flip the marinating chicken every five minutes or so. He made me spend time in the world—with him and with food, but after dinner, when he put on his red Virgin T-shirt and left for the airfield, I'd go back inside. During that time, I still thought that I had to remember everything—and I believed nothing that I remembered. I didn't know that my first summer with Colin was also my last summer with Colin. If I had known, maybe I would have tried harder to be present, to live in the world with him. Instead, a figure apart from myself, I haunted our lives. We wanted to be a great love story, but we had plot problems.

FRAMED BY FLESH FRAMED BY PHOTO FRAMED BY FLESH

FRAMED BY PHOTO FRAMED BY FLESH FRAMED BY PHOTO

As the family record-keeper, my grandmother chose images, glued them to black paper, slid them into protective sheets, bound them between two hard covers, and put them on a shelf: chosen memory. I've noticed that photos with cake props are near-givens for selection: the one-year-old at her first birthday party, hands, face, hair, body, smeared with crumb-clotted icing; the child with the first self-baked cake, presenting it proudly to the camera, to the photographer; the nuptial couple posing, hand over hand, with a knife carving the first wound in a many-tiered cake.

Cakes are important props in American family albums. We love cakes.

Of course, not all the cakes make the cut. I'm thinking of cakes chewed but not digested, the heavy chunks settling in the indentation of the ceramic bowl, thick sediment for bottom-feeding fish, while the icing, made frothy by the additions of saliva and stomach acid, perhaps a scant teaspoon of each, foamed to soft peaks by a fast trip up the esophagus, not *whip* on the blender button, but *expulsion*, and this one-time buttercream is now froth on the surface of the water, clinging to the edges of the bowl, clinging to itself in floating clusters like pond scum. This is the bulimic's cake: you have your cake, of course you eat it, too, but that is not the end of the process. Expulsion. This is a cake that is missing from my body, missing from the picturebooks: *Toilet Bowl Cake—Jill, ages 13–19.*

~

A recent study by Cloitre and others (1996) suggests that women with a history of childhood abuse are particularly skilled at selectively following instructions to remember, leading the authors to speculate that a strategy for coping with abuse "may be enhanced remembering of designated events (e.g., information not associated with abuse) rather than forgetting of traumatic events." Consistent blockage of information about abuse could presumably lead to profound amnesia. (Jennifer Freyd, *Betrayal Trauma: The Logic of Forgetting*)

~

During my first summer out of high school, I enrolled in a video class at the Savannah College of Art and Design and made a short film about bulimia. I thought nobody knew that I was making a film about myself. Except that the film wasn't about me, even. The film was about the *image* that I thought everyone else had of The Bulimic— if, indeed, they had one at all. I didn't want to exhibit any special knowledge about bulimia, because then I risked giving myself away. My take, I decided, would be one of quiet concern and outrage at a fundamental social problem. I did some reading. I discovered that I was unusual in that I never technically binged. Purging was more my deal. I'm not so much into stuffing as I am expelling. One frozen yogurt cone was always enough for me to vomit—I didn't need a whole carton of ice cream. But for the film, I needed a binge scene, or nobody would get it. Who would get "The Bulimic" from a girl running into the bathroom to puke up a peanut butter sandwich? They'd all think she had the flu or something. Where was the drama in that? The buildup? So I went to the Hostess bakery thrift store and bought two bags full of day-old pastries: Twinkies, Ring Dings, Sno Balls. The storyboard ran something like this:

1. close-up of girl's face (wild-eyed, maniacal, stressed out)
2. full-body frontal shot—girl is framed by the kitchen door, scanning the kitchen
3. jump cut to her watch: 4:30
4. shot from behind the girl as she opens all of the cupboards and starts pulling out food (Twinkies, Ring Dings, Sno Balls)
5. splice cupboard-emptying shot with zooms on individual packages of food (as if from her singular perspective)
6. shot of all the assembled food on the counters (emphasize scope, quantity)
7. bingeing scene: alternate shots of two-handed mouth-stuffing with food close-ups
8. shot of girl leaning against the counter, hands on stomach, all the food is gone, and the kitchen is strewn with empty cellophane wrappers
9. close-up of watch: 4:45 p.m.
10. pan shot of girl going into the bathroom
11. back shot of girl falling to her knees in front of the toilet and retching
12. close-up of the girl's face—she is flushed, and there is saliva on her chin; she wipes it away and smiles into the camera. Her expression is conspiratorial
13. final shot: the end of a toilet flush, clean water whirling down the drain, the bowl is shiny, clean, porcelain-white

Thinking about it now, I note obvious problems in the film. Who in the world would have cupboards packed with day-old Hostess products? Certainly not a bulimic. If a bulimic *did* bring dozens of little cakes home, they certainly wouldn't make it from the bags to the cupboards. Also, the point of view is wrong. The perspective is constantly shifting from the girl to some unknown watching eye. (Me watching me? The dissociative aspect? I can't imagine that I was being that clever.)

But this is the thing that gets me: When we were finished filming, my brother's girlfriend left. She took her well-placed mole and her model-thin body with her. I picked up the cellophane wrappers and threw them away, and then I was left with this enormous pile of broken Hostess cakes. Then I did something that I have never done before. I ate them all. At least twenty little cakes. I ate until I was purple in the face. One shoot, and I had become the bulimic I constructed.

~

What the memory researchers can't answer: Why wasn't the slate wiped clean? Why am I not the tabula rasa of the sexual abuse survivors' club? I've read a lot of research on repressed memory and dissociative disorders. I've run studies. I know too much ever to serve on a jury, and yet, if Jake hadn't been there in the beginning to tell me it really happened, I might not believe it, either. It doesn't make sense. If I could remember sitting at the bar while my mother worked, eating cherries and peeling the flavor sacks of juice from the orange rinds, why didn't I remember lying flat on my back on a mattress in a garage? Pinned beneath the tripod of two arms and a heavy torso?

~

The danger of simulation is that we are not consciously aware that we are not seeing. The advantage is instantaneous comprehension, a valuable tool for survival. The disadvantage is that simulated vision has as its source only what has been programmed into our computer: past knowledge. It is incapable of new vision—of creativity. Simulated vision is anathema to the visual artist if not recognized and kept in its proper place. (Keith Smith, *The Visual Book*)

In third grade, Mrs. F, the art teacher, taught us how to compose a face. The ones we made were all wrong, with eyes floating on foreheads, ears sprouting from jaws, and lips pouting like bows on birthday presents or draped across chins like suspension bridges. Mrs. F taught us about proportion. Draw an oval for the face. Over the oval—lightly, carefully, so you don't tear up the paper when you erase—draw a vertical line down the center, and then divide the oval in half again with a horizontal line, so that the face is cut in four equal chunks.

You have laid down the grid and you are ready to work. The eyes don't go so high. You have to leave room up top for the forehead, the bangs, *the brains,* right? Draw the center of the eyes, the pupils, on the horizontal line in the middle of the face, one on either side of the vertical line. Leave the whole top half for brains and hair-do's. Now run your finger back from the outside corner of your eye. You'll end up at the point where the top of your ear attaches to your head, so you know that you want to attach your subject's ear on the same horizontal line as the center of the eyes. The bridge of the nose begins at the intersection, the mouth goes beneath, and voilà. A face (see figure A).

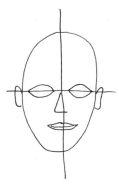

Figure A

I have three primary subjects in my doodling repertoire: a flower, an Arabian horse, and a female face.

The flower came first. In fifth grade, I copied a flower from my reading workbook. I don't remember what story it was for or why the workbook had a flower in the margin or why we even had workbooks for fifth-grade reading class at all, but I do remember liking the flower, and doodling a copy of it into my notebook. I've been doodling that same flower since fifth grade, and while I've always conceived of my flower as a rose—insofar as I thought about the subjects of my doodling at all—I can see that it's a sort of hybrid between a rose and a carnation (the most manipulated flower of all, a neutral, white bread flower, with porous petals, doomed to be dyed to take on the colors of high schools and holidays). My flower is a horrible thing (see figure B).

Figure B

The horse head came next. Sixth grade, I think. My only real childhood girlfriend, Amy, taught me how to draw it. Together, we were horse crazy. In addition to collecting Beyer's plastic horse models, we took riding lessons, and regularly sneaked into a field near her house to attempt to catch, and mount, the fat, mean pony that lived there. When it turned out that the pony was fat because she was pregnant, and subsequently gave birth to a foal (the missing of which event caused both Amy and me great pain), we were beside ourselves with delight. We would train him, but we would have to be sneaky; our time with the ponies was a forbidden pleasure. We told no one. At eleven, I'd been groomed for secret-keeping. If Amy had been similarly conditioned, she wasn't telling, but I know we told no one about the ponies in the field.

Amy lived near my father's house in Connecticut, so I only saw her in the summer—three months out of every year. In the winter we were pen pals, and she sent me envelopes stuffed fat with her own drawings of Arabian horses to decorate my walls. She taught me to draw the horse's eye in the shape of wishbone, not lemon-shaped like a people eye.

Amy and I were young enough to imagine that we would grow up, never marry, and live together on our own Arabian horse farm. She would ride a gray, and I a black. So determined were we to have our shared wish come true, that we once ate a bay leaf each because Amy said that this was better for wishes than being the one to find the leaf in her lentil soup. We ate our leaves straight out of the jar, dry and brittle, washing down the sharp pieces with gulps of cold water, not bothering to chew, trying to sweeten the bitter fragments of green with the lip-licking promise of pastures filled with blue grass and fine, fast horses. . . .

Amy's older sister overheard us discussing our plans one afternoon as we cantered our plastic horses around an imaginary dressage ring framed by d-ring belts, and she hissed through the crack in Amy's bedroom door, *Lesbians!*

Shut up! Amy screamed at her sneaking sister. *Get away.*

I was twelve when I saw Amy for the last time, the summer before my mother moved us to the mountain in Washington. We were both crying as we hugged goodbye. *Don't I get a kiss?* Amy asked. Yes. The last I heard, Amy was living in England on a horse farm, breeding and training dressage horses.

For almost twenty years I have drawn the tapered nose, the flaring nostril, and the wishbone eye, just as Amy demonstrated, and now when I draw it, I begin unconsciously, always in the same order—forehead line, from right to left, nose slope, muzzle, jaw, nostril, lip, eye, ear, forelock, neck, mane, finishing up with a single accessory: the halter. This activity is so unconscious, a memory belonging to my fingers, that I can only draw the horse head facing in one direction. But when the head is there, staring leftward through its single wishbone eye, I sometimes pause to shade the nostril a little darker, and I think: *Amy did it. She really did it* (see figure C).

Figure C

Some time in seventh or eighth grade, soon before we moved to the mountain, a substitute teacher came to our junior high art room with a pile of fashion magazines. Our assignment was to look through a magazine, find a face, and do an enlarged pencil sketch of the face that we chose. Mrs. F: *Fill the page. What's over here? Nothing? There's nothing at all over here in the corner? Go all the way to the corners. Fill the page.* Mine was female, and so heavily made up that I wore my pencil lead flat using the edge to smudge in her dark eye shadow and the blush of her dramatic cheekbones. The image stuck, and the margins of my school notebooks became peopled by a composite physiognomy born of Mrs. F's grid face and the magazine woman. I have drawn this face more often than the flower and the horse put together. I begin with the eyes, moving the tip of my pen from eye to eye for each element: football-shaped outlines, round irises and pupils sporting triangular reflections of light, drooping lids, and fringed lashes. The nose and mouth appear in their descending order, and the oval of the head is drawn in finally to contain the floating features, with special attention to a sizable, one-half forehead for brains, hair, and sometimes hats—an attempt to disguise the pronounced shape of the skull. Without fail, I end with a necklace or scarf to encircle the pencil-thin neck. Accessories vary. Eyebrows are optional. Lips are invariably closed tight. I can't draw male faces (see figure D).

Figure D

My father has covered thousands of pages with coffee mugs, hands, and teaspoons. Morning warm-ups, sketched before anyone else is up: curves in handles, grooves in fingernails, puddles of milk in a spoon's mirror. He shades them all into depth.

In 1988, the last summer I ever spent in the same city as my father, he told me that if I gave him a week, he could teach me to draw better than my brother, despite Ian's dual degree in illustration and computer animation. The key to a good rendering, he said, is to discard all the preconceived notions we have about the shapes of things and really look at them. All our lives we're fed shapes: stars with triangular points, human noses like a ramp turned on end, cat faces with whiskers like a broom. But none of these things really look like that, he said, at least not all of the time. But once we get it into our heads, the image is stuck there. To demonstrate his theory, he showed me how to forge a signature: It's nearly impossible to forge a signature by looking at it straight on and copying a version beneath. The reason this doesn't work is because our brains and our fingers want to form that first capital P the same way we've been forming that capital P for years, so even if we try to copy what we see on the page, our own P creeps into Pete's P. The trick, then, is to turn the to-be-forged signature upside-down. Think of the signature as a curved and crossing line, not a series of letters. Your brain doesn't know what this thing is, so it can work with your hand to craft a facsimile. It's the same with drawing, my father told me. You just have to *look* at what you're drawing, not at the paper. *Give me a week,* my father said.

I never gave my father the week (we don't give each other much), and my brother scoffed at the proposal when I told him about it *(Dad said he could teach me to draw better than you—in a week),* but every time I draw the head of an Arabian horse, which I have been drawing for twenty years now, with the circle jaw and the wishbone eye, just the way Amy taught me when we were eight, I know: *This is not a horse. This is my drawing of a horse head. You don't even know what a horse looks like anymore.* I am reminded of this also whenever I gaze up at a starry night sky. First, my eye sees the picture I've been given since my first peek at good-night storybooks: a black sky decorated with white (or yellow) star shapes and a cut-out crescent moon. In order really to see the sky, I have to tweak my brain manually. I have to say: *Look.* And then I see, or think I can see, the ever-expanding universe highlighted by a three-dimensional moon partially in the shadow of the earth. Not a page in a kids' book, but really the sky. If I don't concentrate, my brain falls back on the image that it has been given: flat cut-outs on black construction paper made huge.

My father has sketched thousands of coffee cups, cups standing alone, supporting a spoon, or held by the hook of his left forefinger: Was each coffee cup *that* coffee cup? That's the exercise.

~

For my twenty-first birthday my mother framed a painting that I had made in Mrs. F's art class: a tempera painting on thick-grained manila paper the color of sand. The painting depicts a girl with a fistful of daisies standing with a snail-headed butterfly at a mailbox. She is a canary-yellow blond, and you can tell it's not a bleach job, because I used the same yellow to render the matchstick fringe framing her robin's-egg-blue dot eyes. A jaunty cherry-red hat juts out behind the circle of her skull. Her nose is a hollow circle, the same blue as the eyes, and the mouth is an inverted red arc. In other words, she is smiling hugely. I know this is a self-portrait, despite the yellow hair, not at all like my brown, because the girl is wearing a Pepto Bismol–pink

T-shirt emblazoned with hazard-orange bubble letters: JILL. Yellow hair, eyelashes, tulip, and sun. Red hat, daisies, mailbox, and mouth. Green stems, tree, butterfly snail-head. Orange JILL, bicycle shorts, butterfly wing dots. Pink T-shirt and butterfly wings. Only one color in two shades—blue: eyes, nose, and flowers. Flesh is the final color. Color explodes from corner to corner. That was Mrs. F's first lesson: *Fill the page.*

Some things I remember like yesterday, without a picture, but maybe it's a composite. Did it happen one time, or fifty? I know I was very small.

I know how big I'm getting by Grammy's belly. When I get to her house, I run to her and stretch my arms as far as I can stretch around her. I turn my head to get a better reach, and my cheek presses against the solid slipperiness of her dress. And it's nice to be here because I know it's Grammy's house. It smells like Grammy, and I breathe deeply, and she calls me Sweetie and says something about You People How Were the Roads and then Umph That's a Squeeze, and I wiggle my fingers on both hands but I can't touch finger to finger, and I let go. Nope, I say. Not Quite, Grammy says, but Close. Not Too Close, Mom says, and she gives Grammy a squeeze too. Umph You People Are Going to Squeeze the Stuffing Out of Me.

~

Here's one memory I know I created from a photograph. *Photographs promote forgetting.* Walt Disney World, Orlando, Florida. I am three, and my brother is seven. There are painted wooden stocks set up for photo opportunities. My brother locks his head and hands in place, strikes a pose, the lugubrious pose of a prisoner, wrists hanging limply, and someone snaps a picture. I tell this story as if it's my memory. I claim that I yelled, "Get him out! Get him out! He's stuck in the stockade!" (My brother's part: "Stocks, you idiot.") I explain that I was more upset by this than I was by my trip through Magic Mountain, and my mother's story of me there is one of ceaseless screaming. I say that I mistook the stocks, with its hole for Ian's head, for a guillotine. The propellant of my memory is my concern that Ian was going to die, lose his head. I want this memory because it demonstrates my concern, even at age three, for the welfare of my brother. I can't find this photograph. I see this memory in the frame of a photograph. I have decided that I created the memory from the picture, but I can't find the photo, and this disturbs me. Perhaps I created the photograph from my memory.

~

After I graduated from college, I worked for three years in a psychology lab at the University of Oregon in Eugene. In the lab we studied the way memory works.

Until just about the time I started working there, the lab had been primarily a cognitive research lab. The main area of study was something called representational momentum. In the simplest of terms, "rep mo" is the effect of moving something forward in your mind, because your mind has registered this forward-moving effect, even once the object has stopped. This mechanism explains how a leopard, for example, is able to anticipate the continued motion of the antelope she is hunting and pounce in the right place. In other words, the momentum of the antelope is represented in the leopard's mind, and she is able to predict where the antelope will be microseconds in the future. I spent a lot of time in a small, dark, stuffy room struggling to program an ancient Hewlett-Packard computer in Pascal for a rep mo experiment in which a glowing, green birdie flew around the dark screen in a circular path. After flying around a couple of times, the birdie would stop, disappear, and then reappear in one of seven "test" positions. The subject's task was to push one of two keys: "different" or "same." I would sit in this darkened room for hours at a time, watching the subjects repeat variations of this task for a mind-numbing number of repetitions; as you've probably gathered by now, the subject would misremember the final position of the birdie several positions farther along the path than it actually was when it stopped. After a day of six to eight hour-long sessions, I would misremember my name and have a raging migraine headache in the bargain.

The lab was run by Dr. Jennifer Freyd—that's Freyd like the chicken in the bucket, or the way my brain would feel after watching the lighted pixels of an animated bird scurry around a circular path all day. If you read newspapers and watch television news, you might know the name. The year before I was hired on in the lab, Jennifer, who had already begun to develop her theory of "betrayal trauma" to explain abuse-related amnesia, regained her own memories of having been sexually abused by her father, Peter Freyd—who vociferously denied Jennifer's allegations. Jennifer's mother supported Jennifer's father, asserting that if there had indeed been abuse in their house, she certainly would have been the first to know. Thus, the family was divided, and in what was initially purported by the elder Freyds to be an attempt to reunite their family, they joined together with psychologist Ralph Underwager to form a national association called The False Memory Syndrome Foundation. FMSF is a group dedicated to spreading the message that most allegations of childhood sexual abuse are false. For the record, there is no such "syndrome" listed in any edition of the *Diagnostic and Statistical Manual of Mental Dis-*

orders. In any case, no matter what their motives, the elder Freyds clearly had a vested interest in silencing both Jennifer and the research we were doing into the cognitive underpinnings that might explain the repression of traumatic memories. Memory is political, whether you remember or forget, believe or don't believe, and in that lab, we dug in on the frontlines of what was dubbed by the media the "Memory Wars."

∿

J. Geraci [the interviewer]: Is choosing paedophilia for you a responsible choice for the individual?
R. Underwager: Certainly it is responsible. What I have been struck by as I have come to know more about and understand people who choose paedophilia is that they let themselves be too much defined by other people. That is usually an essentially negative definition. Paedophiles spend a lot of time and energy defending their choice. I don't think that a paedophile needs to do that. Paedophiles can boldly and courageously affirm what they choose. They can say that what they want is to find the best way to love. I am also a theologian and as a theologian I believe it is God's will that there be closeness and intimacy, unity of the flesh, between people. A paedophile can say: "This closeness is possible for me within the choices I have made." ("Interview: Hollida Wakefield and Ralph Underwager," *Paidika: The Journal of Paedophilia*)

∿

When I quizzed my brother about the incident with my Baby Alive doll, he fired back with this exhaustive inventory of teenage weaponry: "We used to make bombs made out of butane canisters and gun powder with a cannon fuse—we'd seal up the end with wax, and perforate the outside of the canister, so when it blew up, there'd be shrapnel. We'd make them in ***'s garage, and then we'd usually take them out into the dunes to blow them up—sometimes we used fuses, sometimes electrical detonation, and we'd usually have something to destroy—plastic army guys or Coke cans or something. Sometimes, we made tennis ball cannons, and they would shoot them up really high, but every kid I knew was into the same stuff, even with the explosives and the weapons, you know? Clubs with spikes, bobos, throwing stars, brass knuckles. . . . Now they've got Quake, so kids can rip people's heads off on the computer instead. It's just directing violence at imaginary enemies or intruders. It's not like for us it was about killing people, you know, it was just about the excitement of how big a hole we could blow in the ground."

Her head wasn't blown off. She was just a little black around the mouth. And she never ate again.

My brother's burning didn't make him afraid of fire or water or spreading molten lava—not that he ever encountered an active volcano, but if he had, he probably would have tried to poke a long stick into the glowing liquid fire just to see how quickly it would ignite.

When Ian was about fifteen, my mother had a boyfriend whose truck had blown up on the Plum Island bridge in Newburyport, Massachusetts. My mother told me that when he climbed from his burning pickup, he was on fire. Nobody drove up the bridge to help him— they just stopped their cars at the bottom and gawked: *Look! A man on fi-ya! Oh my gawd. He's on fi-ya!* I heard that after the explosion he had walked down the bridge alone to get help, and for all these years, I have pictured him staggering down the bridge, blazing with flame, legs stiff, hair and coat and shoes aglow, arms stretched straight in front of him, a combination of Frankenstein's monster and the wild-headed Heat Miser from the holiday special. But I suppose that's not possible. That's not a walk you could survive, and he had. He didn't look that bad to me, but my mother insisted affectionately, lustily: he was a *changed man.* Being that close to death had changed him, he said, and she believed him. He'd found a certain kind of spirituality. They had a shared experience, my mother mooned—she and the man who had been on fire had both known what it was to burn. Adding to my mother's theory that our lives and the burned man's miraculously preserved life were inexorably linked was this strange fact: the truck conflagration happened on July 22—the same date Ian had been burned.

I can't believe that even still I'm such a bitch about this—I mean, that poor man, I'm sure he *was* changed. What a terrible thing. But I never liked this guy—before or after the burning—and I always had the feeling that he knew I was onto him. The burning had changed him, of course, but it did nothing to alter the fact that he was a chauvinistic prick and that he mirrored in both stature and demeanor the big-balled tomcat he brought with him when he moved in. My live-in man vote was for the red-haired fisherman, but he'd already sold his boat and headed west in the school bus.

Man and cat were my dual nemeses. Rough-coated and tag-eared, the cat had a perverse, hip-swinging strut undoubtedly produced by the wide arc his rear legs needed to take in order to accommodate his gargantuan kitty testes—with each step, a rear paw flicked sharply to the side in a kind of testosterone two-step. He was a loathsome, smelly, arrogant beast who actually had the cajones to spray on my pillow one afternoon when I was at school. So while I was battling the cat *and* my poor mother, who was responsible for bringing the cat into our house in the first place, the man who had survived the burning truck was trying to help my brother come to terms with his identity as a burn victim.

Ian would have none of it. One afternoon the boyfriend asked Ian to join him for a support group meeting—to help him cope with the scarring, other people's reactions to him. Ian refused to go. "Why should I?" he said. "I don't have any problem with it. I've always had scars. So what?"

⌒ Isolated Monkey

An observation from the famous Harlow monkey experiments: "When normal monkeys were introduced to the isolated monkeys, the isolated monkeys withdrew to a corner or rocked back and forth for hours. If a normal monkey approached an isolated monkey, the isolated monkey would sometimes bite itself until the normal monkey would leave it alone. The isolated monkeys' problems continued into adulthood." (Jennifer Freyd, *Betrayal Trauma: The Logic of Forgetting*)

Acting out. The worst thing I could possibly say to my brother. Circa 1976.

> *I wish you had died.*
> *What?*
> *When you were burned. I wish you had died.*
> I can never take it back.

Acting out. The worst thing I could possibly say to Colin. Circa 1989.

> *I wish you would just leave.*
> *What?*
> *I'm not worth it. I can't do this. I wish you would just go.*
> I can never take it back.

Acting out. The worst thing my brother could possibly say to me. Circa 1998.

> *I don't want to talk about it, Jill. I don't want to think about ***. I don't even like to think about when we were kids anymore. Before you told me, I thought it was fun.*

I hear this, and I want to scream. I get off the phone, and I scream and scream.

There are gaps in the fairy-tale love story that Colin and I shared. Holes that I, as the in-love and well-loved narrator, can tumble through if I am not careful. Colin is still alive in this story. He is not yet a dream.

The Prozac calmed the bulimia, but still things were bad—still I was feeling phantom flesh pressing onto my body in the night, still my corners were filled with malevolent shadows, still my mind was echoing with voices and a buzzing, a scratching, a cacophony of noise that I could hear but could not understand.

Without the bulimia I was without outlet. I didn't know what to do to feel better. Throwing up wasn't good enough anymore. I did what I did with the blade from the blender that afternoon because I didn't know what else to do. I was carving sentience into my flesh, needing to know if I could feel the cut. I did not want to die.

When Colin found me with the blade, and the lines on my wrist, the flesh parting reluctantly, and the blood, just a soft trickle of blood, we both cried. I don't know what else there was to do. Threats and promises do nothing when you're just looking for a way in. I was reminded of the grade school playground game with the name I can no longer remember: Wimp or Coward or Pussy. Something like that. This was the game: Find an opponent. Press the fingernail of your pointer finger into the flesh on the back of your other hand. Rub up and down. The fingernail should be aligned vertically, so that it serves as a cutting edge, not just a scratching one. Begin rubbing at the same time as your opponent. Don't stop. Don't stop until the blood comes to the surface. Don't stop until you are digging into raw flesh, rub after rub. Don't stop. Don't stop. Don't stop until your opponent stops, and when she does, you win. This is the game I played with myself and the blender blade on a day in late October 1989.

I did not want to die. In two weeks, Colin would be dead. I would not.

~

On that day, Colin and his visiting family—sisters and brothers and nieces—were over in the field across from our house playing soccer in the sunshine. I stood at the window and watched them playing: running for the ball, tackling one another, rolling in the grass and laughing and laughing and laughing.

I remember a feeling of panic and this thought: I must cut myself. Not for the blood, not the blood, but for the opening.

The chef's knife from the kitchen drawer wasn't sharp enough. Hardly made a dent in my flesh. Sharp. Sharp. What will be sharp? I ripped open cupboards and drawers in the frenzy of the search, testing every blade on the soft flesh of my inner arm. Dull. Dull. I lifted the lid off a stainless steel Oster blender.

Inside, the three joined blades bloomed like a menacing tulip. Gorgeous. I reached in and touched the tip of my finger to a sharpened petal. When I pulled my finger out, I saw a red ball of blood growing. I locked myself in my bedroom. Plucked blossom. Sharp blade. Happy family in the sunshine.

I can read my scars as I can those on my brother's body. The blender scars are no bigger than a couple of short lengths of dental floss. There are two, on my left wrist. I am right-handed, so of course I used that hand to angle the blade, aim the blade leftward. The two lines are perfectly parallel, which I can appreciate still, but one is so short—only half an inch long. Much shorter than the other line. These lines on my body are tiny. I did not want to die. They glow white when I am cold, making me afraid of myself and my impulse to carve entrance: a raised, luminous warning not to let anything, or anyone, stay for too long. When my skin is warm, these scars are nearly invisible, and just today, ten years later, I remember what Colin said to me as he held me, crying, "I'm sorry. I'm sorry. I'd forgotten how bad it could be."

～

I loved to watch Colin's hands, especially when he was driving—the fingers of his left hand curled loosely over the smooth arc of the wheel, the fingers of his right hand draped over the gearshift as insouciant as Sunday afternoon sex. I used to tell him that I wished I could slip parts of my body into that shifter—fingers, belly button, tongue—to feel that hand on me.

I have a picture of Colin's hand on the steering wheel—in an envelope, not in an album. In the window behind him I can see through the reflection of his profile to the road beyond. I can see right through him.

~

As a child, Colin liked to draw pictures of big trucks and boats. He liked things that went fast. The interesting thing was his method. He began at the front. Drawing a truck, he would begin with the beam of the headlights, and work his way backward: headlights, grill, hood, windshield—all on a perpendicular plane, all in excruciating detail. He never sketched an overall plan for the truck, an outline to provide a frame for his details. So, often, Colin would work his way back to the middle of the truck's load and run out of paper. If it was a farm truck, transporting pigs, he might leave dripping nostrils, a snout, some eyes, ears with whiskers, and then: the edge of the paper.

After the accident, Colin's mother made a photo album for each of us—all the best pictures of Colin from birth to death. On the final page, she pried apart the plastic sheet protector and slid in a photocopy of the newspaper article: *Crash near Tillamook kills three.* I picture her smoothing the wrinkles out of this final page, at least eight times. One time each for her six surviving children, once for me, once for herself. Smooth. Snap. There. Done. I wonder whether she stacked the pictures and did each album individually, or whether she did them assembly-line fashion. In which case, there she was at the end: *kills three, kills three, kills three . . .* at least eight times. *Theobald and Bock were wearing seat belts. Downey was not.* I wonder whether she thought, each time, as I did, *Colin always wore his seat belt.*

When I received my album from Colin's mother, I was grateful. I had never seen many of these pictures of Colin as a baby, as a little boy, as a muscle-bound teenager. Why would I? There was no rush. I turned to the last page of the album, the one with the accident article, and I peeled open the plastic cover, the plastic she had smoothed, and I pulled out the article. I folded it carefully and put it in a box, but I didn't want it in the album as the final chapter.

⌐⌐

The article appeared in *The Oregonian*, page A25, next to an advertisement for Meier & Frank's 3-day sale and an article about logging and angry environmentalists. The date was November 10, 1989. Colin had been dead for two days, and somebody read it aloud in the kitchen:

CRASH NEAR TILLAMOOK KILLS THREE
Dead were working for Virgin Lightships, a blimp company
TILLAMOOK — Three members of a British blimp company's flight crew died and another worker was injured when the van

in which they were riding pulled onto U.S. Highway 101 south of Tillamook and collided with an oncoming tow truck Wednesday night, authorities said.

The driver of the van, Andrew Theobald, 28, of Ruthin, North Wales, United Kingdom, was dead at the scene of the crash at 9:20 p.m. Also dead at the scene was a passenger, Colin Stewart Downey, 22, of San Rafael, Calif. Another passenger, 28-year-old Lawrence R. Bock of Marion, Kan., died later at Tillamook Community Hospital. Theobald and Bock were wearing seat belts. Downey was not.

Another passenger, Christopher Patania, 25, of Ypsilanti, Mich., was transported by ambulance to Emanuel Hospital & Health Center in Portland, where he was listed in critical condition with multiple fractures and abdominal and head injuries Thursday afternoon.

The van was owned by Virgin Lightships, a British blimp company. Virgin was on the north Oregon coast to test a blimp it bought from Seattle's American Blimp Co.

The driver of the tow truck, 46-year-old Don Burden of Tillamook, owner of Burden's Towing, and an unidentified passenger suffered only minor injuries and were treated at Tillamook Community Hospital and released.

The accident occurred at the intersection of Highway 101 and Long Prairie Road, a straight section of highway about a mile and a half south of Tillamook, said Sharon Weber, a spokeswoman for the Tillamook County sheriff's office.

The tow truck was the largest in the Burden's Towing fleet and is designed to haul tractor-trailers. It was pulling a motor home southbound on a flatbed trailer at the time of the accident.

The tow truck was headed south when the van apparently turned left through a red blinking light into its path. Officials in the sheriff's office said the van apparently didn't stop at the flashing light.

Thursday, red-eyed employees of American Blimp and Virgin Lightships tried to carry on without their co-workers. American Blimp, which built the colorful advertising blimp, had contracted with Virgin, the buyer, to provide a flight crew for testing the craft.

Blimp crews worked quietly Thursday to inflate the blimp, which was moved from Seattle to Tillamook last week to continue Federal Aviation Administration certification.

Virgin Lightship's employees were too upset to talk about their friends and co-workers.

"We're all in shock," the American Blimp president, Jim Thiele, said of the close-knit group, "but we know they would have wanted us to carry on, so we're here."

He recalled, "We said goodbye here, and a few minutes later our lights went out for a moment, I guess when they hit the power pole," Thiele said.

"The night before inflation is a nervous time anyway; a time when you think about all the things you might have forgotten. With this, I don't think any of us got any sleep last night."

The accident is still under investigation.

～

I believe photographs promote forgetting. . . . The fixed, flat, easily available countenance of a dead person or an infant in a photograph is only one image as against the million images that exist in the mind. And the sequence made up by the million images I will never alter. It's a confirmation of death. (Marguerite Duras, *Practicalities*)

～

Photographs pretend to allay one of the haunting fears that follow a death: I will forget. I will forget the eyes, nose, chin, shoulders, hands, legs. I will forget what his feet looked like in shoes. I have used photographs over and over in this postdeath ritual. I stare at the still until I can conjure up motion, make the specter move the way he would have moved.

I don't have Colin on video. That would change things because then I could hear him speaking, and I think that the voice is the hardest thing to recreate in memory. I've lost his voice—not the words he would say, but the sound: cadence and timbre. I would know Colin's voice if I heard it, of course, but I can't recreate the sound in my mind.

In the day after Colin died, I wished for three things. First, I wanted him alive. Then, if having Colin were impossible, if he himself could not be yearned back from the dead, I wanted both to be pregnant and to discover an unerased message on the answering machine. Both were the same wish: to have something to cleave to. When my menstrual blood came later that month, weeping out from between my legs, asserting that the cycles of my life would go on and on, no matter what my will, I mourned the void in my womb. I mourned the baby that might have been, could have been. Mourning is done in pieces, in bites of This Could Have Been. I cannot remember the sound of his voice in my ear.

∽

"You didn't really want that baby."

"I did."

"No, you wanted a baby version of Colin. You wanted rumpled dark hair and brown eyes that could look straight through your skin."

"I wanted that baby."

"You say you 'wanted something to cleave to.' A recording, a baby. *Cleave:* to adhere, cling, or stick fast. *Cleave:* to split apart. A word that embodies its own contradiction. You wanted 'something to cleave *to*'—to stick to you? Or something to cleave *you*? You did not want a baby."

"I would have learned."

∽

Jill Writes in Her Journal

January 14, 1990
I haven't been able to write for a week because:

a. *I'm too confused to know what to write*
b. *My writing skills have deteriorated and I don't know how to write*
c. *I've been drunk*
d. *I've been asleep or*
e. *I haven't felt like doing anything at all*

Jill Writes in Her Journal

February 16, 1990
Why do I keep having these "Colin's dead" dreams? Why can't he be alive—at least in my dreams?

Jill Writes in Her Journal

February 20, 1990
Tillamook, OR. Today I found out that nobody who knew Colin ever saw his body. The police identified him according to his clothing and personal items. Tom didn't see him, Alex didn't see him, Floppy didn't see him—nobody who had ever seen his face alive saw him dead.

～

After Colin's accident I didn't scribble a word about him anywhere but on the muted green pages of the lab notebooks that I used as journals. Then, five years after his death, I set up camp at a writer's conference on the banks of the McKenzie River in Oregon. On the second day of the conference, I lost my wedding ring.

Colin and I weren't married when he died. On the night of the accident I was wearing only an engagement ring—smooth yellow gold planted with five tiny sunken diamonds—but on the day we returned from burying him, I went to the jeweler and asked him to put the ring together, the engagement ring and the wedding band we'd already had forged, as we would have done if Colin had not died. There was no ceremony. I paid the man, took the ring in my hand, thinking how it was heavier than it had been before, nearly twice the weight, and part way to the door, stunned, my feet stopped moving forward, and I slid the ring onto my left hand. How anxious the man in the shop must have been for me to finish my walk out that door. I don't know how long I stood there in my own private marriage ceremony—just me and the ring, with Colin nowhere to be found—thinking *I cannot believe this. What is this? I cannot believe this. I cannot believe this.* In the early days of grief things tend to repeat themselves, taking longer to sink in than in happier times, and so five years after Colin's death, I'd shifted the ring from my left hand to my right, but I was still wearing it. I didn't know how to take it off, I guess. And then I went to this writers' conference, where I was staying in a tent, and one morning I lifted my hand to unzip the tent's door, and the ring was gone. I wrote this story at the conference as my search for the ring unfolded. This is what I made of it. These are the first words that I could write:

THE RING

The ring has become the story. I rub my neck which aches from the rhythm that I have fallen into since I felt my naked finger brush against the next and willed my reluctant hand up before my eyes where I confirmed it: My ring was gone. Not forgotten on a soap dish in the restroom to be returned to and claimed, not tucked away in a pair of socks in my top drawer at home, not locked up in the fireproof vault in my grandmother's closet. Just gone.

I am not writing the story. I am trapped in the story.

I am The Woman Who Lost The Ring.

I am in its rhythm: step and look, step and look, crouch to the ground, feel the nubs of dirt with my right hand as my fingers squeak across the green blades of grass, repeat with the left, step and look, step and look, crouch, feel right, feel left, step and look. . . . I am aware of the terror that whirls behind my eyes that are sore from looking, ache deep into the back of my skull from looking, but are afraid to close, afraid to look back into the terror. So they pull my whole body forward in the rhythm of looking.

The ring is such a crucial link in my life now that it's . . . I can't say gone, but somewhere else. ("Just somewhere you're not used to having it," a woman waiting in the line with me for scrambled eggs and cantaloupe this morning assured me.) Now that I look down at my left hand and see only the white band of skin on my tanned finger where the ring should be, I wonder how I ever was so foolish to wear the ring, especially after what happened, especially given my history with losing.

I remember the time when that ring became a part of me as if I'm painting a picture with the richest, and brightest, colors of my life, that window from age nineteen to twenty when the experience of loving and being loved so completely transformed my life that I felt as if I glowed yellow. I was happy, and I hang on to the stubborn conclusion that if it hadn't been for the accident, that love would have stretched across my entire life.

"Do you know what I find interesting about this story?"

"No. Yes. Probably. You're going to say that I wasn't as happy as I say I was here, and that's true, I know that's true, but I think I *felt* happy, or at least I felt as though I should have felt happy—or something like that."

"Right. Go on."

"Remember, I was writing a *story*. . . ."

My grandmother sat across the kitchen table from us, Colin and me, and laid the rings onto the Formica with the precision and brevity of a practiced card dealer (which, indeed, she was). Three rings. All of them flashing their diamonds. This was serious business. I had been groomed for this moment.

"Go ahead and pick one," my grandmother said, lighting up another Benson & Hedges and letting it dangle from her mouth, sticky with Maybelline's Magnetic Mauve, while she slid the rings toward us like plastic poker chips.

My mother stood over us. "Now, you're not supposed to lose this," my mother said, looking down at me sternly as I tilted my hand from left to right, catching the light of the overhead lamp.

"No kidding," I said. "I thought I was supposed to toss it down the drain."

"I mean it, Jill," she said, looking at her mother for backup. "This is a *very* special ring that your grandmother is giving you, and it's about time you learn to take care of your things and *not lose them.*"

I didn't know that the ring was in Colin's pocket that evening on the beach in front of the See Vue motel in Yachats, Oregon. If I'd known the ring was in his pocket, I would have been nervous; I wouldn't have been so easily inspired by the smell of the sea and begun casually talking about the time that my mother's boyfriend covered our Christmas tree with live lobsters. I'll skip the actual moment of the proposal both to keep it for myself and because it was so romantic in an utterly clichéd sense as to be somewhat sickening to the outsider. Let it suffice to say that, back in the room, we made love on an Oriental rug laid over the shag carpet, and I hit my knee—hard—on an oak rocking chair. Then we took a bath together and watched the ring glitter beneath the water.

Everyone else was already at dinner when I realized the ring was gone. *Breathe,* I commanded myself. *Relax.* Maybe you should eat something first, you need to eat, and then you'll be able to deal with this. But my heart and brain were locked together in a tango of panic.

I knew Colin was really dead when I called my mom at 5:30 in the morning and she said into the phone, "My God. No. Oh, my God, Sweetie. Stay there. I'm coming right over. I'll be there. I'm coming." Then she hung up. Before she said that, I had been thinking that it was too early in the morning for her to come over. I had been calling her to let her know what had happened—Colin is dead; they said a car accident—but I didn't know she'd come right over. I thought it was too early.

The morning after the accident, as Colin's parents and his brothers and sisters and their children arrived in Eugene one at a time, someone went to the store and bought a paper, reading it aloud in the kitchen while someone else fried bacon: "Crash near Tillamook kills three." And then there was a list of names. "Also dead at the scene was a passenger, Colin Stewart Downey, 22, of San Rafael, Calif. Another passenger, 28-year-old Lawrence R. Bock of Marion, Kan., died later at Tillamook Community Hospital. Theobald and Bock were wearing seat belts. Downey was not."

"Colin *always* wore his seat belt," I whispered, shaking my head from side to side, and slid my back down the refrigerator until I reached the solid linoleum of the kitchen floor. I started to scream. My mother gave me a bath, holding my head in the warm water, rubbing in the shampoo, wiping my eyes with a washcloth, stroking my back as I leaned out of the bath and over the toilet bowl. I retched green bile and watched it glow against the white ceramic bowl, forgetting what I was supposed to do next, while my mother held her hand on my wet back, trying to absorb some of my pain through her palm.

I am in the rhythm of the ring. But I am not alone. One by one, women join the search. Step and look, step and look. What were you wearing? Have you looked in your car? between the seats? the showers? the pool? your bag? your towel? you *shook* the towel that you were using?! you *shook* the towel? Oh Jill. . . . we'll find it. Don't give up. And we fall into the rhythm of the ring. Step and look, step and look.

Two days after the accident I was still sitting in the closet in a pile of Colin's dirty clothes. My mother wanted me to eat something.

Colin's mother suggested gingersnaps, so somebody went to the store and bought some for me. My mother held one of the smooth, round cookies in the darkness in front of my face. I opened my mouth for her, because I couldn't think of a reason not to. The porous bottom of the cookie stuck to the mucus on my lips, and the cookie stayed in place when my mother took her hand away, but I couldn't bite down.

I couldn't swallow. I wanted to see Colin's body. If they had let me see his body, I might have been able to hang on to my belief that there are things in this world that endure as solid and knowable—like a spoon clinking on the rim of a ceramic mug, a ball of wool socks found by touch in the back of an underwear drawer, the milky sweet-and-sour smell of a baby's head, or even the warm, blood-pumping, human body of someone you love, and the way crashing metal can make that body turn cold.

I was twenty. I didn't know yet that losing one person can make you afraid of losing everyone, but I think that's why nobody would take me to see his body—the funeral home director said Colin's body was "unsuitable for viewing," and nobody believed that I would be satisfied to see just one hand.

I want to interview Naomi, the poet who lost the camel charm at the conference the year before. She sits at a table in the dining hall eating gingerbread, fruit, and yogurt—hungry from singing. She pulls out the camel for me to see. It is a small golden camel, thin, much smaller than my ring, with a basic dromedary shape: single golden hump, golden head, and most critically to the story itself, two sets of tiny stuck-together golden legs.

"We need Jeanette," she insists. "It's really Jeanette's story. She is The Finder of Things."

At that moment, Jeanette enters the dining hall.

I want to know how the camel was found, how long it was lost, how hard the camel was hiding—I am eager to draw comparisons between this camel and my ring. After all, the camel now swings happily on a sturdy chain around Naomi's neck. The story comes together in the rhythm of things lost.

"I found it by the pool, in a crack, standing straight up," Jeanette says.

"*Upside down*, straight up," Naomi corrects. "Upside down."

"Yes," Jeanette says, "in the crack, upside down, just one little foot sticking up from beneath a few pine needles."

"Now, wait a minute," I say. "*Ruth* said that the camel was under a *big* pile of stuff."

As if waiting for her beat, Ruth walks into the dining hall and hears her name.

"Ruth! Ruth! Ruth!" everyone shouts.

"Oh no!" Ruth says. "Are we telling the raft story again?"

"No," I say. "The camel story, the camel story."

"It was virtually unfindable!" Ruth exclaims.

Before we headed to California with Colin's ashes, my mother took me to the student health center to see my old psychiatrist. I didn't have to say a word. Dr. A led me through the pretty room with the couch and the overstuffed chairs and into a side room lined with white cabinets and containing only a long, aluminum table on wheels. I remember leaning over that shiny metal table with my pants pulled down to my thighs. Supporting my weight on my elbows and touching my lips to my own cold reflection, I wondered vaguely why I couldn't tell where the needle was piercing my skin and how I would know when it was okay to feel again.

"All done," she said, snapping the rubber gloves from her hands.

We took Colin's ashes to the ranch where he had spent his childhood. I barely remember it now. The images I do have are like photographs: the caretaker's wife handing me a plate of pancakes and sausage in a barn set up like a banquet hall, patting my hand, saying, "It's okay, dear. You're young. There will be others. Promise me you'll be happy." Colin had been dead two days. I didn't promise anything.

I remember watching the butter melt a soft spot for itself in the center of my top pancake, knowing that I was going to have to throw up again.

The writers' conference where I lost my ring is held every year at a monastery called Saint Benedict's, owned by an order of Dominican monks, on the McKenzie River in Oregon. On occasion, I'd seen one of the monks walking around the grounds, arranging a sprinkler head or going into the chapel, but I'd never had a compelling reason to try to talk to them before I lost the ring. I went looking.

The sign on the door said, "We're in the front (back!) of the house." There was an arrow to let me know exactly what that meant. I started in the direction of the arrow. Another sign, this time on a post stuck in the lawn: "Private. Staff Area." Oh God, I thought, then quickly corrected myself, Oh Goodness (I heard my grandmother, whom I'd seen actually go to church only once, on Easter, scolding, "Never use the name of the Lord in vain," and then to my mother, "Honestly, these kids have had no proper religious education"). I stared at the sign on the lawn, reminding myself that if I did get to talk to them, I would avoid saying God or Damn. I walked past the sign and peeked around the corner, saying in a high, shy voice, "Hello?" and waiting to be recognized.

Two men were sitting in white plastic chairs, eating one of those snack mixes with pretzels and little chunks of salty green and orange things, glass tumblers within reach on a table.

The one closest to me turned his chair a bit, and I jumped at the opening. "I'm so sorry," I said, "I wouldn't bother you except that. . . . I hope I'm not interrupting or anything." I breathed in nervously and got a good whiff of whiskey. I looked at the glasses, brown liquid with a clear layer on top where the ice had melted and the water had risen to the surface. I breathed again. Jack and Coke. I was relieved. "I wouldn't bother you in the evening like this," I said, "but I've lost my wedding ring."

The faces of both men deepened with compassion. Wow, I thought, maybe this losing a wedding ring thing is worse than I thought. We made our introductions, and Father Anthony, a man with pale blue eyes and a thick gray beard, offered me a chair. Then he held out the blue plastic dish with the multicolored snacks. "No thanks," I said. "Just ate."

Brother Dan started asking me questions: Was I sure I hadn't taken it off before I left home? When was the last time I could really remember having the ring on? Had I already looked in the pool? Was I sure it wasn't at home? (He repeated the few questions about which he felt most strongly.) A mosquito landed on the side of Brother Dan's bald head.

"Of course, you know who you need to pray to, don't you?"

Uh oh. Here it was. "No," I said.

"Ahhh, . . ." he said, sitting back and rubbing his belly. "Saint Anthony! Saint Anthony, the finder of all things lost."

Then he started telling me about all the things he had lost in his life and how Saint Anthony had helped him find them. Father Anthony pushed the snacks toward me again. I wondered whether the mosquito was starting to suck blood out of Brother Dan's head. I wanted to say something, but I couldn't.

"Of course, you also know, Jill," Brother Dan continued, "that if you pray to Saint Anthony and you find the ring, you'll have to convert."

"Mosquito," Father Anthony said, gesturing toward Brother Dan's head. Brother Dan slapped the shiny surface of his head, and the mosquito dangled there by one squished leg.

"You'll have to convert," Brother Dan repeated. Then he took pity. "Just kidding," he smiled, winking at Father Anthony, holding up his glass and looking back at me. "Hey, can I get you a drink?"

The ashes of a six-foot, two-inch man are not light. "Can I carry the box for a minute?" I asked Colin's sister Dyan. We climbed the hill that looks over the river and the barns: four remaining brothers, two sisters, one mother, one father, me, my mom. I was surprised by the weight of the box. My elbows stretched with the weight, and I held it against my stomach, hard, feeling my hipbones come forward to touch the cardboard box with a step, touch, step, and touch again. I stared at the word on the top of the box: CREMAINS.

"What the *fuck* kind of word is that?"

When the metal detector didn't work—imagine a woman at a writers' conference with a beeping metal detector, imagine how you would hate her—I decided to take to the pool. I had been bold enough to swim in the pool on the day that I lost the ring, and so it seemed a reasonable place to look. Cold flesh shrinks, and my shrunken finger could have let the ring go. Father Anthony and Brother Dan came to the pool to help me search. Both of them wore jeans and flannel shirts. I was wearing a bikini, and might as well have been naked. I stayed in the water for as long as I could stand it, diving for the things they pointed out at the bottom of the pool.

"There," Brother Dan said. And I took a breath, dove deep. A dime. "Anything that sparkles, I guess," he said. He was trying. We were all trying.

"Here's something," Father Anthony said. Pulling another breath deep into my lungs, knowing the icy water would yank it from my throat, I went back down to the bottom. A leaf. The water was deep there, nine feet at least, and the light distorted a dead brown leaf into something shining.

By the time I finally climbed out of the pool, blue with cold, shivering, I had brought to the open palms of the waiting monks a dime, a leaf, a penny, a barrette, more leaves, a stick, and a stud earring. Standing on the rough concrete by the pool, I tried to cover my jutting nipples with my folded arms, all the time acutely aware that:

1. I could cover my nipples, but my pubic hair was still showing,
2. cold flesh shrinks, and
3. I hadn't found the ring.

"Maybe if you write finding the ring into the story, then we'll know where to look," someone suggested helpfully.

"You know about the silver dollar, don't you?"

"No," I said, "I don't know that one yet."

"This one really works." The woman stood in front of a clear cooler filled with water and containing floating slices of cucumber and wedges of lemon like tropical fish. "You need to picture a silver dollar in your mind." She held her palm out flat. "Then, you need to put whatever you lost onto the silver dollar." She pinched the fingers together in the other hand, gripping her invisible something, and placed it deliberately in her palm, on top of the equally invisible silver dollar. Then she threw both hands up in the air. "Then you forget about it," she said. "And the next time whatever you lost comes into your mind, it will be right there."

After the first night I began flushing the suppositories. The psychiatrist at the university counseling center said I would need something to calm me down, help me to hold down my food, prevent me from becoming dehydrated. She wrote me a prescription for fourteen suppositories. Maybe after fourteen days it's okay to cry. I don't know. I do know that after the first night I started flushing them down the toilet so that I could know he was there when he came into my room at night and pressed his hand on my cheek, maybe not his hand, but himself, something soft and real on my cheek, and through the pressure, "I'm here, Jill. I'm okay. I love you." Not words. Just the message, filling my body. It wasn't my food I needed to keep down. It wasn't even water. It was this feeling. Without it, I would have died.

The women's voices levitate me. The lost ring, and its rhythm, begin to feel less like loss and more like magic.

I'm thinking of putting together an anthology of lost stories. Since I became The Woman Who Lost The Ring, everyone has a story to tell. "*You're* the one?" she'll say, and then she'll offer her piece of hope, her story to beat the last. There is the woman who lost her contact lens while she was skiing, stopped in her tracks, and ordered her companions to go get some Hefty bags from the lodge. They filled six bags with the snow from around the woman, took it home, melted it, and *found the contact lens*. Then there's the woman who went camping alone for a week in the wilderness and lost an earring—looked everywhere, couldn't find it. One year later, she went back, started gathering wood for the fire, and *found the earring*. Another woman held her hand across the table to me, displaying a thin gold wedding band. "I found this one in the garden after five years," she said.

"Yours?" I asked, genuinely impressed.

"No," she said.

Step and look, step and look. The rhythm of the ring is teaching me the texture of the ground. The smooth grass, the chunks of dirt, the rocks, rough and smooth and crumbling, the needles from the trees, sharp and broken. Composting. I'm learning to watch the ground. Step and look, step and look. Sometimes I think that I see something glitter, and I fall to my knees.

~

"Well, aren't you going to say anything?"

"Yeah. I like it. Except maybe the end when you fall to your knees. It seems kind of defeatist, or healy-feely or something."

"I agree. But, if I remember correctly. . . ."

"You say that often: *If I remember correctly*. What is *to remember correctly*?"

"If I *remember correctly*, then I remember to the best of my ability with no intention to bend my recollection of events and feelings as I experienced them."

"Always as you experienced them."

"Of course, and in this case, I remember, to the best of my ability, that I intended the knee-falling as a kind of combination of prayer and thankfulness. And the vigilance of looking, of course."

"So, did you find the ring?"

"Oh! Yes! Well, I didn't find it, but about a week after I'd left the conference and returned to Eugene, a woman from the conference showed up at my lab in the psych department. She said that after I'd left she'd pitched her tent where my tent had been because she felt as though she was the one who was supposed to find the ring, but, she said, she'd found only a forgotten tent stake, and she held out a closed fist to me, and I held out my palm, and plunk. There was the ring. But I never wore it again. I told myself that I was putting it into the safe-deposit box because I couldn't take the risk of losing it, but that wasn't it, because when I'd decided that the ring was really gone, I interpreted it for myself in a spiritual frame: Colin had taken the ring to teach me another lesson."

"What lesson?"

"Not to cling to material objects. After Colin died, the funeral director guy in Tillamook gave me that horrible little white paper bag with all his 'personal effects.' I remember everything that was in that bag by touch, as if I'd been blind on the day he gave it to me. The leather of his wallet was polished to a smooth curve. Like a shell that had been caught in the tides of his body. There was a lot of money in his wallet, and blood had seeped into the paper. Not from the folds in the wallet, but from this crack in the leather at the place where the wallet folded. The blood was still a little wet. And his ring was in there—sterling silver, with bumps around the outside like a message in Braille. The ring had been a gift from me—an engagement ring. I wanted to wear it, but it slid off my thumb, so I unfastened my watch, put the strap through, and buckled the ring to my wrist. Tight. So that the bumps in the ring made indentations in the soft flesh on the inside of my wrist. And his lucky rock—a shiny, smooth, silvery pebble. That made me crazy. *His lucky rock. His fucking goddamned lucky rock. How could he have his lucky rock and be* dead?"

"Maybe he was lucky. Maybe there are worse things than being dead."

"Right. Maybe there are. But don't ever suggest that to someone the day after they find out that somebody they love is dead. Not *Maybe there are worse things than being dead.* Not *At least he didn't suffer.* Not *Time will heal.* Not any of those things. You should know that."

"Was that everything that was in the bag?"

"Everything that was Colin's. But in the bottom of the bag there was all this crap. Debris from the accident, I guess. Pebbles, dirt, glass chips. They must have just scraped everything up off the pavement and popped it in a bag."

"So why did you tell me all that?"

"*Because* I cared about that ring on my watchband as much as I cared about living. Or more. Actually, definitely more. So, one morning in Costa Rica, about four months after the accident, I woke up and felt my wrist, as usual, and my watch—and the ring—were gone. Not on my wrist. Poof. Gone. I was heartbroken. I felt as if I was losing him all over again. But then I had this feeling, all over my body, this feeling that Colin had taken back the ring, that he didn't want me to cling to it."

～ Grieving in Costa Rica

After Colin's death my mother would have taken me back into her womb if she could have figured out a way to do it. I took on my grieving as a full-time job, and my mom took on me: I moved home with her. She fed me, she bathed me, and she drove me to appointments. She did everything for me. One day, in the spring of 1990, I realized that there was no reason for me to get out of bed. She was killing me. I got on a plane and went to Costa Rica.

～

In Cahuita, Costa Rica, in a reggae coffee joint on the beach, I met a black man named Daniel with a hole in the back of his green cloth jacket who didn't seem to like me. "The hole is from my trip to Nicaragua," he said. I laughed. He didn't. He looked me up and down and said, "The green bills have all the power. When U.S. money fails, all money fails. The U.S. doesn't fight any wars on its own land. They don't have to. They have arms in all other countries." The year was 1990. The Iran-Contra deal had been in the news for a few years. Before we left the *casita*, he said, "Do one dance if you are sexy, Soltera. Dancing needs no lessons. You must feel the music." I refused.

The next day, on a black sand beach, I saw Daniel again, and he took my hand and led me into a still, saltwater pool. (Remember, I was twenty years old, grieving, as malleable as soft clay. Frameless. I did as I was told and walked where I was led.) When I was standing ankle-deep in the lukewarm water, Daniel told me to look down at my feet and see my reflected image. "Speak more slow, girl. Each word is a meditation. Meditate on each word. That is the language. Slow down, Sweet. Watch out for Mr. Alligator." Daniel's kisses came with the same thick weight as his words. On the night I spent with Daniel and a full moon on the beach, he said to me, slowly, each word a sentence, "Make sex with me, Soltera."

"Make *love* with you."

"Yes," he said.

I did not. Daniel persisted, "Love again, Sweet. Love yourself. Be happy, and he will be happy. He is watching you and cannot be at rest until you are happy. When you are happy, he will see—*She is happy.* Peace will be in his heart when it is in yours." I walked down the sand to the water and stepped in up to my thighs. Air and water felt the same. I swam out, against the waves, following the lighted path that the full moon had painted across the water. In the morning, when I woke up in my hammock back at the *cabina,* I noticed that my watch was gone, and with it, Colin's silver ring that I had worn on the band since his death. That morning, a sloth cast a shadow over my wet body in the outdoor shower. I stood naked under a cold trickle and watched him for an hour. He was as slow as grief.

When I saw Daniel for the last time at the bus stop, he called me "smart girl" and seemed somehow glad that I was leaving, glad that he would never have to love me.

On the bus, careening away from Cahuita, I wrapped my fingers around my bare wrist, where the ring had once been attached, and it occurred to me that Daniel might be wearing Colin's ring. Daniel might be Mr. Alligator sporting a shining hoop of silver. Bumping along past banana trees whose fronds waved in the steamy ocean air, seeming to wish me farewell, this didn't seem like such a bad thing.

~

I didn't make sex with Daniel in Cahuita. I liked him too much. I waited a few weeks until I met a blond, blue-eyed, loud-mouthed *norteamericano* in the airport in Managua. We didn't, any of us, have visas to be in Nicaragua, but the plane needed repair, and the next flight out wasn't scheduled until the next morning. There we were.

The airline had us bussed to a hotel on the outskirts of Managua. We passed gutted buildings and half-naked children who held baskets full of colored gum and reached for the windows of the bus, shouting: *Chicle! chicle!*

At the hotel, I shared a room with the blue-eyed man. I don't remember choosing. He ordered piña coladas with paper umbrellas and led me out to the hotel's faux lagoon with its kidney-shaped pool and palm trees. The world seemed to have tilted off its axis. I sat in a reclining deck chair and held the cold glass against my bare stomach while chlorine fumes stung my eyes and the blue-eyed man courted me with tales of his life as a merchant seaman. Because of his stories, a few umbrella drinks later, when we were floating in the tepid pool and I felt him harden against my submerged thigh, I didn't move away. "You could go insane out there, but it's so beautiful. At night, when all the other hands are down below or in their bunks, I go up on the deck with my harmonica, and there's only the sea and the music. I could stay there all night."

The next day we caught our repaired plane out of Managua and checked in at a *pensión* in Guatemala City, where the blue-eyed man had again booked a room with a double bed and a luxury: a private shower. The sheets on the bed were soft and yellow, and when we had sex for the first time that afternoon, I held on to that image of the solitary man on the deck with a harmonica and tried not to think of Colin. I couldn't do it a second time. Colin's face was everywhere, so as the afternoon sun melted shadows into the buttery sheets, I gave the blue-eyed man a blowjob to get his hands off my body. When he came, I turned my head to the side and spit the bitter semen onto those golden sheets as if I were depositing a bit of gristle into a linen napkin. The blue-eyed man didn't notice. He said, "Wow. Where'd you learn to do that?" and we went out to a bar, where I got so smashed that I drank tequila from a shattered glass. Somehow my throat wasn't cut when I swallowed.

~

I have three photos of the blue-eyed man. In each of them he's flipping off the camera. I took the pictures.

~

I have a recurring Colin dream. The "action" of the dream varies— we're grilling kabobs, or riding in an ambulance, or hanging out in a hotel room eating chocolate—last night, nine real-time years after his death, he was writing out a check for me to use to pay the rent. I took the check from him, kissed him on the mouth, and then thought, *Wait just a minute, here. What bank is this? He can't write a check. He's dead.* This moment of realization is the dream feature that has remained consistent all these nine years. I say, "Colin, what are you doing here? I thought you were dead." And he replies, always smiling, sort of smugly, like he's pleased by his own cleverness, "Yeah? I *am* dead." As if that's supposed to make some sort of sense to me. As if I'm supposed to maintain my suspension of disbelief in a dream where the primary character admits to being dead. Sometimes I go with it. After all, he doesn't look dead. He looks great. And it's so wonderful to see him, so fleshed out and warm and kissable. (I've tried, at these times, to make love with him, but it never works. He disappears.) Other times I persist in my line of questioning: "If you're *dead*, then what are you doing *here*?" Again, more or less the same reply: "I came to see you." Every time, he explains somewhat impatiently in a yeah-yeah-let's-get-on-with-it kind of way. These dreams wouldn't be as strange if they were intermingled with other Colin dreams, but they're not. These are the *only* dreams I've had about Colin since he died. Before last night I hadn't dreamt about Colin for more than a year.

~

A couple of months before Colin's accident, we took a weekend trip to Bainbridge Island in the Puget Sound. We'd forgotten how decidedly unromantic bed and breakfasts can be—even those that provide a claw-footed bathtub right in the bedroom next to the bed. We tossed and turned most of the night, too warm to sleep, too inhibited by the sounds of our sleeping neighbors to have sex, until Colin proposed that we drag a blanket out onto the back lawn, beyond the gazebo. We made love there, in the cool air, and it was lovely. The next day we wandered up and down the beach and shot a whole roll of film with my Canon. I didn't develop the pictures when I got back to Eugene. I forgot about those pictures, and the camera, until after the accident, and when I remembered, it was with a burst of joy: Here was something preserved. I found the camera, flipped the lever, began turning to rewind the film on the roll, but there was no tension on the lever. It was as if I was winding nothing at all. Somehow the tail end of the film had become detached from the reel, I thought, and I got in my car with the camera and drove to the nearest camera shop. I asked them to take the whole camera into the darkroom, roll up the film, and develop my pictures. When the camera shop man emerged from the back room, he was laughing: *There's no film in here. You were shooting with no film. You're going to have to do it again.*

~

There is also no photograph to support the story that my mother began telling about a week after Colin was killed. The setting is Eugene, Oregon, where we are all living in the fall of 1989—Colin and I are living with his sister Dyan and her two daughters on a suburban cul-de-sac, and my mother is living alone in a more bohemian neighborhood in a small house with a wood-burning stove and two giant cottonwood trees in the backyard.

As cottonwood trees grow older, they are like humans in that they also grow considerably more brittle, and winds that would only rustle the leaves and sway the branches of more limber trees snap off huge limbs of the groaning cottonwoods. Anthropomorphically speaking, during a nasty winter storm in which an older maple tree might slip on the ice and get a colorful bruise, the cottonwood would break a hip. Eventually, no amount of preventive trimming can save the cottonwood that grows in a populated area. An old cottonwood is a safety hazard.

In my mother's story, Colin is spending the day with her while I am off at my classes. They are splitting and stacking wood in the shed. In my mind, the wood in their hands is a fallen branch from the largest cottonwood, although of course that's the sort of detail that concerns no one anymore. My mother's story is shorter than my introduction:

So he said, *"I'll tell you how to take care of her."*

And I said, *"What? Who?" At that point I had no idea what he was talking about. We were just stacking the wood, and he said this casually as we passed each another, our arms loaded.*

"I mean Jill. There's a book you should read, so that you can understand it better."

And then he said it again: "You'll have to be the one to help her when I'm gone."

And I remember thinking: Of course I will, but where are you going? Why won't you be helping her? I mean, not that I didn't want to, but he seemed to be doing such a good job, with the bulimia stuff and everything else. That seemed to be working, and I just can't remember exactly what he was saying, but I know that I was thinking: What about you? Where will you be? And then, later, I thought he must have meant while he was on his trip to England, but now . . . now, with everything that's happened, I know that he meant now. He knew that he wasn't going to be around much longer.

～

"Colin was like your babysitter. He took care of you. For chrissakes, he even counseled your own mother on how to take care of you. He was like a fully functional mother for you."

"I know. If he had lived, we would have had to transition."

"Transitions are your worst thing."

"I know."

～

We have a series of photographs of the day that we had to have the giant cottonwood cut down to a stump. Branches had been falling, the neighbors were talking about lawsuits, and we didn't know what else to do. The first photo is of my mother and me—we are holding hands and watching the cottonwood go down. The shot was taken from behind us, so you can't see our faces, but I remember that we were crying. There is another picture of Uncle Mark with a chainsaw. He is cutting the tree into manageable pieces so that we can use it for firewood. So the cottonwood won't go to waste. So it didn't have to die for nothing.

All of the other hippies were heading to Max Yasgur's farm in Sullivan County, when Mark set out in the opposite direction, bound for Berkeley. Along the way, when he'd run into buses full of the Woodstock-bound, they'd say, "You're going in the wrong direction, man!" and Mark would shake his head, flick an ash, and wish them all good luck.

There's a page in the family picturebook to document the impending departure of my grandmother's son, Mark, from their home in Fishkill, New York. The photos appear typeset, as though they should be read from left to right on the page.

My grandfather, Ben F. Ingraham, the principal of Wappingers High School, is glued to the upper left. The photo has been trimmed along the right-hand side. A white border frames him on the top, bottom, and left sides. On the right side, his arm is trimmed off so that the same amount of arm is missing on both sides. My grandmother, despite the notoriety of her aesthetic failings, strove for balance in the composition of the family albums. On the left border, there is a stamped date: JUL 69. (I will be born next month. Sixteen years later, my grandfather will have a massive coronary on the toilet. His son, Mark, will find him there, pull his body onto the floor, and attempt to revive him with CPR. He will not succeed.) However, here, in the album, Ben Ingraham remains a portrait of straight lines. His back is pressed up against the beige wall of the family dining room, and his shoulders, carved out of the stiff fabric of a steel-gray flannel suit jacket look so straight that I can imagine his body as one of those painted, plywood props for picture-taking at the zoo or amusement park. A tanned, stern face juts out uncomfortably, just daring my grandmother to take a picture for which he is not prepared and posed.

Ben Ingraham is a thin, precise man, and he likes to wear the starched white collars of his dress shirts tight on his neck. However, after forty summers out in the backyard laid out flat on a cot and slathered in Johnson & Johnson's baby oil, the skin on his neck, though undeniably bronzed, is loosening, slackening. The slight roll of empty flesh that hangs disobediently over the collar of his shirt is a source of great embarrassment to him, but what can he do? Positioned, he nods a nod that would be imperceptible to anyone but a wife who has been trained these same forty years to perceive just that. He is ready. She counts: *one, two, three, cheeeeeese.* He does not smile. He feels his thin lips sticking to his teeth in a perfect, horizontal line and wishes he had a drink to wet his teeth. The flash of reflection on his brown-framed glasses occludes the dark marbles of his eyes with what I imagine to be the backward image of my rounded grandmother hiding her face behind an Instamatic camera.

The next photos are of Mark himself—a son who has been more embarrassing to Mr. Ingraham during the year 1969 than the loose skin on his neck. (Mr. Ingraham doesn't like to be embarrassed. He's the kind of man who stomps on milk cartons and cereal boxes before folding them into the well-rinsed trashcan. He likes neat garbage, and trash disposal is his specialty. Instead of putting the can out the night before pick-up, as his untidy neighbors do, he gets up at 6 A.M. on garbage day to drag the can to the curb for the 6:30 pick-up. He pulls aside the curtain at the sound of the approaching truck to make sure the garbage has been safely taken away, and immediately retrieves the can and tucks it into the garage. The day that his son appeared on the front page of *The Fishkill Times* with a photo of the car he had stolen and crashed into a garage in downtown Beacon, Mr. Ingraham rolled up the paper and stuffed it in the bottom of the can.)

The two photos of Mark are not well framed, and I suspect this is due to my uncle's failure to cooperate. Failure to conform. Failure to pose. Failure failure failure. By now, my grandfather is back in place on his side of the couch, drinking muscatel from an insulated water mug decorated with mallard ducks. He cannot bear to see his only son slouch. In the first photo, Mark's body is in profile, and he is slouching, looking at something that the camera can't see, looking— it occurs to me now—as though he's staring down the Mark in the next frame, looking to pick a fight with himself. The Mark in the next photo is ready to run, and the fingers of his left hand are pinching together as if he were trying to grab an imaginary joint. These two pictures of Mark are pasted side by side, a series of mugs, but the pictures are cut. Something, or someone, was cut out of each of these pictures. Mark is reworked, reframed, and glued beneath a plastic skin.

~

Mark Brian Ingraham was born on March 9, 1948, in Poughkeepsie, New York. That same year General Electric packaged an otherwise useless silicone substance in a plastic egg and marketed it for children; this material could be bounced, stretched, and pressed onto inky newsprint to pick up images—images that could then be stretched until the original image was unrecognizable. Silly Putty was an instant success. The next year George Orwell published *Nineteen Eighty-Four*, and Mark took his first steps in a country that was reading and wondering about the notion of a totalitarian state run through mind control.

Soon after Mark's birth his father left to serve overseas in the Korean War, and Mark spent the first three years of his life under the loving and watchful eye of his older sister, Martha. Their mother, Beatrice, who was given the home-baking ease of Pillsbury cake mixes the same year that she gave birth to her youngest child, will say later that these years when the kids were little were the happiest times of her life.

~

Mark was a troublemaker from the start. In kindergarten, the teacher sent him home because he was using an L-shaped building block as a gun; he insisted he was an outlaw from the wild, wild West. In 1964 Mark got his driver's license. Within months he got a ticket for going *under* the posted speed limit on Main Street in Beacon, New York. It seems that he was being escorted out of town by a motorcycle cop on a Harley, and Mark discovered, much to his glee, that if he went slowly, the cop's bike would start to wobble. Slow enough, and the Harley might go down. It did. Mark loved this story. How could he resist? The cop on the fallen hog was Mark's nemesis: Officer Hal Brilliant.

A few months later he was stopped again, this time for going over 100 miles per hour on the way to the drag races on the edge of town. The officer—not Brilliant this time—squinted into the interior of the car as he wrote out the citation: no visible drugs, no alcohol, just a couple of stupid kids going too fast. As he handed Mark the ticket, he said, "Young man, do you understand the seriousness of this situation?"

Mark reached over to the glove box, snapped it open, and pulled out a stack of citations about a half an inch thick. Nodding grimly, he placed the new ticket on top of the others and tapped the edges to line up the corners. Then he ripped the stack in half. "Yes, sir," he said. "I believe I do."

Mark was in the tenth grade.

At the end of that year the principal of his high school, Mr. Ben Ingraham, was forced to kick him out. After leaving Wappingers High School, Mark went to a school for "problem" teens and then on to the Peekskill Military Academy; the latter institution, which had first opened its doors in 1833, closed down for good the year that Mark enrolled. My grandparents never found another place that would take him, and Mark took the test and got his GED. Without a formal education, Mark learned to disassemble a car engine, clean all its parts, and put it back together. He learned that bat shit is a miracle fertilizer and began taking to his friends' attics, armed with a baseball bat and a garbage bag, to gather pounds and pounds of the precious guano. He learned that he could live well, and happily, out in the woods of the West, where he was ruled not by the iron fist of some authority figure but by the fickle hand of mother nature. Mark didn't need predictability, structure, or any institution; he needed freedom. For twenty years he lived on the tops of mountains in little cabins with open-air shitters. He was happy, and my mother was happy because he was happy. If our family had one collective wish, it would be that Uncle Mark had never left the mountain.

Mark was my only uncle, and our family's bad boy: an outlaw, an embarrassment, an adventurer, a criminal, a mountain man, a drunk, a hero—depending on whom you asked and when. Cut out of the same flesh that forms the rest of us, lubricated by the same blood (although, near the end, his was carrying two strains of hepatitis), Uncle Mark was the Ingraham who made headlines.

He never *learned his lesson.* When a man goes into prison fighting for freedom, he comes out of prison fighting harder. If he comes out at all.

~

Mark served his first jail sentence when he was sixteen years old and spent the rest of his life either avoiding or battling the system. I'm not like that. I buckle. If I'd been in Berkeley in 1969, serving a sentence on a narcotics charge (he'd been busted with some speed in a plastic baggie), and the guards ordered me to cut my hair, I would have cut my hair. Not Mark. For his defiance he earned three long months in solitary to grow his hair longer, and when he came out, he said, "At least I got to be alone for a while."

Through his rebellion, Mark defined the morality of our small family. When he was sixteen, he "borrowed" the family car, led the local police on a high-speed chase through the streets of Fishkill, and made it home in time to park the car in the garage, climb the trellis to his attic bedroom, and tuck himself back into bed, clothes and all, by the time the police arrived at the house. My grandmother, going to the door in her bathrobe and slippers, insisted that Mark had been sleeping for hours, and opened the garage door to prove that the car was safely parked. The cops felt the hood. It was burning up. Mark was busted. After a three-month sentence in the local detention center, my mother tells me, Mark came whistling home, singing a song he'd learned from one of their kids' records, "The policeman is your friend! La la la la la. . . ."

The way Mark told the story, and he was quite the storyteller, he was just having a little fun, and the small town police didn't understand his humor. I believed him. I always believed him. Consequently, despite the fact that I'm too chicken to park illegally, good and bad have never been equated with legal and illegal in my mind. Nobody ever told *me* to find a policeman and tell him my phone number if I got lost. Instead, I grew up scanning the streets for cops, the fuzz, pigs. My job was to report the smell of bacon.

~

Mark wrote a story about a chameleon after he was released from jail in 1970. The paper it's written on has been torn from some kind of journal; the ballpoint ink is alternately red and black. The three sheets are filthy, the ink is smeared, and my mother has been moving this story around with her for almost thirty years:

> Ian was a boy who lived in a grey house with a red door in
> the middle of a very busy block. He was a beautiful child with
> long curling blonde hair and forest green eyes. Ian's parents,
> relatives, and friends said they loved him very much. During the
> day there was school, and in the afternoon there was baseball
> down behind the tall white building with the fantastic day-glo
> colored windows. He loved to walk in the wood by the creek.

Amazed, he saw white fluffy clouds, light blue sky, and green and brown trees. There were golden fields and flowers of every color he'd ever seen or heard and the darkest bluest water. Ian would wonder what it was that made everything as perfectly beautiful as it was. One exceptionally sunny day while Ian was hiking through a cluster of maples, he heard what he thought to be a very tiny voice say, "It's a fine, fine day for a walk in the woods." He looked down, and there amongst the clover and ivy surrounding a rotting stump, he saw a bright orange strip. He stooped to see and found a small lizard. "We haven't seen nicer for over two weeks," replied the boy. The tiny lizard and Ian became fast friends and spent the rest of the day playing by the creek. This lizard was a chameleon, and chameleons have the magical powers to turn any color they want. When the little fellow was in the grass, he quietly became a shining green, if he were on a tree trunk he would miraculously turn a glorious brown, yellow, orange, or red depending on the color of his setting. He named his magical lizard Happy. Happy and Ian talked of all good things in the forest and exchanged stories of their personal adventures. Happy choked up as he told of the harm gasoline engines do to the air, water and soil. He said with the population growing the way it was and with the attitudes of the people always wanting to build on, cover over and destroy our vulnerable earth child, that in twenty years there would be no more natural resources or woods or clean water, and then no nothing. From that day on it was always Happy and Ian together doing all they could to nurse their polluted area back to health. Ian's rainbow buddy would sit on his shoulder or hang on his shirt and blend in so well with what he was wearing that he was never seen, and Ian was always thought to have been alone. Ian's parents were deeply concerned about his lack of productivity and his always being so happy all by himself. His parents and friends began to treat him with a new kind of fear. Ian and Happy would take long walks out of town into the great rolling green hills, free of buildings, garbage and people. It was euphoric out there where he and Happy could actually smell all of nature's colors. Happy would get on the ground and leap from side to side, changing color as he went, and Ian would laugh until his sides ached. His elders now resented his continuing good humor and labeled him a disgrace. His abnormal behavior had been the talk of the town. A cop named George walked a beat on the sidewalk just outside the woods. He was big and soft and clean shaven. George never looked into the trees because he saw more of what he wanted to see in the concrete. He hated the routine of his boring life. One day Ian and Happy burst out of the forest laughing not far ahead of the sorry soldier. George ran up with hatred bubbling in his heart and spun Ian around as brutally as he could. It happened so fast that Happy flew off and hit the pavement. George saw him as he bounced on the sidewalk (you see, chameleons can't turn grey). The pig lunged forward with a gurgling cough and squashed Happy right down level with and dead to the ground. Ian's heart broke and likewise his mind. He flew at George's throat and clamped his teeth down tightly over his windpipe. Shaking his head viciously, he tore huge pieces of tendons, purple veins, and fat from the monster's ugly neck. Hot blood was pulsating into Ian's eyes and mouth as they both collapsed. The happy smile was erased from Ian's face forever and ever Amen.

~

"Gruesome. Did Mark name the character of the boy after Ian your brother?"

"Yeah, isn't that weird? I mean, I guess he thought that he was writing a kind of fantasy children's story when he started out, but it's so grim in the end. Kind of twisted. Ian had been born when he wrote it. He was around. But Mark was the little boy who lived in the gray house with the red door. That was the Fishkill house—the one with the picturebooks in the attic. What about the end, though? That's the part that gets me: Ian consumes the cop."

~

When I'm not carrying something, when I feel light, I sometimes fear the disintegration of my body. I could lose the weight of my skin, its subtle but constant pressure holding me in. Then I would fly to pieces. I once was in love with a man who said he couldn't compete with a ghost, the weightless apparition of a dead lover hovering above our bed. Then I made a switch and loved a man who left me for my own lightness; when he said, *You don't understand my dark side because you don't have one,* I would have laughed if my lungs hadn't been compressed by the weight of his leaving. I am gaining. My next boyfriend accused me of craving the heart weight of chaos, and when it did not occur naturally within our relationship, within my life, he said, I would manufacture some: pick a fight, pick at my face, make something, anything, ugly and unbearable. I resisted his analysis so vehemently that I had to get out. He was right, of course. I need something to carry—and I cannot hold that weight in the flesh of my body.

⌒ *Days on the Wall*

And this is the story of how Uncle Mark ended up in Kentucky.

In the fall of 1992, there was a big marijuana bust in Northeastern Washington State—the biggest outdoor growing bust in that part of the country ever, as a matter of fact. The story was all over the papers. Reporters couldn't believe their good fortune. Rows and rows of mature female plants, high-grade Indigo hybrids, covered with green, purple-tinged, hairy buds provided photo ops for local papers that would have turned the staff photographers at *High Times* green with envy. But the full color photos weren't the best part.

The marijuana had been grown between rows of corn on a ranch that was struggling to make ends meet in a county where, quite frankly, grains weren't the highest-grossing cash crop anymore. The farmer had a pre-bust name that made headline writers feel tingly all over: Bud King. Of course, folks in the farming community were shocked, or so they claimed in interviews, and Bud King didn't take long at all to figure out that the best thing for him to do was to strike a hasty deal with the federal prosecutors and give a full confession. In an act of dramatic revelation, he used a backhoe to unearth his buried treasure, $637,000 in cash, and revealed that this was not the first year of the operation, but the fourth. Two other ranchers who were involved—brothers aged seventy-one and sixty-seven—also cooperated with the investigation immediately. That's when the papers came out with the story about the strange and now unhappy alliance between the hard-working second-generation rancher who was at risk of losing his farm, and the first-generation hippies who had led the desperate ranchers down the primrose path (and whose parallel threat to livelihood wasn't mentioned in the reports).

Growing the marijuana in his cornfields wasn't Bud King's idea, despite his headline-making name. Bud King knew corn and cattle. His buddy Ernie Anderson, however, in addition to having a good grasp on the fundamentals of agriculture and animal husbandry, had befriended a group of hippies who lived up on the mountain adjacent to his land. In the fall they bought hay from him for their horses; in the spring they helped him move the cattle to summer grazing land. Spending all this time with the men from "the Hill," Ernie Anderson had learned that they had some agricultural know-how of their own. For argument's sake, let's say it was Ernie who made it all possible.

Times were rough for the hippies, too. The four hippies came down from the mountain because the simplicity of their lives had given way to technology—not their own, but that of surveillance equipment in the nineties. The government was using infrared in the airplanes that buzzed low over the mountain from July to August. The risk was too great. Their friends were going to jail. The infrared cameras picked up the heat of the developing buds hanging over a patch of cool, watered earth like lights on a Christmas tree. Somebody got the idea of growing the plants with other plants, legal ones, plants that would need irrigation. Fast-growing corn was an obvious choice. The corn stalks would provide not only the physical cover of their broad, drooping leaves, but also share water with their new, but not unwelcome, neighbors from the North. The corn in these fields had never been so well tended. The first three years went smoothly, and everyone was rolling in green.

Even after a seven-way split, four hippies and three farmers, each man received more than two hundred thousand dollars each year. Of course, all the money was in cash, and none of it could be taken to the bank. In years past the money reaped from a good season with the much smaller mountain patches could go into Mason jars or steel ammo boxes and either be buried under a specific fir tree out in the woods or stuffed under a bed with the dust balls and dirty laundry, depending on a particular hippie's caution.

But now the money was overwhelming. Too much. Nothing was off limits anymore. Spokane's Hilton became a popular party spot. Purple felt bags with gold Crown Royal lettering carpeted the floor of the suite. Women in tight skirts used razor blades to shape mazes of cocaine on gilded mirrors that they took off the walls. The phone in the suite rang constantly. Everybody wanted a piece of it. The hippies didn't wait for the city to come to them; instead, they came down to it, and the ride was fast and furious. One by one, they shaved their beards and cut their hair. Time for a change for these old hippies, they said, laughing and toasting their good fortune with another shot of Crown Royal straight from the thick-glassed bottle. One by one, it seemed, they forgot why they'd moved to the mountains in the first place.

Besides burying it all in a big hole out in the field and lying on his tax returns—*Come on now. What was he supposed to do? Report $637,000 in drug profits?*—I don't know for sure what Bud King did with his money those first three years. I don't know him the way I know the hippies—in fact, I don't know him at all—but I've read enough in the newspapers and thick stacks of FBI reports to patch the holes with a few fictional details and come out with a workable narrative. The thing to know is that someone wasn't happy. Somewhere, there was ill will and bad blood.

In those first green, green years following the hippies' descent from the mountain, maybe Bud King paid off some big loans that he'd had to take out on his land. Maybe he came closer to fulfilling his dream of securing the future of a working ranch for his two sons. That much anybody could have figured out from the papers. But I also imagine that there were earlier, more visible signs of Mr. King's inexplicable prosperity. Perhaps he also hired men from town to come out to repair fences and put new siding on the big cattle barn. Maybe he got a satellite dish and a big screen television, and on Sundays he and his two grown sons gathered around to drink Rainier beer and watch the Seahawks. Maybe the reception was perfect. Maybe the neighbors were whispering about Bud's good fortune in a year when other farmers were forced to sell off parcels of land to make ends meet, but nobody thought to suspect marijuana plants in the cornfields. So far, the plan was perfect, but sudden success can make people wary, and Bud King's neighbors weren't happy—something wasn't right, wasn't fair. They would be watching.

The FBI wouldn't reveal to the newspapers the name of the informant, but after the bust the country learned that in May 1992 somebody had seen an old red flatbed pickup truck with a blue tarp over the bed, tied with yellow nylon rope, pull up at the gates of Bud King's ranch. The gate was locked, wrapped with a thick length of chain and hooked with a weighty padlock. The lock was new. The unnamed informant watched a man get out of his truck, climb the aluminum gate, and walk down the road toward the ranch house. He didn't know what he was looking at when he lifted a corner of the tarp and saw that the bed of the truck was packed solid with cardboard flats full of six-inch seedlings, but he knew it wasn't corn, so he went straight to the police. "On account of the fact," he may have told FBI agents who rushed to the area to take his official statement, "on account of the fact that I knew that man was a stranger, not from around here, and the fact that Bud King just got that new satellite dish up at his place when all I got is rabbit ears and that doesn't help the reception much at all. Well, just a bit. Anyway, I've been living here all my life, and I knew them plants weren't corn." The FBI report left out some details that I now imagine: the informant tilting back his chair, pulling the bill of his cap down tight on his forehead, chewing on a toothpick and smiling contentedly as he wrapped up his story of a warm June day and a red truck and a bed of young plants. Maybe the FBI agents, eager to get the initial report back to Washington and start regular funding, didn't notice. Maybe they didn't care. Maybe they knew all they needed to know about how another person's success can breed resentment.

It doesn't really matter what they knew or thought. Based on this informant's statement, the bureau assigned a handful of full-time agents to the case at taxpayers' expense. It was an election year, and I'm guessing that the Bush administration was desperate to make a killing in its ongoing War Against Drugs. Consequently, the agents assigned to the case were under strict orders not to make a move until the plants were mature. Wet and heavy. The plants would be weighed straight out of the ground, roots and all; the federal agents could then calculate the weight of the plants into street value for premium bud. The estimated value released to the press, just two months before the general elections, would be in the tens of millions. The American public would go crazy. Stepping-stone drugs. The disintegration of America's youth. Damn hippies. ("But what about that farmer?" voters might wonder. "Is his name really Bud King? Do you think the hippies held a gun to his head?"). Just say no. Summer of 1992, election year, and everybody had gotten greedy.

Agents from the Federal Bureau of Investigation teamed up with agents from the Spokane Regional Drug Task Force and made their first visit to the King ranch on May 28, 1992. There, they found a small wooden corral where "numerous potted plants were observed"—in fact, Agent Bedford reported an estimated count of three thousand plants. A green leafy sample was collected at this time, and on June 23, 1992, the Washington State Patrol Crime Laboratory "revealed that the sample removed form the corral was marijuana, a controlled substance." During their initial corral investigation, Detective Poindexter and Agent Bedford also observed "several inflatable owls which were attached to strands of string over each sheet of plywood."

Knowing that the blow-up guard owls were also in place, the agents settled in with their binoculars to wait out the summer.

~

On September 4, 1992, at approximately 5:30 A.M., I and members of the Spokane Regional Drug Task Force went to the marijuana field and discovered approximately 345 marijuana stalks which had been cut and placed in stacks in the northwest corner of the marijuana field. The branches and leaves had all been removed and all that remained was the main stalk. Also observed was a large ball of red twine as well as pruning shears. There were also several plastic chairs, plastic tarps and numerous beer cans. A marijuana stalk was taken for evidentiary purposes which subsequently tested positive as marijuana. Task Force members and myself searched for any cut corn stalks and were able to determine that harvesting of the corn had not commenced.

Because the participants have begun their work as early as 5:25 A.M. on the morning of September 2, 1992, appear to be harvesting the marijuana, and may discover the surveillance being performed, and may attempt to destroy evidence, it is requested that a warrant be issued for execution at anytime day or night. (Special Agent David Bedford's affidavit)

~

Finally, on September 9, 1992, acting on the authority of a "federal destruction order" signed by Federal Judge Quackenbush, federal and task force agents made their long-awaited move onto the King ranch for the "arrest and eradication of the marijuana field." Mark was not in the field that morning when the first arrests were made at 5:30 A.M.—his whereabouts and eventual capture are another story—but suffice it to say: they got him.

On the day "Operation Bud" was busted, agents counted sixty-five hundred marijuana plants in those cornfields. The eradication process that Judge Quackenbush had ordered took days, and a close-up of agents tending a flaming mountain of weed was placed proudly in the newspaper.

Ultimately, the seven defendants in the marijuana-growing "conspiracy"—three ranchers and four hippies—were sentenced according to the number of plants found. The defendants from the hippie mountain were forced to plead guilty to possession of one thousand plants each: trace a finger from the drug *(cannabis)* on the x-axis, and another finger from the number or weight on the y-axis *(1,000)*, bring those two fingers together, and you've got the number of years that a human being is sentenced to serve in federal prison—unless, of course, he or she becomes an informant. In Fed Math, that means the equation now looked something like this:

(# of Plants - Rat Points) / # of Co-Conspirators = Prison Years Served

In drug cases, it is not the elected judges but the prosecutors who make the calls. Despite the mandatory minimums, the prosecutors can maneuver to give another value (number of plants) to the judge for each defendant; in this case, each of the farmers, even Bud King, on whose land the marijuana was grown, received six months to five years in prison. Each hippie received five to ten years. A couple of them were willing to bargain a bit. Mark got all ten—he wouldn't rat on anybody about anything. Neither threats nor enticements would convince him to give the FBI any information about the men with whom he'd been working.

I can't help but admire this. As I said, Mark molded my sense of morality. His final prison sentence began officially with time served in the Spokane County Jail on March 1, 1993. The charge: Conspiracy to Manufacture, Distribute, and Possess with Intent to Distribute over 1,000 Marijuana Plants. The sentence: 120 Months; 3559 SRA; 5 Years Supervision; $50.00 Felony Assessment.

⁓

3/3/4
Hi Jill,

Are you OK? Your answering machine is doing strange things. And it won't let me talk to you.

Ah! I remember I was once crazy.

Looking forward to Sunday—we'll have croissants and mocktails.

love, Mark

⁓

A photograph is a trace of appearances seized from the normal flow of the eye. (John Berger, *Ways of Seeing*)

The photo arrests time.

Arrest: v. 1. To stop; check. 2. To seize and hold under the authority of law. 3. To capture and hold briefly (the attention, for example); engage.

⁓

All the photos we see have been filtered—framed, shot, selected for a photo album, an exhibition, a magazine advertisement. I don't like the posed, Old West pictures of Mark and his last on-the-outside girlfriend. I've never seen her in the flesh. They met only months before he went to prison for the final stretch, and the core of the story is that he loved her and she betrayed him. (I offered my anger and my loyalty, but Mark wouldn't take it: "Bitch," I said. "Shut up," he answered.) So I can't show the pictures or give a name, but I will say this about the Old West pictures: they disturb me, embarrass me. I want to put them back into the box and pretend that I never saw them. If I'd never seen them, then I wouldn't need to put them into the photo album of this book. I threw them back in the box. A small poof of dust rose. The faces I didn't want to see stared up at me from the bottom of the box. I picked them up again. Threw them back. I did this three times, and finally, the artist won over the niece, and I tucked them into the back of the album, where I have to see them every morning.

And, in the end, it's not the gun, the spread thighs, the booze. It's the expression on Mark's face. He looks mean. The image we all create of Mark is that of the big-hearted outlaw. We never talk about the cold-hearted criminal, but he's here in this trio of studio pictures. Of course, Mark is posing. They both are.

It's not enough, then, to say they both are simply very good impostors of themselves. I don't want this to be my Uncle Mark.

I look more closely and determine that I lied. It's not only, or even mostly, the expression, but the dimpling of flesh on her thigh. Not all over, but in that one point, where the tip of his black gun presses the flesh through her fishnet stockings.

∼

Every photo is a construct. An element of the prison photos: in none of these pictures are we surprised. Prison waiting rooms are no place for candid snapshots. This is all about posing.

∼

Grammy and Mark were only two hours away from each other for the last three years of her life. She was in Eugene with my mother and

me, and he was in the federal pen in Sheridan, Oregon. Only a two-hour trip by car, but Grammy saw Mark only once, during visiting hours.

I wasn't there, and my mother can't remember the actual time that they spent together with Mark in the prison, except to remark that Grammy was already in her wheelchair with the attached auxiliary oxygen tank, and that it must have been quite a coup just to get past the visitors' checkpoint with its relentless metal detector and tight-assed guards. I know that I never made it through fully dressed. Once, stacking various items of apparel on the counter of the guard stand— Birkenstocks, belt with buckle, silver bracelet, overshirt with metal buttons, I joked—*I feel as if I'm playing a game of strip poker with a fixed deck. By the time this thing stops beeping, I'll be butt naked.* (Okay, maybe my joke was less than lighthearted, but they had me, right? I was standing there in my bare feet, pulling the barrette out of my hair, laughing, and the guard didn't even crack a smile: *Step through, ma'am.*) Which brings me to one more thing about the Sheridan FCI. After you make it through the metal detector, you are stamped on the flesh above your right thumb with ink visible only in the black light of the prison checkpoints. Then you wait in a holding area like a farm animal before the next set of computer-locked double doors, and in this space, there are two things: a plaque celebrating the FCI

Employee of the Month, and a full-length mirror with the message *This is the image you will present today.* Redressing, I always wondered whether this prop with its quasi-motivational message was intended for us, the visitors of felons, or for would-be employees of the month. Perhaps both.

But my mother can't remember waiting with my grandmother in this area, or being inside with Mark, and I can't remember ever hearing about it either. *I just know that it was too hot in the car. The sun was beating down on her, so we came back along the coast, stayed in a motel in Yachats, went to the sea lion caves the next morning. That was the sad part. You know how there are all those stairs there? To get down into the cave? Well, she was in her chair, so we had to take the elevator, of course, and she kept saying how she wished she could take the stairs. And then when I was wheeling her down that steep ramp to the platform where you can get close to the sea lions, I had a hard time keeping a grip on the handles, it's so wet down there, and I kept thinking that if I lost her, she'd go crashing away and launch right over that chain-link fence and onto the rocks with all those fat, barking, stinky sea lions. It was horrible. And I have a picture of her there, along the coast, but there aren't any prison pictures. I can't imagine why we didn't take any. Why are there no pictures? I just can't remember. You know how Grammy could be so nonemotional. The antithesis of me. We only tried it that one time.*

With no visits, Grammy and Mark filled the rest of that space with letters, pictures, even a by-mail game of Jotto (a game that loses any appeal it may have in real time when each turn is divided by a three-day postal delivery). But they gave Jotto their best shot—when you're both on the inside, you run out of things to talk about.

∼

Writing and fiction, my grandmother told me, should be *entirely fabricated.* Less than a month before her death (her mind was sharp until the end, just her body had gone to mush), I had a momentary lapse of reason and gave her "The Ring" to read. She called me and demanded to know why she was *painted as such a sordid character.*

What? Why? Because of the bright lipstick and the cigarettes? She told me that I remembered it wrong, that it didn't really happen that way. And did I have to include the brand of cigarettes, for heavensakes? *Don't you have any imagination?*

~

And so I have flirted with the possibility of anonymity—better than even a foreign language, the possibility to write *as far as you want,* and not have to live with the consequences. (Nicole Ward Jouve, *White Woman Speaks with Forked Tongue: Criticism as Autobiography*)

~

Mark Writes to Martha from the Sheridan FCI

The other day I was out walking around the farthest corner of the track. It was sunny and hot. A farmer was plowing a nearby field. I noticed that he had left his two young children to wait for him in the shade of a tree just beyond the fence. To me, it was like a scene out of a fairy tale. I was transported beyond the prison walls to a place where life went on in a normal fashion. I stared at those children, almost in disbelief. They were real. And then they waved to me! They saw me! I was still real, too. I hardly knew how to respond. I knew I shouldn't wave back, but I had to. So I did. Immediately the bells started clanging, and I was sent inside to be punished.

~

We're here. You're here. We're all real.

~

"So, for Mark, this was a moment of corroboration?"
"Yes, I think so. The wave was the corroboration. . . ."
"For which he felt he would be punished. . . ."

"Yes."

"If Jake corroborates, as you say, . . . backs up your story on that time in the back of the garage. . . ."

"Many times."

"There you go. You see? Each time? Each time separately? If Jake corroborates those many times, or even only one time, in the back of the garage. . . . Does it matter? If you're so keen, so dependent, on corroboration, then what about the rest of this book? You can't remember anything without corroboration? Memory can't come without corroboration? Whatever happened to putting together the pieces? Building the picture? Can't give anything but my own version, so deal with it. But here, with this issue of corroboration, you give yourself over. You give your story over. And what about ***? What if *** showed up to tell *his* side of the story? Would you suddenly be discorroborated?"

~

The FCI Sheridan Commissary List from May 1995 includes a category called "Stamps & Debit Credits ($19.20 Stamp Limit)." Near the bottom of this category I find what I'm looking for: "Photo ticket (Limit 20). . . . .$1.75."

"Catch that guy's eye," Mark had said to me one Saturday afternoon in the Sheridan visiting room. "I've got tickets that we need to use."

In the picture I am wearing the blue dress that I wear later in Mark's pirate gardener collage. My mother and I look at Mark, and Mark stares straight ahead into the eye of the camera.

Later that week, after we'd spent our photo tickets, Mark called on the phone: "The guy who took the pictures says he'll give me two cartons of cigarettes for your address. I'm thinking about it."

"Funny."

"Oh, come on now, would Uncle Markie sell out niecey that way?"

"Two whole cartons? Who would pay that much for an address? You flatter me."

"Yeah," he said. "You're right. Only one carton for the address. The other one is for a picture. Of course, he's just saying that. I'm sure he's got all the pictures of you he needs."

"Mark! Gross. That's gross. Thanks for the image."

"That's what he told me to tell *you*."

~

The visits to Sheridan were easier when I went along, my mother told me, and now that I have the pictures arranged in my own album, I can see that she was telling the truth. Mark and I didn't talk about whether he planned to drink when he got out. What difference did it make? Better to play Guess-the-Crime, coffee poker, joke around. I could save my crying for the parking lot when we were climbing into the Subaru, planning what we could make for dinner, knowing that Mark was inside, bent over, getting his anus probed for goods we had never delivered.

⌒ *Days on the Wall II*

On my grandmother's first day in the nursing home, a few days before Christmas in 1994, she said to me, "What I need is a good heart attack, you know?"

"It's a tricky thing to hope for," I said. "But I'll try—if I have to hope for something."

Grammy lifted her hand slowly and patted the top of her head. She hadn't had a hair appointment in more than a month. "Oh, sugar," she said. "I must look a fright, huh?" She did look wild. Her usually tightly curled white hair, stained yellow in the front from years of smoking, was frizzing out like a baby duck's.

"I take that back," she said. "First, I want a good hairdresser; then I want a good heart attack."

When Grammy, Mom, and I moved to Eugene in 1987, my grandmother bought a bachelorette apartment in an "adult community" with people her own age. These were Grammy's golden years. Eight of them. Do not be fooled, this was not a place of dull tea parties and civilized games of bridge—these people partied, some of them for the first time in their lives. My grandmother was the founding mother of Saturday poker games, and near the end of her time there, a bachelor down the hall named Eddie was luring her down to the recreation room under the guise of teaching my eighty-two-year-old grandmother to shoot pool. I caught on to their real game, though, when I bumped into Eddie in the elevator one afternoon after Grammy returned from her first heart surgery, and he said, "Say hello to that grandmother of yours for me, will you? How's she doing? We're all thinking about her. Tell her, will you? We miss her. She's such a cute little tomato. Don't forget to tell her Eddie said hello, will you?" And when I repeated that last part to my grandmother, she giggled, almost blushed, and said, "Oh! That was definitely Eddie. He's been teaching me a little pool down in the rec room, you know." We knew. And she smiled, a great big smile that pulled the wrinkles in her cheeks up like a drawstring, "Ahh. . . . Have you seen his car down in the garage? It's a convertible! A big, bone-white, beautiful convertible."

I wasn't around on the night that Grammy went into the hospital, but Grammy told me later that she gave in and called the paramedics when she was sure she couldn't take another breath. Her doctor, looking appropriately concerned, told us Grammy had congestive heart failure and that she was garbling her words because of the large doses of drugs they were giving her to drain the fluids out of her lungs. Drip. Drip. Drip. I sat in the blue vinyl chair by the dividing curtain, fiddling with the clear plastic oxygen tube that ran along the metal railing at the side of her bed and watching the catheter pull the water from her body. Then it made sense to me. I leaned closer and listened to her take a sleeping, gurgling breath. Inhale, exhale—every breath sounded like a kid blowing bubbles on the surface of a glass of Pepsi with a straw. Oh, Jesus. My grandmother—librarian, card player, record-keeper, *grandmother*—was drowning in herself.

In the hospital Grammy tried hard to die. My role, it seemed, was to facilitate this healthy dying, and I would say things to my grandmother that my mother could not say by herself without choking on the spit that rose up in her throat: "Gram. We love you, and we'll miss you terribly when you go, but we're ready when you are. We don't want you hanging around here for us. When you're ready, you go. We'll take good care of each other." My mother would nod, and cry, and squeeze Grammy's hand until she said, "Ouch. All right, already," or started to snore, depending on what drugs she was on at the time. She started having waking dreams, like the one in which she saw a nurse walk into her hospital room stark naked. "What? What?? What are you doing? Put some clothes on, for heavensakes!! It's not like you've got anything to show! I don't want to see that saggy bosom! Get *out* of here!" We took these as signs of a supernatural ability to see through clothing, signs that she was beginning to cross over into another consciousness, and we apologized to the nurse in question. But Grammy pulled out of those days, much to her dismay, and giggled wickedly about the incident with the naked nurse. She had survived her allotted twenty-one days in the hospital, and the administrators assigned a caseworker, who met us in the hall in front of Grammy's room and told us, "Your mother is a management problem. As a hospital, we're simply not set up to handle chronic conditions on a long-term basis. We need the bed. Tomorrow, we'll do a thorough assessment and then we'll make a decision." The caseworker tapped her pen on the clipboard. "There haven't been any signs of delirium or dementia, is that correct?"

"No!" my mother and I answered together. The caseworker stepped into my grandmother's room to introduce herself to her new client, and I heard my grandmother say, "Well, hello. You're not going to take your clothes off, too, are you? Did you know that we have a naked nurse on this hall?"

In those last few days in the hospital, after the pen-tapping caseworker, we held nightly emergency meetings at my mother's house, during which we drank a lot of red wine and tried to feel better. The wine helped. We thought about buying another house, one that was big enough for us to live in with a room for Grammy. We thought about the costs of hiring a day nurse while the two of us went off to work. We thought about the costs, and we drank red wine, and in the end, we called a company that moves people into nursing homes, bed and all. Before she knew it, Grammy was living in a nursing home, requesting a good heart attack, and she hadn't even sat up.

The nursing home smelled like death. Or something after. Decay. Or worse. Death in life. Dirty diapers and mashed potatoes, stale breath and candied yams, Jergens lotion and hamburger casserole. Breath that rattles around in old, cigarette-stained lungs for too long before it finds its way back out through the slack, dry lips of a dying man. The smell I could stand, after olfactory fatigue set in, but the sounds made me crazy.

My favorite patient was a man named Stan Parker (I learned his name from the brass-colored plastic tag in the slot by the door of his room). Stan was one of only two men on Grammy's hall, and he couldn't walk, or crawl, or move at all of his own volition, but the nurses would prop him around the room in various positions to give the impression that he was leading a normal, mobile, animated life in that ten-by-ten-foot space. Like changing window dressings or a series of framed photos, each peek into Stan's room revealed a new view: now here's Stan on his bed, curled on his side, now in a wheelchair with a dinner tray, now propped up on pillows in a recliner in front of the television (the programs of choice: *Wheel of Fortune* and *Hard Copy*). Stan had a trademark scream: "Oh my God, oh my God, oh my God, oh my God!" with increasing tempo, until it sounded like, "Ohmygod, ohmygod, ohmygod, omigd, god, god, goooooddddd. . . ." Then silence while he worked up the energy for another chant. One time, when I was walking past his room with my dog on a leash, he stopped mid-chant and hollered, "Hey! That's my dog! That lady has my dog!" In a place where nearly everything had been lost, the residents of the nursing home were inclined to point fingers, lay blame, pick out the thieves. Reciprocal filching was standard. One woman who motored around the halls in a wheelchair, using her slippered toes to scoot herself along, made a habit of coming into my grandmother's room and taking a pair of leather loafers out of the closet, claiming that my grandmother had swiped these nice shoes from her room while she slept. She always left the toe-worn slippers in their place.

After Grammy went into the nursing home, I took to eating After Eight mints for breakfast every morning—accompanied by a café latte. I must have felt ill by 9 A.M., but that's the merciful thing about grief: you start to lose feeling. This time I couldn't feel my gut. My oral fixation went through the roof. I bought variety packs of Carefree gum at Costco and chomped through them at a rate of three to four packs per day, consuming two pieces at a time. I was the chameleon-tongued woman, changing tongues to fit the flavor: spearmint-blue to peppermint-green and back to bubble-gum pink. I also chewed pen caps, mangling them into plastic wads and spitting them across the lab. And I had to stop using pencils altogether because once I had ripped the metal ring and the eraser off with my incisors, I'd move the pencil back to my molars and munch down through the painted yellow wood like a beaver. All this I did more or less unconsciously as I struggled to concentrate on work.

I lost my capacity to think. I'd get in the elevator and forget where I was going. I'd get in my car to drive to the store for some more gum and before I knew it, I'd be sitting at the stoplight a block from the nursing home. Following the route in my mind. Straight, left, reverse. Brake? I liked to think that if an undergraduate on a moped had streaked out in front of the car during this time I was driving on autopilot, I would have braked.

One afternoon in late April I brought my dog in to visit the nursing home right after we'd been for a run at the track. I remember my outfit—glistening black Lycra running tights and a ratty pink tank top—because when I entered the room, my grandmother looked up from the canasta game that she and my mother were playing and said with delight, "Look, Martha, it's the strumpet!"

"The *what?*" I asked.

"The *strumpet,*" Grammy repeated, enunciating carefully, as if I'd failed to understand her the first time. "*Strumpet,*" she said again, clearly enjoying the crisp, final "t." "As in: prostitute, whore, tramp, hussy, slut. Often used to describe a woman of ill repute. Strumpet."

"I get it, Gram. Glad you like the outfit." I snapped off Tango's leash and plopped down on the tile floor to stretch my legs.

"She doesn't really mean it," my mother said sympathetically, plucking a card from her hand to discard. "She just says that to shock you."

Grammy laughed. "I do too mean it," she said. "If your grandfather were here, he'd call the sheriff. Come to me. . . ." she intoned as she drew a card from the pile. "Ahh!" She laid her hand onto the table in fans of white, black, and red and set a triumphant final discard upside down. "Look at that. *Five* canastas, and two of them naturals. Now I can die." She leaned back in her blue vinyl chair and closed her eyes. "And then, you know the first thing I'm going to do? I'm going to run up the stairs!"

"Stairs?" I asked. Grammy had never shown any particular religious tendencies, and I was surprised by this attention to ascent. "To Heaven?"

"No," she said. "Maybe. I don't care what stairs. I just want to run up the stairs. Any stairs. I used to love to run up stairs, and I can't even walk up them now." She hummed happily and mumbled, "Yup. First thing I'm going to do. Right up the stairs." Her fingers shook as she led them in a climbing motion, knuckles as knees, up a tiny imaginary staircase.

One morning, six months after Grammy had gone into the nursing home, my mother called me at work.

"I've been thinking," she said, "and I have an idea."

She sounded happier than I'd heard her sound in weeks. Lifted.

"Okay, okay," she said. "What do you think of this. We'll bring Grammy home. We'll just bring her home. We'll get her out of there." Pause. "We'll kidnap her!"

"We'll *what?*"

"We'll kidnap her, and we'll just stop giving her all those medications that are keeping her alive. We'll let it happen naturally. We'll just let her go naturally. Peacefully." She sounded like a hum. She was losing her mind. I was afraid she would do this. Lose her mind.

"Mom," I said. "Mom. I like the idea of bringing her home. I really like that idea. But, Mom, we can't just stop all of her medications. Just like that. Boom. What if she doesn't die? What if she can't breathe?"

"Morphine!" my mother shouted. "Morphine! We'll just give her morphine when she's in pain, or when she has air hunger."

She'd thought of everything. I knew that she'd been up all night devising this plan. I could picture her drinking Merlot out of a yellow coffee cup, leaping up every time she had an inspiration. Getting happier. Maybe dancing a little. Maybe singing along to Nina Simone:

Ooh ooh, child, things are gonna get easier. . . . Free. Grammy would be free of what my mother called that "old, troublesome body."

"Mom," I began again. I don't know when I got to be the practical one in the family. Amazing how life flip-flops on itself. Mother-daughter-mother-daughter. We're a family of planners. We make lists to remind ourselves to brush our teeth in the morning so that we can have the satisfaction of a task completed. "Mom, we can't do that. We just can't do it. Listen. Listen. We don't know what would happen without the medication. Anything could happen. It could be terrible. We can't do it. What does Grammy think of the idea?"

My mother started to cry. I'd fucked up her whole plan—her plan to save Grammy, the world, herself. So she got mad.

"*You* don't see her, Jill. Not like I do. You're not there. You don't know what it's like in the morning when she wakes up, if she's slept at all. She can't even go to the bathroom. Nothing *works* anymore. Nothing works, and you don't see it."

"Okay, Mom," I said. "Why don't you take a break? You stay home tonight, and I'll go over and spend a few hours with her, okay? I'll make sure she knows that we're ready to do whatever she needs us to do to help her out of this mess. I'll talk to her about it."

"Okay. All right," my mother said. "But I was going to sneak in some food for her. She hasn't been eating anything except what I bring her. She says she doesn't like the way they mix everything together. She just isn't eating."

"I'll bring her something good. I'll make her a grilled cheese sandwich. Something simple that she'll like, okay?"

"Okay. Thanks. And I'll just stay here." A pause, but no click. "But remember that you have to be a little sneaky. Some of them don't care. They know it doesn't matter. Not anymore. But some of them are sticklers for policy, so you just have to be careful. Okay?"

"I can handle it, Mom. Take a bath or something."

"And you'll talk to her? About bringing her home?"

"Yes, Mom." It is not uncommon for my mother to repeat everything at least once before hanging up, especially in times of high stress.

"She likes white bread and plain yellow mustard. Nothing spicy."

"Yes, Mom. I can make a sandwich, okay?" I said too sharply, and I could hear her starting to cry again on the other end of the line. "Oh shit," I said. "I'm sorry. It's just that I've got it all under control, okay? I can do it. Just rest."

"Call me?"

I put my head down on my desk, feeling the smooth paper of the calendar pad against my forehead. Terrific, I thought, my grandmother's dying, my mother's losing her mind, and I'm studying the brains of undergraduates. Fucking terrific. I mean, if I didn't wonder about my own sanity, would I have any interest whatsoever in anybody else's?

On the corner of the pad I made a list for the grocery store, tore it off, and stuck it in the front pocket of my jeans. It turned out that Grammy didn't need Mom's plan. Instead, I killed her with a grilled cheese sandwich.

I pulled into the parking lot of Albertson's supermarket at four o'clock. My mother had reminded me that the dinner trays came around at the nursing home between five and five fifteen, and I wanted to be there on my covert operation with Grammy's sandwich before she came face to tray with whatever it was the dietitian had planned for the evening repast. As I parked, I imagined a grayish beef patty, curled ribbons of soggy coleslaw, and a side of sugar-free green Jell-O. I didn't like to go into Albertson's with its bright lights and over-packed, over-colorful aisles. Usually I shopped at the health food store where my mother worked, but I couldn't bear to go in there and answer well-intentioned inquiries into my grandmother's health—*Umm. . . . She's dying. She's going to drown in herself. Unless my mother takes care of her, first*—besides, I needed white bread.

Time was slowing down. I locked my car and crossed in front of the traffic in the parking lot. The hot asphalt seemed to adhere to the soles of my shoes, and every step was an effort. I stepped onto the black, corrugated mat of the automatic door and waited for an uncomfortably long time before the door hummed open and a rush of air-conditioned coolness sucked me into the store. Building up speed, I snatched a red plastic basket from the rack, hooked my bare arm through the cool metal handle—For Your Shopping Convenience—and made a beeline for Dairy.

My list was organized according to food group. In four and a half minutes, I was waiting in the Express Lane—*12 items or less*—and glaring at the woman in front of me who was cheating the system with her presumption that three cans of Chicken of the Sea tuna could count as one item. Less tuna, fewer *cans* of tuna, I thought, but for some reason the grammar game didn't comfort me. So I tried math. Sometimes when I'm stressed, I count, add, multiply, and divide. I was about to tell Tuna Lady that three cans didn't count as one item in my Express Lane when it flashed through my mind that Grammy could be dead before I got to her room with the sandwich. I was running out of time. Then I realized that "item" scrambled becomes "time." And the woman in front of me had two too many. My heart raced like a kitchen clock when the cookies are already burning. I didn't have time for this. My grandmother was dying. *Don't you know that she could be dead before I make it to the nursing home?* Melodramatic? Perhaps. But possible. I had a conversation with myself in different voices—inside my head, so that nobody would think I was crazy. Nobody but me, I pointed out. These were the big issues, but instead I fantasized about confronting the Woman with Too Many: "Ma'am, excuse me, were you *aware* that there are *seventeen* grams of fat per serving in that container of Ben & Jerry's, which, for your information, is supposed to serve *four*, not one, which makes for a whopping *sixty-eight* grams of fat, and at nine calories per gram that's 702 big, round, sloppy *fat calories*—are you aware that no amount of tuna packed in water is going to make up for that?" I smiled to myself, trying to focus my eyes on a kid at register four who was gnawing on a Cap'n Crunch box.

Another five minutes passed before I made it to the cashier. I had six items on the belt: extra sharp cheddar, sliced sourdough bread, French's yellow mustard in the squeeze bottle, a pack of Carefree, a single stick of Land O' Lakes that I ripped from a carton of four, and a six-pack of O'Doul's non-alcoholic beer (which did count as one item, by the way, because they were connected, and I would have got her Budweiser in the tall cans, that's what she wanted, that's what she asked for, but I couldn't stop worrying about drug and alcohol interactions, and I didn't want to be the one to kill her). I didn't *know* then that you can kill your grandmother with cheese. The cashier couldn't get the UPC code on the beer to scan. Slide. Slide. Slide. No beep. I guess you don't have to be a fucking rocket scientist to work here, I thought sweetly. Type the fucking number in. I'm going to scream. I'm going to count silently in my head, I thought, count each item, and when I get to ten, I'm going to scream: one, two, three, slide, four, five. Tap-tap-tap of the code being typed into the register. Loud beep.

"Twelve twenty-three, please." I didn't have to scream. You wouldn't have the guts to scream, really. "Paper or plastic?"

I stood in the middle of my kitchen holding the brown paper Albertson's bag. Time was speeding up, and I struggled to remember how I'd seen my mother make a grilled cheese sandwich. *Butter each piece of bread on both sides.* The butter was still too hard, and I ripped a hole in the first piece of bread. Goddamn it. I tossed the bread in the garbage. Plenty of bread, not enough time. Taking a paring knife from the drawer, I carved slivers of butter from the end of the stick, forming a small pile of butter shavings on the cutting board. Carefully, very carefully, I stuck the mini-pats of butter onto the bread with my finger tips. Never has a grilled cheese sandwich been so lovingly fondled. Four twenty-five. My grandfather didn't want anyone to touch his food. I never got that. He wanted them to make it for him, but he didn't want them to touch it. I held a few pats of butter between my palms to warm them for ease of sticking. I slit the cheese package, sliced off five pieces of cheddar, and arranged them on the bread. God knows what my grandmother did to my grandfather's food when he wasn't looking. She told me once that if you drop the turkey on the floor when you're basting it, just pick it up, put it back in the pan, wipe off the dust with a sponge, and baste it some more. Who's going to know? If you make a big stink about it, nobody will even eat the turkey that you got up at 6 A.M. to make the stuffing for, she said. Keep quiet about it, and nobody will know. I set the assembled sandwich down on the cutting board and lit the flame under a small cast-iron pan. High and fast? Low and slow? I went for medium medium.

Through extensive conversation, I convinced myself that when I got to the nursing home, Grammy's room would be empty. The nurse would say, "You're Beatrice Ingraham's granddaughter? I'm very sorry to have to tell you this. . . ." And she would be. Very sorry. I burned the sandwich on both sides. Grammy liked things crunchy. Before the nursing home, when she could still get out to shop, her favorite culinary treat was a bag of chicken wings from the deli at Safeway, burned to a crisp in the toaster oven. She liked black foods in general. She even liked black jelly beans. On this issue, we parted ways. I flipped the charred sandwich onto a sheet of foil and folded up the edges quickly to hold in the heat.

I drove to the nursing home with the hot sandwich, growing soggy, and the cold beer, getting warm, in the passenger's seat. Five o'clock. Dead. Dead. She's going to be dead. Cancel. Cancel that thought. Shut up. She's fine. What are you trying to do? Bring on her death? Are you trying to *cause* her death? That's the way to do it, you know. Just create it with your negative thoughts.

When I got to the nursing home, I hurried down the hall to Grammy's room, past the white plastic receptacles in the hall: LAUNDRY, DEPENDS, TRASH, HAZARDOUS MEDICAL WASTE. When I reached her room, I said please please please don't be dead and looked at the ornament my mother had hung on the door—a laminated photograph of a stuffed crescent moon that she had created out of some Fiberfil and a nylon stocking—chubby cheeks, bright smile, and all.

A golden tassel hung from the moon's chin and swished back and forth across the door as I pushed it open, forcing a cheerful "Hi there, Gram!"

My grandmother was not only alive but dressed and sitting up in her chair by the window. A covered plate sat on a yellow plastic tray on the small table in front of her.

"Ahh!" Grammy said, smiling. "What do you have for me?"

"A greasy sandwich and a couple of beers," I said. "So, how ya feeling today?" Once I could see that she was alive, I started to get particular.

"I told you not to ask me that question anymore. I told everybody not to ask. How do you *think* I feel? When I was in the hospital. . . . Oh, *when* was I in the hospital? The nurse told me that as long as things were going in, going round and round, and coming out, I was doing okay, you know? Well, they're not going round and round anymore. How do you think I feel?" I leaned over to give her a kiss on her cheek. Her skin felt like tissue paper against my lips.

"Sorry, Gram. I forgot. I promise I won't ask anymore," I said, giving her arm a little squeeze just above her wrist and noticing another deep purple bruise spreading up her arm like a birthmark, only it had never been there before.

Grammy scooped an ice cube out of a plastic cup with her trembling fingers, put it in her mouth, and crushed it noisily between her teeth. She didn't like to eat much anymore, and she'd always liked black coffee better than water, but she'd become addicted to ice-cube crunching since she'd arrived at the nursing home. "Well," she said. "Where's my beer?"

I gave her a beer and the sandwich.

"Grammy," I said, molding, squashing, and remolding the tinfoil into shapes while she worked on her sandwich. "Did you know that Mom wants to kidnap you and stop all your medications?"

Her eyes got wide in mock horror.

"She means well," I continued. "I mean, I'd do it, too, if that's what you wanted. We love you. We love you, and so we want you to know that whenever you can't stand it anymore, when the pain gets really bad and you can't stand it, we'll do whatever we can to help."

"Thank you, Dr. Kevorkian," Grammy said. "I'll keep that kind offer in mind. But do me a favor?"

"Yeah?"

"Don't do anything until I say so, hmm?" She chewed on a bite of sandwich, her lips closed tightly, rotating in a clockwise direction. She was a careful, methodical chewer, I thought. Like a cow—sweet, slow, and contemplative. Only when she was chewing. "Can I offer some constructive criticism?"

"Too black?"

"No, soggy. Just a little soggy. You put it into the tin foil too soon, you know? When you put it in the foil, you need to poke some holes. Next time just poke some holes, and it'll be fine. You know what your mother does? She just brings the whole cast-iron pan with the sandwich in it."

"The whole pan?"

"Yup." Grammy took a sip of her beer. "Mmm." I reached across the table for the bottle. "Hey! That's mine! Get your own!"

The door opened, and a head peeked around the door. Grammy held the beer in her lap, and I snatched the metal cover from the untouched dinner plate down over the half-eaten sandwich. The head said, "Hi, Beatrice. Did you do your puffer?" An arm reached around with a watch on the wrist, and the head nodded toward the time. "Six o'clock."

"Ha *ha*," my grandmother laughed, reaching out and tapping the inhaler on the windowsill. "Already did it!"

Before I left, I performed all the evening settling-in rituals: helped her into her nightgown, changed her loafers for her slippers, made sure that both the remote control and the cordless phone were within reach of her spring-operated, plastic-handled, long-armed mechanism that the physical therapist had given her for reaching the hard-to-reach, straightened out her oxygen cords, and gave her a big, sloppy kiss. "Good night, Gram. I love you."

"Thank you, Sweetie. Hey, wait. Where's my grabber?"

I handed it to her and smiled. "Oh, yeah. Sorry. Guess that'll help, huh?"

Grabber. Puffer. Grammy was looking better than she had in weeks, and she'd eaten her whole sandwich, soggy crust and all.

The morning after the grilled cheese and beer party, my mom called me at my lab. "This is it," she said. "Oh. I've got to go. They're here. The nurses are here. They're trying to get the IV hooked up for the morphine. We've got to get this IV hooked up. I've really got to go."

"Well, what is it?" I asked. "How do you know? What's wrong? Can she breathe? Is she drowning?"

"No, it's not that," she said. "Oh, wait. No, this side. When the other nurse was in just now, she said this side. She talked to the doctor. Jill? Jill, are you there? It's some sort of blockage in her intestine. She's all swollen. Oh, the poor sweetie, she's so swollen. She says no heroics. When I got here, they were going to take her to the hospital and try surgery, but Dr. O said she wouldn't make it. She doesn't want to make it. Jill? Are you there?"

"Yeah, Mom," I answered.

"Oh, I've got to go. . . ."

"I'll be right there." I could hear Grammy moaning. Click. Intestinal blockage. The grilled cheese sandwich. Oh, Jesus. I choked and spit up half-digested After Eights into a paper Starbucks cup. I typed an e-mail to my boss: *My grandmother is really bad. My mom says she's dying. I'm going over there right now. I'll call you at home when I know anything. Right now, I just don't know when I'll be back.* It took me a long time to type those five sentences. I logged out, grabbed my backpack, locked up the lab, and headed for the nursing home. We'd known about the congestive heart failure. We were prepared for my grandmother to go by air (not enough) or water (too much) but not like this. This wasn't part of the plan. It took my grandmother two days to die.

We set up camp in Grammy's room. My mother settled into the brown chair by the window, where she could crack the curtain for light, and she sewed faces onto stuffed nylon balls, showing me each face as it was "born." Whenever Grammy shifted her foot under the sheet or made any kind of noise, my mom would be on her feet and at Grammy's bedside like a superhero in a cartoon whooshing through time and space.

On that last afternoon a man on a riding mower came to mow the lawn outside Grammy's window, and I was annoyed, afraid that the noise of the mower would disturb Grammy's rest. The windows were open, and she took a big sniff, smiled, and said, "Lawnmower."

That was her last word.

Grammy slept, head back, white hair springing to all edges of the pillow, mouth open, trying to breathe, gasping, gurgling, slowing down. We had turned off the bright overhead light. Now, the only light in the room was a reading lamp on the table by the window. My mom sat under the light, holding the nightgown that we cut off Grammy the morning before, and a sewing needle. She hadn't taken a stitch in more than an hour. I moistened a mint swab in a cup of water and tried to wipe some of the drying saliva from Grammy's lips and tongue. She didn't wake up. She wasn't waking up anymore. I put the swab back in the cup. "I love you, Gram. I love you, love you, love you."

"Do you think we should call the boys?" my mother asked. She meant Mark, who was of course locked up at the Sheridan FCI a couple hours to the north, and Ian, who was three thousand miles away in Atlanta. The boys. "Oh no, I can't. I can't do it." She started to cry again.

"I'll call," I said. I looked at my watch. Nine o'clock. "Do you want me to call?"

"No," she said. "We'll just call them when it's over. What would we say? We don't even know. They'll just feel bad that they're not here with us." I kissed the top of her head, and her scalp felt hot and damp on my lips. The waiting games that part of you never wants to have end can be so long.

At ten o'clock the evening nurse came in to check on Grammy. She was wearing purple tights and a flowered tunic under a white lab coat covered with pieces of medical tape and adhesive prescription labels. I knew that her name was Jane. She was Grammy's favorite. "Oh, damn," she said. "I'm going to miss you, Beatrice." And then Jane put another dose of morphine into Grammy's hand. "This vein isn't going to take much more of this," she said. "I hope we don't have to start a new one."

Before Jane left the room, she taught me how to count Grammy's respirations. "She's slowing down. It's the morphine. The morphine will just wind her down." Then she lifted the blanket off Grammy's feet, pressed her thumb down on Grammy's toe, released quickly, and counted. "See?" Jane said. "Her circulation is dropping. You can watch how long it takes for that print to fill back in. You'll know it's soon when her feet and hands start to get cool."

Grammy was getting cold and turning blue. She died in pieces, from the outside in.

We decided that we'd better call the prison to tell my uncle, so that he could be with us, so that he could be thinking of his mother while she died. My mother took the cordless phone into the bathroom and let the heavy door click shut behind her. I heard sounds but no words. When she came out, her voice was shrill and shaky, but she wasn't crying: "They won't get him for me. They won't let him call. They said that the best they could do was send the chaplain down to see him. I said no. No. Don't send the chaplain. I don't want him to find out from the chaplain." So my uncle knew nothing until he was surprised by his number coming over the intercom the next day—*Inmate # 07157–085*—calling him to the visiting room, where my mother and I were waiting, holding hands. When he came through the doors, scanning the room to find the visitors who had come unannounced, nobody said anything. But he must have read his mother's death off our faces, and my mother held her little brother, squeezed him, shaking, until the guards intervened and told them to find a seat in a hurry.

At eleven o'clock Dr. O finally arrived. He said, "At this point, she's only alive for the living. I'm going to write a prescription for morphine every half hour."

My mother was inspired. She clapped her hands. "Let's go for it," she said. "Okay, thank you. We're going to go for it. We're just going to go for it."

Finally, we were going to help Grammy die.

In the last hour I took it all back. I squeezed Grammy's toe and counted, too long, while the blood returned to fill the circle. I panicked. My mother stayed calm. She stopped crying. I started. "That's it," she whispered to Grammy, stroking her hair, holding her hand. She pressed her lips against Grammy's forehead. I counted breaths. Not enough breaths. "Half an hour," my mother said to me. "It's time again. One more. Jill, get Jane." I got Jane, but I couldn't talk to Grammy anymore. I couldn't tell her it was okay. I couldn't tell her that I was ready for her to go—because suddenly I wasn't.

When my grandmother stopped breathing, finally let out that last breath and didn't try again, I held my breath with hers.

My mother whispered, "Good girl, that's it, let it go, we're okay, let it go."

I waited, counting slowly: One Grammy Breathe, Two Grammy Breathe, Three Grammy Breathe . . . Ten Grammy Breathe, Please Breathe. She didn't. I let go of her hand and waited for her blood to color in the prints left by my gripping fingers. The outlines didn't smudge.

My mother slid her hand behind Grammy's ear and began to slip off her oxygen tubes. "We can get rid of this horrible thing," she said.

"No! Wait. Just wait one more minute. We need to make sure. Just one more minute."

We waited. Each of us laid a hand on Grammy's head. Cooling. I willed her to rise up between us.

"Okay," I said. "Go ahead."

My mother pulled the plastic tubes out of Grammy's nose. I took my hand from Grammy's head and clicked off the buzzing oxygen machine at the foot of the bed. Stillness.

I returned to the head of the bed and looked down at my dead grandmother. I wanted to see a look of peace on her face, but her mouth hung open from her body's last efforts, just minutes before, to get air. I put my hand under her chin and pushed her mouth closed. Her face, including her lips, was all one color: pale gray. Ghostlike. I released my hold on her chin, and it slowly dropped open to gravity.

"Oh, my God," I whispered. "Oh, my God. What do we do?" I had no idea what to do.

"I think we pray," my mother said. Birthing coach. Sweating. Bone-tired.

"We don't know any prayers," I said.

"We don't need to know a prayer. She'll hear us."

We knelt down on the cold tiles, our hips touching, folded our hands on my grandmother's cooling sheets, and prayed.

"The stairs," I said. "Maybe she's running up stairs." And I prayed for that thought to slide down my clenched throat and settle into the place that felt so hollow in my chest. I held that thought in my mouth like a cherry cough drop, sweet and melting, and my mother's warm hand slid across the sheets and closed over mine.

For three months in the fall of 1995, Mark was not permitted to receive guests in the Sheridan visiting room. He'd been bad, very bad. In his words, included on the Incident Report under the category Comments of Inmate to Committee Regarding Above Incident, "I must be guilty if they say I am." Apparently, Mark had smoked some pot (he never would tell me where he got it), and he had been caught: *On 09–06–95 results were received from Toxicology Laboratories indicating Urine Specimen #EOOO57843 tested positive for Cannabinoids. Records reflect Urine Specimen #EOOO57843 was provided by inmate Mark Ingraham, #07157–085. Medical staff advised that inmate Ingraham was not receiving an authorized medication which would test positive for Cannabinoids.* I've got a whole file of paperwork on the "incident," reports in a rainbow of colors, a different color for every tangentially involved individual who could possibly give a shit about the fact that Mark had smoked "three hits" of pot.

I remember how relieved we were when we finally received the robin's-egg-blue copy in the mail: "Cannabinoids? That's it?" The prison held a Discipline Hearing concerning the "incident," at which Mark was presented with a list of Inmate Rights—among them, *The right to present a statement or to remain silent. Your silence may be used to draw an adverse inference against you. However, your silence alone may not be used to support a finding that you committed a prohibited act.* I smile to see that the space for the inmate's signature has been filled in by a staff member's scrawled "refused to sign."

That's my Uncle Markie. In 1970 I would have cut off my hair. In 1995 I probably would have signed. I wouldn't have wanted to sign, but I would have signed. Markie Boy was the rebel I always wanted to be. Mark was *admitted to Administrative Detention.* He was in the hole for thirty days. Mark said he never minded the hole. It was quiet there. Too bad he couldn't have his leatherworking tools. Mark's counselor spoke up for him at the review: "He is an orderly in the Unit (2B). He is a good worker and never causes any problems. This was really a surprise. We asked for leniency. He is not a problem."

～

Things Overheard on the Inside: An Excerpt from Mark's "Jail Talk" Journal

I'll get out the peak of July, then it'll be winter, no fall, winter, fall. Wait. Which way do they go?

～

9/17/95 SUNDAY 'ROLL TIDE'
Dear Jill,

Hi. An epic letter and wonderful story. . . .

Well I'm the proud owner of an orange jumpsuit. I've been in the hole since the 6th, sentenced on the 14th—which is when my time starts. I got 30 days segregations, 27 days good time taken away, 90 days no visits, lost my room, 1/2 my property, etc. etc. All because my urine was found to be tainted with a trace of cannabinoids. !@#$*%^!!!

Hey, the Crimson Tide is doing good huh? Of course I don't know what happened yesterday. The Ducks are kicking ass. You really know how to pick 'em. Around here it's rest, rest, rest! I'm glad you enjoy your purse. She grabs the purse and crosses many state lines. That's a federal beef.

AND NOW THE SEQUENCE OF EVENTS IN NO PARTICULAR ORDER

I'm glad to hear Tango is recovering from ringworms, next it will be the hairy snakes. You school teachers are a sick bunch, but loveable. Are you sure that "glint of recognition" in the eyes of your students is not the realization that the class is almost over? Ah, to have a teacher like you to break.

"Mom, send me an iron."???? It would probably be cheaper for a new one at K-Mart. I'm glad you told her you had the board. Women. . . .

No tobacco, no coffee, no music, no crafts. . . . woe is me. I
was holding onto the bars and doing little jumpies on my toes
and I think I sprained my knee and threw my hip out.

These one-inch pencils take a little getting used to. The 3-inch
toothbrushes too.

Well you guys try to behave yourselves down there.

Love, Mark

TOMORROW AND TOMORROW AND TOMORROW

CREEPS IN THIS PETTY PACE FROM DAY TO DAY.

B. F. I. + W. S.

~

A taste for alcohol and its effects is not uncommon in my family,
but in a family of hard drinkers, Uncle Mark is the hardest—or rather,
was the hardest. He claimed that he never did acquire a taste for the
distilled mash that can be made from mess hall prune juice, and even
the best smugglers have trouble fitting a fifth of Crown Royal in any
of the usual hiding places.

We've all got our drinks of choice. My mother rarely starts cooking
dinner in the evening without popping the cork on a bottle of red.
She's a Burgundy woman. My brother likes whiskey and Diet Coke.
My grandmother drank Schlitz. Grandfather kept that gallon jug of
muscatel under the kitchen sink most of his life, and downgraded to
Budweiser in the tall cans, two at a time, when his doctor advised him
to quit drinking. For my part, I was twenty years old before I figured
out that I could drink without blacking out; I thought buzzed, drunk,
high, and hammered were synonyms for no lights, no memory, no
way to know when to stop.

Myself? To this day, I confess, I'm a vodka girl: tasteless, odorless,
barely there.

~

I have been living with the assumption that *** is dead. I have
coveted this belief out of cowardice. If I go looking for him, and I

find out that there is no death certificate, that instead there's an address for him somewhere in Massachusetts, that *in fact,* he's still living in the garage behind his mother's house, just a line of footprints in the sand from *my mother's* old house, then? Then. Then what? If Jake can say, Yes, it did happen, then, isn't it equally plausible that *** could say, No, it didn't happen? And if it did, it's only because you were a slut and asked for it. More than asked for it, you instigated it.

I would be uncorroborated, and I'm a coward.

~

*** had a mother, too. She was a shadowy figure and not often home, and when she was, it was startling—as if the overstuffed, cigarette-burned chair in the dark corner had decided to begin breathing. Her habits were strange—she was often gone all night, and when she was home in the day, she never even cracked a blind. The house was either totally dark or lit only by a dim, artificial glow—was it blue? Maybe the light from the television only? That's how I remember it, but I couldn't have been in there more than five times in all those years because *** stayed in the garage almost always.

On one of the few occasions that I actually saw ***'s mother in the house, she was eating Frosted Flakes. I remember that she added sugar to the pile of papery flakes, two or three teaspoons at least, because I couldn't believe it—we weren't allowed sugary cereals, so this was a shocking thing, and I watched to see if she would eat it, and she did, of course, sitting in her chair, an amorphous lump of crunching, and if she talked then, I cannot remember what she said because I was so focused on that chewing. I know that the bottom of that bowl must have been thick with the melting grains, and I remember the sound of her licking up the last of that sugary sludge and how I felt an ache in my teeth and an anxious longing—for so much sugar? for a path through the dark to the door?

The truth is that I was terrified of ***'s mother. I never understood completely what it was that she did when she was not in the house, but she was some sort of nurse, and her patients were crazy.

Now I understand that she must have been working with the criminally insane. I know they were people who had perpetrated something unthinkable—like ax murder or eating the tender hands of children.

***'s mother told us things—such as, if you wrap a baseball bat in a towel and beat someone to death, there will be no bruises. I believed this absolutely until just this moment of writing it down: but how could there be no bruises if a body has been bludgeoned *to death?* (Maybe I remember this because *** talked about it often— the anonymous murder, the possibility of killing without consequences. I don't remember. I told you, the mother was a shadowy figure.)

***'s mother also told us about the man with the giant cock, huge and pendulous like that of a horse. He wouldn't keep it in his pants— not ever—and he liked to whack things with it. He'd walk down the hall, she said, thwack, thwack, thwack against the wall, the way kids do at school with their hands, rhythmic and bored; but this guy used this huge, floppy penis, and when someone tried to move pass him, he'd hit them with it, thwack, thwack. There was no controlling him, she said. If I told you whether she laughed or groaned when she said this, I'd be making it up. I don't know.

*** had a mother, too.

~

In 1995, after my grandmother died, my mother took a trip back to Plum Island to visit her friends. This is part of the letter that she sent to report:

*I saw our old house—which seemed much the same as ever (I hope to have some good pictures for you of it all). 12 years since we've been there—12 years that we lived there. Truly a dear old spot. A place that will always be "home." Maybe the place you spend the most time in when your children are small + "growing up" is what makes it seem home-y. Mother told me not long ago that was her favorite time of her life. Anyway, it was very lovely there and did remind me of happy times. In driving down Jackson Way, I did see Gay (the woman who had bought Donna's house) + also Mrs. *** in her doorway. I saw no sign* *of* ***—*nor did I ask*—*I was startled enough to see her appear! I spoke with the mailman who always lived on the corner in the big house near ours.* . . .

She didn't go in. She didn't find him. She was *startled enough to see her appear!*

◠

I have never gone back to the island in Massachusetts. I live with my assumption—which is fed by what I know about ***'s relationship with drugs, alcohol, and motorcycles—that *** is dead. How do we expect things to look when we revisit them twenty years later? Do we want a whole new world? So that we can rest comfortably in the illusion that the world we knew left with us? That it is ours and ours alone?

◠

Your Grammy Sarah, my mother always says, *was a hard mother to have.*

And then India chimes in: *He's not a monster, Jill. You can't just come here and say he's a monster.*

◠

The vision that I hold in my mind of *** is actually one of him walking away. The distance he is covering is the one between my bedroom window and the back of the garage where he lived, a distance of about fifty yards, a field of sand and sea grass away. And I've never thought of that before: I could see the back of ***'s garage from my bedroom window. The whole time, always, he was right there. From the back he looks so old and ugly. He is shuffling, as if his feet are too heavy to lift from the grip of the sand. Because he is not wearing a belt, his jeans are sliding down his hipless body. The crack in his ass is a secret I know and the image of him I hold in mind. Walking away.

◠

Mark Writes to Martha from the Hole: Sheridan Federal Correctional Institution

SEPTEMBER 1995

9/6 WED 7:00 P.M.

Dear Martha,

Well they took away my pen and exchanged it for a real short pencil. Those tailored khakis I traded in for an orange jump suit. I'm styling now. I can see where news from my segregation cell will be mighty scarce. This is just a note to say don't expect calls and/or cards for some time. A urine specimen was returned here which claimed I had cannabinoids in my blood. Probably left over from the 60's back in Berkeley. I lose good time, visiting, phone, etc. etc.

Mark

⁓

MON 9/11

TOMORROW AND TOMORROW AND TOMORROW

CREEPS IN THIS PETTY PACE FROM DAY TO DAY

B. F. I.

Breakfast in bed this morning, lunch and dinner also. What a life. I got a hold of a good book—*The Star Rover* by Jack London. I had never even heard of it, which for a London fan is pretty amazing. Secrets of doing time in solitary confinement. Try it. The book, of course. There is a McMurtry book called *Dead Man's Walk* a prequel to *Lonesome Dove*—back when the boys were just getting into rangering. These guys would *love* to see a guy lose it in here, so I'm trying not to.

Love, M

⁓

WED 9/13

Hi Mop,

They took my celly out last night and left me in a cell alone.
The first time I've been alone in 2 ½ years. I stayed up late
reading *The Star Rover* (great book) unable to sleep. I doubled
up the mattress and hardly knew how to act. I'm sure I'll get
somebody today, but I'm hoping not. The window does not open
and it faces the afternoon sun. I bake. . . . Got your letter today
and don't worry I'm not going to lose my cool here—I refuse.
Geiger is the only place I know where you can wear your own
clothes. What suitcase-pack are you talking about? Of course you
can use what you want, but what is it?

Love, Mark

~

There comes a point when secrets don't help anymore. Secrets become laughable, unkeepable, unbelievable. In 1996 my live-in
boyfriend of two years broke up with me, moved out, and fell in
love with another woman—not necessarily in that order. Denying
any infidelity, he told me with a straight face that sometimes love
just changes, people change. I didn't believe him. Not very often, I
thought. It's not very often that people change all that much. But
I guess he figured that there are some secrets that are still worth
keeping.

When he said this—*people change, Jill*—his eyes couldn't stay focused on mine. I watched his eyes shift, slide from their focus on my
face, across the lawn, and pull back in to settle on the brown glass
lip of his beer bottle. Sitting on the cement steps of our rented house
in Tuscaloosa, Alabama, we had this same discussion at least twenty
times before he finally left. It was July, and we sweated, flicked fire
ants from our bare toes, and drank cold beer.

"It's this fucking state," he had said. "It's the climate. If we'd stayed
in Eugene, we'd probably still be all right." We had moved from Oregon to Alabama so that I could go to graduate school.

"You're right," I said. "It's just like everybody says down here—it's not that you're fucking someone else, *it's the humidity.*" I wound my hair up on top of my head, away from the sweat of my neck, and leaned back against the screen door.

"I don't know why you say that," he said.

"You didn't have to come here with me. It was a choice," I said, lifting my bare leg away from the steps and picking off the flakes of gray paint that had peeled away from the step and stuck onto my sweat at the back of my thigh.

～

During the break-up, I drank a lot of vodka, switched from Gordon's to Absolut, figuring if life sucked, why not have it suck and be broke, too? What difference did it make? The truth is, none at all. I don't remember that it made any difference. I'd start drinking at exactly three o'clock in the afternoon, almost, not quite, but almost what we call in my family "a respectable cocktail hour." I knew that at three o'clock he was getting off work, going out behind the restaurant, standing in the shade of a dumpster, and smoking a cigarette in the company of a woman for whom his feelings had not (yet) changed.

During this time, I understood in my bones the feeling of dependency—on a substance, on a man. When the clock struck three, I'd pull the icy bottle of Absolut Citron out of the freezer and drink it straight out of the bottle, thick as syrup, and cool as a popsicle. Not my first flirtation with addiction—what the mind forgets, the body remembers.

I consider forgetting about this father-finding, baby-having, security-seeking bullshit and just going it alone, whatever and whenever I please. No babies. Not in bubbles, not in my body. Not now, not ever. Because I can't ignore the obvious fear: Could I carry a baby? Could I hold her in my body? Feed her from my flesh? Support her growing weight in the shell of my skin and bones? Would I be able to give over my hips to be her cradle? Adding on to what I have only just come to accept as my own? Could I stand it? What if, what if, what if, in the sixth month of gestation I panicked: *Get her out of me. I cannot carry her. I cannot. I cannot carry her.* A baby cannot be vomited.

~

In March 1997 Uncle Mark was transferred from the federal penitentiary in Sheridan, Oregon, to a prison hospital in Lexington, Kentucky—he'd hoped to escape the rain with the move, but during his first week there, there were three solid days of wall-shaking thunderstorms. The weather center put out a tornado warning. Mark reported, disappointment thickening the tone of his voice, that the prison itself sustained no structural damage. I pictured him there preparing for the best—a tumbled wall, a swollen creek—building an escape dinghy with a bed frame hull, a garbage-bag sealant, a prison-issued sheet sail.

~

The reception was never good when Mark called from prison. I never had that wonders-of-modern-technology feeling that he was right next door. So close. No. He always seemed so far away. Often the yelling and screaming of the other prisoners in the background made it hard to hear.

"Jesus, Mark, what the hell is that?"

"Oh. Nothing. Just another stabbing."

I hoped he was kidding. In our family, we'd learned to make jokes about almost anything, funny or not, but after five years inside, Mark sometimes lost the edge on his wicked sense of humor. He'd just had a birthday, and I knew that attempts at birthday cheer would make me feel like an idiot, but I couldn't help it.

"So. . . . Did you have a happy birthday?"

"Oh, ye-e-e-e-es," he said. "Oh, yes, the best fucking birthday I've ever had. Cake. Candles. Party glasses of Crown Royal all around. Did you get that Crown Royal like I told you?"

(Four years earlier Mark had issued a request from prison for me to buy a case of Crown Royal, so that when he got out it would be nicely aged. As well-aged as he would be. My mother thought he was kidding. I knew he was dead serious, but sometimes it was hard to tell with him. In the waiting room of the Sheridan FCI, bathed in a liquid stench of microwave popcorn, shitty diapers, and cheap perfume, my mother had squeezed Mark's hand and forced a small laugh. She clung to the hope that he wouldn't drink when he got out. If he got out. Mark had directed his order at me: Get the Crown Royal.)

"Oh, yes," I echoed his sarcasm. "Got it up in my attic now. Coming right along. Yum. Yum."

"Good."

Pause.

"So. . . . How many days are you getting off for all your good behavior lately?"

"A year and a half total. Course I've lost some of that already. Fifty-four days a year. But you only get that if you really suck ass."

"You've never been good at that. Sucking ass." I relished the sibilant quality of the phrase as it moved from tongue tip, to teeth, past lips.

"No, I've never acquired a taste."

We laughed. On the phone, eventually, we laughed a lot. I hopped from topic to topic, risking touching on something that'd piss him off, hoping to stumble onto something that might make him happy.

"Mom said you can have money at this new place."

"Yeah. I've got some change in my pocket right now." I imagined him fingering the loose coins in his pocket, but I couldn't hear any jingling over the din of the other men.

"Cool. Well, that's something, huh?" (At Sheridan, Mark had been sent to the hole for three days because they'd found a quarter in his locker during a search.)

"All they have are candy machines. I don't like candy, but I buy it sometimes just because I can. Which is sick. They don't let you save up enough to get anything good."

"Like what? What do they have that's *good?*"

"I don't know. I haven't found it yet."

"Oh, terrific, Mark."

"What? I'm without connections. I don't know anybody yet. I'd just as soon not know anybody."

"With that attitude, you'll never know anybody."

"You're right. I've got the wrong attitude. I've got a terrible attitude. I need to go hang out in a dark corner, on a dark night, with some dark people and get more into the mainstream of prison life here."

"Right. That sounds a lot better. I like the sounds of that."

Mark chuckled. He loved that shit. He loved knowing that I had absolutely no idea in hell what it was really like for him on the inside. So he baited me.

"Oh niecey, don't worry. I'm actually used to all this shit. Most of the guys in this place are just starting their time, with little short sentences. I'm old hat. Niecey?"

"Yeah?"

"Get the Crown Royal."

⁓

"Did you ever get it?"

"No."

"And?"

"I'm sorry. I'm sorry that I didn't. We pretended and pretended that when he got out he wouldn't drink. We'd all quit. Nobody would be a bad influence. What a joke. I wish I had gotten the Crown Royal. I wish I could have said: *Mark. I got it. I really got it. It's waiting for you.*"

"To kill himself with?"

"Jesus. No. Yes. I don't know. It doesn't matter. It would have been something for him to think about, so much time for thinking. . . . those gem bottles of dark amber, lined up side by side like salvation in my attic. Something that he knew would wait for him. Wait for him and only get better—mellower, better integrated. But you know what? You know what bugs me? I found out that whiskey's not like wine. Once it's sealed into the bottle, it doesn't continue to age. Mark knew that, I'm sure. I could have put that Crown Royal in the attic ten years or ten days before he got out of prison, and it wouldn't have made any difference."

"But you didn't."

～

Mark couldn't sleep in prison. Inside, he told me, it is never dark, never quiet, and he developed something he called "tickley feet." Trying to sneak up on sleep, he would crawl into his narrow bunk, barely big enough for a man who was six-foot-two when he wasn't slouching, and close his eyes. But as soon as the world in his head darkened, faded to gray, a prickly feeling trickled down the arches of his feet. Lying on his back, he tried to rub out the tickling on the sheet, like running in place, like he could have run right through the metal frame on the bed above him, through his snoring bunkmate, through the roof, out into the air. But the running didn't help the tickling. The friction of his feet on the coarse sheet only made it worse, and the tickling spread through his ankles, moved into his calves, and settled into his knees. His knees vibrated and jerked—a white-coated doctor with a pointed rubber hammer tapping and testing, tapping and testing. Over and over, Mark's reflexes responded.

Prison doesn't take away the body's instinct to run. Once Mark called me to report that he hadn't slept in a week. The body remembers everything, even when we think we have forgotten. Flesh responds.

～

Mark Writes to Warden Beeler

LEXINGTON F.M.I.

I am a medical transfer from F.C.I., Sheridan, Oregon. I now reside in the Antaeus unit. The policy of deciding the order of dining by the unit's rank in sanitation inspection I think is an unfair one. Admittedly, Antaeus is usually situated last. This means that at an

average of 4+ hours a day, Antaeus inmates are locked in their unit
28+ hours a week longer than some others. This means 28+ hours of
lost time on the yard, in the library, wherever. The menu is many
times missing the best parts and we have very little time to eat.
Antaeus is the medical unit and many inmates, like myself, are not
able to kneel down under beds and raise our arms above our heads
to clean. I'm here for a knee replacement and my right shoulder has
a severed nerve and doesn't move. Yet when I look around this unit,
I feel quite physically fit. It seems to me unfair to punish an entire
unit of physically handicapped inmates for perhaps only certain
areas of sanitation problems. Thank you for taking time to listen.

◠

Mark Writes to Martha

SELMA, OREGON (CIRCA 1973)

Dear Mop,
    The Birds are singing, the flowers are in the millions, the
creeks are up, and the buds are bursting. Happy Spring.
        love, Mark.

◠

Sometimes I close my eyes, lay my head on the desk, under the
lamp, and if I concentrate, the heat from a bare bulb can feel like the
sun on my face. I wonder if Mark ever tried that.

◠

When I was eighteen, I lost my taste for doughnuts on a houseboat
moored in Shasta Lake. Under a tree, looking down on the man-boy
who yelled my name from boat to boat, I was alone with no photographer, and my body knew its own story even before the rape, even
before the doughnuts: *Here, Jill. You get first choice.*

◠

Writing autobiography, I sometimes confuse my life with the fictions I have created. Writing can become like a photograph in the family album. Do I really have a memory of standing in my grandmother's rose garden, wearing my favorite purple dress? Or have I built this memory from the picture? In my fiction, there is a recurring image of a little girl who doesn't want her baby bunny. I almost believe this girl to be me—she could be me, except for the part about the safety scissors. I don't think I had any.

~

I found them when I was swinging in our curved, wicker hanging chair, pumping my legs, and listening to the chain slide and rub through the ceiling hook: *Careful! Don't kick that box!* my mother warned. When I jumped down from the chair and opened the flaps of the box, I found two baby bunnies. They huddled together in the corner of the box, and the sound of their tiny claws scratching on the cardboard was no louder than the sound the crickets made as they tried to crawl up the side of the Chinese take-out box, where my brother trapped them each week to feed to his pet tarantula, Spike.

One bunny was brown, and the other black. I named them Chocolate and Licorice, but my brother changed the black one's name to Tar. When Chocolate was small, so small that she could sit in my hand, and her ears were as thin as paper, so thin that I could see the pink veins inside, I had a terrible thought: if I wanted to, I could cut off her ear with my school scissors. If I wanted to, I could; she was that small. I remember thinking that the cut-off ear, paper thin, would probably stick like tissue to the short blade of the round-ended scissors with the bright red plastic handles. I remember that thought because after that I didn't want the bunny anymore. I didn't want to hold her in my hand. She was too small and soft.

I didn't cut off the bunny's ear, but what I did do was much worse—slower, crueler. I didn't like having the rabbits. I didn't like to hold Chocolate when she was little because I was afraid that I would hurt her, maybe accidentally, maybe on purpose. I hated her vulnerability. Maybe Chocolate knew that.

By the time Chocolate was mature, she wouldn't allow herself to be held. When I reached my hand into the chicken-wire hutch to dump the green feed pellets into the bowl (a chore I would complete only following dire warnings from my mother), Chocolate would turn into the Tazmanian Devil: a whirling dervish of tooth and claw. I would pull back a scratched and bleeding hand, and she would stare me down with cold eyes, licking the dirt and blood from her front paws. Only when I closed and latched the door would she allow Tar to emerge from the sleeping box in the back of the hutch. She protected Tar fiercely—Tar was timid, soft, until the morning I found her frozen and dead. I had forgotten to feed them the day before, the cage was dirty, and the water in the bowl was covered with a sheet of ice.

Chocolate stopped being mean; with nothing to protect, she became timid. She mourned Tar. My mother's boyfriend at the time, a carpenter I didn't like, made me a cross to erect in the sand over Tar's grave—he burned in her name and the date that she died. I knew this was wrong, and I wanted to tell him that I didn't deserve the ceremony of the cross, but I didn't know him well enough to tell him.

~

When I began this book, Mark was alive. In order to revise, to bring it all up to date, I could probably just go through and change all the tenses:

Mark says. Mark said.

Mark sees. Mark saw.

Mark fears. Mark feared.

Mark could die. Mark died:

Today Mark dies,

Yesterday Mark died,

Mark will die,

Mark has died

is dead.

Get the Crown Royal

August 1997 was big for our family. In order of impact: Uncle Mark died in federal prison after serving only half of a ten-year sentence, Ian got married, and I turned twenty-eight. My brother married his then-pregnant girlfriend in the dining room of their house on August 16. A cowboy minister they'd found through the Atlanta yellow pages officiated. Because mine is the only birthday that Ian can ever remember, he chose this date for his wedding, figuring that then he'd be able to remember both his sister's birthday and his wedding anniversary with a single synaptic effort.

During the brief wedding ceremony, Ian's German-born bride misheard the cowboy minister when he said, "hold him in my esteem and love," and parroted back her vow to "hold him in my steamy love," while my confined dog scratched relentlessly at the bedroom door, and Uncle Mark's ashes rested serenely under the coffee table at the feet of the cowboy's emphysema-wracked wife. Between the coughing and the scratching and the cardboard box under the coffee table, I didn't know whether to laugh or cry. I did both. In the photos, though, we are smiling, and the wedding couple holds the knife to cut the cake I made for them: three layers, cream cheese frosting, and a toy bride and groom.

~

Mark Writes from Prison: Sheridan FCI 1993

> Bake me some cakes and put them in a pile,
> Be very careful and slip in a file.
>
> Make me big tarts, but remember the law,
> Be clever, discreet, when you add the hacksaw.

Now shape long rolls with love and plenty of butter,
Holes I'll make with the hidden glasscutter.

Apple's okay, but I like cherry pie,
Be sure in the middle you stash the hair dye.

To wash it all down put a key in my tea,
That fits the car in the lot that's waiting for me.

~

We did not plan for the prison break to go this way. Uncle Mark had told me to find him jetpacks. He had broached the plan when he was still at the prison in Sheridan, Oregon. Microwave popcorn, shitty diapers, Old Spice—all three mean the visiting room in the federal pen to me. The air would be so warm and thick with fake butter and perfumed human bodies that I felt as though I had to chew a few times before taking in a lungful.

Prison is a hard place to breathe, and the more you think about it, the harder it gets. In prison, Mark managed to keep breathing for five years. I don't know how.

That day in Sheridan, Mark hatched his jetpack plan over a chicken parmesan sandwich and a paper poker cup of black coffee. Prison visiting rooms are all about food. Food is something you've got to have, inside or outside, and even a row of vending machines behind a strip of red tape creates a workable domestic space—soda, coffee, juice, ice cream, cold sandwiches, hot sandwiches, burgers, burritos. Prisoners aren't permitted behind the red line, so visitors take requests, pump in quarters, wait to heat sandwiches, get everything just right. In a situation where there is nothing else you can do, a beef and bean burrito in a plastic wrapper with a plastic package of salsa from the box above the microwave can seem like a gift.

My mother returned from the microwave with a chicken sandwich for Mark. The sandwich was tucked into a gray, institutional paper towel, folded over in triangles at the base of the sandwich, like gift wrap. "Careful," she said, handing him the sandwich, "it's molten."

The chicken parmesan was Mark's favorite. Barbecue was only a backup when the machines were out. Mark stuck his finger down inside the sandwich and wiggled it. "Molten, eh?"

"Oh," my mother moaned, snatching back the sandwich, "is it still cold in the middle? I'll take it back. I'll give it another zap." She made her way back to the microwave line. It was a Saturday, and we had five hours. She could afford the time to make it perfect.

"See that guy? The one waiting for the girl at the Coke machine?" Mark asked.

"Yeah," I said. I turned in my hard plastic seat to get a better look: standard khaki uniform, short gray hair.

"What do you think?" Mark asked.

"Not a drug dealer," I said. "Bank robber?" Guess-the-crime was a favorite game of ours. It's not as easy to tell a white-collar criminal from a crack dealer as you might suppose.

"Nope. He's the Tylenol murderer," Mark said. "Killed his wife. We've really been upgrading around here."

"Who's the woman?"

"Probably his girlfriend."

"Do you think she knows? I mean, hello, . . . excuse me. Were you *aware* that your boyfriend is the *Tylenol killer?*"

Mark smiled, leaned forward to put his elbows on his knees, and said in a low voice, "Did you bring the jetpacks?"

"What? Packs of what?" my mother asked, returning from the microwave and catching the tail end of Mark's sentence. She gave him the sandwich. "Here, try this."

"The what?" I echoed.

"The jetpacks. I told you. Jetpacks. Get them."

Between bites, Mark painted the escape scene. He would strap them on, he said, and fly right over the double fences of the prison yard. The twin coils of razor wire, glinting under the light of the moon, would be lovely—their knife edges as pretty as tinsel on a tree. With a jetpack, he said, still whispering out of the side of his mouth, turning away from the disco-ball ceiling camera, he could be free. I never knew if he was joking. He must have been, right? I didn't get the jetpacks.

~

Mark was transferred to the federal prison hospital in Lexington, Kentucky, in March 1997. It took my mother and me five months to make a plan for a visit together. We flew separately and met at the Lexington airport. "Could you see it?" my mother asked. "Mark said if you look off to the left when you're landing, you might be able to see the lights of the prison. I wanted to wave and say, 'Hello! We're here! We made it!' I sent him the itinerary. I'm sure he was thinking of us landing. He was probably waving."

As I said, we didn't plan for the prison break to go this way.

When we arrived at our motel, a Days Inn in Georgetown, the desk clerk told us that we had four messages: my mother's boyfriend, my roommate, my brother, and the chaplain at the Lexington Federal Correctional Institution. A message from the chaplain. We took the key to the door of our room. My mother said, "The chaplain. That's bad." Then we said nothing. If we were quiet and didn't speak, if we didn't make a noise, maybe death wouldn't hear us. Maybe our hearts wouldn't finish the journeys they were making from our chests to our throats and finally out through our mouths.

Somehow we got through the door. I called the prison. My mother sat on the edge of the bed and watched me. The voice on the other end said, "I'm very sorry to have to tell you this." I didn't blink. I watched my mother. "Mark has passed." In my panic, searching: passed an exam? passed a gallstone? passed through the walls of that goddamn prison?

"When?" I whispered.

"Two o'clock. Would you like to talk to the chaplain?"

"No." I covered the mouthpiece with my hand and looked at my mother. "He's dead."

"No," she said. "No. We just got here. We came to visit. No. He knows that we're coming. No, no, no. . . ." Her words became a wail, a chant, the sound coming from a place so deep inside her body that I didn't even recognize my own mother's voice.

⁓

Sitting on the quilted polyester bedspread, holding the heavy phone in my lap *(who haven't we called who needs to know?)*, I felt like a psychologist watching a grieving patient begin the process of mourning. Maybe I thought I was some kind of expert. Maybe I thought death gets easier with practice. Denial. Bargaining. Anger. Denial again. The stages of grief aren't like items on a list to be checked off. We live through them, then we move on to something else, then we return to a place in our grief we haven't finished with yet.

In the wake of the world-stopping, gut-numbing news, I didn't know how my mother would live without her brother—and neither did she. "I can't," my mother repeated. Shaking her head, she paced back and forth in the space between the end of the two full-sized beds and the long dresser. Door to sink, and back again. "I can't. I can't imagine a world without Mark in it." I sat on the bed and watched her.

"I know," I said. "I know."

A few hours into the evening, my mother made up a story whereby Mark could still be alive. For the time that she took to tell me her thought, she was smiling, happy—she'd found a solution to the un-solvable: "This is just like him, that rascal. He's not dead. What if he's not dead? What if he figured out a way to stage his death? So the prison would *think* he was dead. But really he's on a plane somewhere right now. He's free. And we'll be planning his funeral, and then, out of the blue, we'll get a call and it'll be Mark. What if he's not dead?"

"Mom. He's dead."

Her smile dropped off her face. I might as well have slapped her— or killed Mark myself. And I guess, in that frozen moment of grief, I had. She glared at me, and her face contorted with anger. "How do *you* know?" She screamed at me, and then, changing only the inflec-tion, she screamed again, "How do you *know?*"

"I guess I don't," I said. I didn't. "I'll call them. Tomorrow I'll go look at his body. You don't have to. I'll go. Then we'll know. Then we won't always be wondering."

~

The first night in the Days Inn we stayed awake, numb and sick, wondering what Mark would want us to do. That's what you're supposed to ask, right? What would he want? You're supposed to pretend that's what you're figuring out, pretend that's possible, but I couldn't quiet the voice in my head: *He doesn't care. He doesn't care. He's dead. Dead people don't care.*

He had never requested cremation, but we needed him to be portable for the journey. If we left him "whole," we couldn't take him on a plane with us; instead, his coffined body would be sent back through the prison system and shipped across the country to Washington State, where he would be buried. Finally, we decided, we had to go ahead with the cremation. We couldn't let him go back through that prison; we needed to take him with us.

We didn't plan for the prison break to go this way.

I never got the Crown Royal. I never got the jetpacks.

~

The people at the funeral home didn't want to let us see him. The prison hadn't told them that there would be "a viewing." "Not a viewing," I instructed. "We don't want you to do anything to him. Don't do anything. We just want to take a quick look."

Two hours later we were shown into a back room at the funeral home. It was him. He was wearing a hospital gown, but I didn't believe that it was the one he'd died in. There was no blood. He looked so clean, hands folded demurely over his stomach. Mark, in life, was anything but demure. His eyes were closed, and his skin looked shiny, but the tattoos, a black peace sign inside his right wrist and a bare-breasted woman surrounded by wild animals on his left forearm, were all Mark. Despite the unnatural hand folding, the fingers were Mark. The nail beds were Mark.

"He doesn't look fat," my mother said.

"What?"

"He said not to be surprised if he looked fat. He doesn't look fat."

And that was it. If we'd stayed a moment longer, I would have touched him. I didn't want to touch him. I knew he would be cold. I hadn't come here to see my Uncle Mark. I'd come to verify that it was his body. It was.

~

We just wanted Mark back. The only charge that was paid above and beyond "direct cremation" was a rush job on the incineration because we wanted to catch a plane the next afternoon. I have since learned that it takes a body only an hour and a half to burn, faster if you're a hot burner due to plentiful body fat (like a steak, I suppose), and given that the "rush job" was completed in just over twenty-four hours, I'm not quite sure of their methods. I use the passive voice in discussing payment because *we* didn't pay anything to the Kentucky Mortuary for cremating Mark's body; in death, the Bureau of Prisons becomes suddenly benevolent. Apparently, an institution that pays inmates a standard salary of seven *cents* per hour for jobs ranging from landscaping to furniture-making, and more seriously, can't seem to provide adequate medical care for the living, is suddenly rolling in funds when it comes to disposing of dead bodies. We were told by the funeral director that the prison would pay for whatever mode of disposition we chose.

~

When we met with the funeral director for the second time, to pick up Mark's ashes, my mother said to him, "I just wanted you to know something." Her eyes were swollen to a squint. More tears gathered and came down her cheeks. I reached out and squeezed her hand, thinking, *He's not going to care*, but listening to her anyway, knowing that she would regret it later if she didn't tell him. "I know that Mark came from the prison and everything, but he wasn't some terrible criminal. He wasn't a murderer or a robber or a rapist." She paused. "He was a marijuana grower." She enunciated these words slowly, as if to make sure that the man understood. She didn't say "pot," as she normally would, she said "mar-i-juan-a"—one soul-saving syllable at a time. "He was a gardener, you know?" She smiled at the innocent sound of the chosen word. "He wasn't a criminal."

"Doesn't matter to us," the man said. I was right: he didn't care. He wasn't evil or callous, it's just that it didn't matter to him. A dead body is a dead body is a dead body when you're a funeral director. "We treat their families the same no matter where they come from."

"I'm not talking about us," my mother said, knowing that she'd been misunderstood. "I'm talking about him. I wanted you to know that about Mark. He wasn't a criminal."

~

Twice now I have made a long journey with someone I love wrapped tight in a plastic bag and nestled into a cardboard box. The first time I was startled by my lover's still-weight: a young man, surprised by death, burned to ashes, is still a thing of substance. The second time, a fool in thinking I was a veteran in this business of death and cremation—death is not something that gets easier with practice—I anticipated the strain in my muscles when I finally held my uncle in his box. But I learned that the bones of a fifty-year-old man, too long behind iron bars, have already begun to disappear. The second time, with my uncle, the surprise was in the heat. My hands were damp from the cool Kentucky rain, and when I reached out to take the box from the man in the parking lot at the funeral home, the cardboard felt hot and dry. "My God," I said to my mother, and I smiled. "He's still warm." I handed the box to my mother, and she carried it to the car and climbed in. I turned the key in the ignition, and my mother patted the cardboard box and smiled: "We've got him now. Let's get out of here."

~

After we returned the rental car and checked in at the Delta counter, my mother said, "Well. I guess we should go to the bar and have a drink."

I smiled and said the sort of thing that people always seem to say right after someone dies, "Mark would like that." We went to the lounge and chose a table in the corner. I had Mark's ashes in a pack on my back. I slid my arms out of the straps and sat him in a chair at the table. "There you go. Been awhile since you had a drink, eh? What'll it be?"

My mom smiled. She looked relieved that we'd made it this far. "He'll have a Crown Royal. Bloody Mary, for me," she said. "Extra horseradish."

"Got it," I said, walking to the bar. I reached around to my back and touched a wet spot on my shirt. Mark's heat had made me sweat.

∿

I had to take the pack off to run it through airport security's x-ray machine. I didn't say a word. I looked over my shoulder as we walked toward the gate and saw the security woman pointing and whispering.

I laughed. "I guess they probably think we're crazy."

"Pretty smooth," my mother said. "Quite the escape."

Maybe it was the booze, and maybe it was the situation, but we laughed all the way to the gate. When you can laugh—laugh.

∿

We had to walk across the tarmac to get to our plane. Mark was in my backpack, and my mother reached over and patted the pack. "Here we go, Sweetie," she said. "You're free." In that moment, feeling that warmth on my back, taking strong steps toward the plane, I felt a surge of joy. "Fuck, *yes*," I thought to myself and to Mark. "This is it, Markie Boy. We're out of here."

∿

We have learned that the prison lied. The day after Mark's death we went to the prison to pick up three cardboard boxes, sealed with duct tape, containing everything he had been allowed to hold on to: sweat clothes, photographs with pinholes top and center, a box of colored pencils, a shaving kit, postage stamps, running shoes, books. We didn't want to leave any part of him on the inside. The prison personnel—the warden, the counselor, the ward supervisor—repeated this phrase: "He just collapsed. He was vomiting blood, and then he was rushed to the hospital." *Rushed to the hospital.* How long did he suffer? *Rushed to the hospital.* What time did you say he collapsed? When was he taken? *Rushed to the hospital.*

Mark was not *rushed to the hospital.* Instead, he was left alone in a room with a bedpan. Twice, a prison employee changed the pan for him. The blood was spilling over the side of the pan and onto the floor. He was making a mess. Over the course of three hours, Mark filled three pans with his blood before he was *rushed to the hospital.* I can't stay with this image for long. I get dizzy, and my typing fingers freeze. And the thing that hangs me up, the thing I can't let go of is this: if he was vomiting up blood, if he was vomiting blood and no one was helping him, why did he do it in the pan? How can you have the presence of mind to aim for a pan when you are puking up blood alone in a prison?

Other prisoners smuggle their stories along with their condolences out from behind the prison walls. Along with news of the horror of Mark's last hours, we learn this: Mark ate a good dinner that night. He played an "old man's game of bocci ball" and told everyone who would listen that his sister and his niece would be coming the next day. The prisoners tuck this good news in with the bad, all the time wondering: Who will be next?

~

My mother saves things. She saved the scrap of paper that we scribbled notes on when we talked to the prison chaplain on the phone from the Days Inn. It's a pale yellow check-in slip, perforated on each end, and my mother says that she can't believe that her name is signed on the sheet. Written just like everything was normal. Also on this sheet, over the pale type, I have written in deep black ink: *75 S—exit 120—R—Stop—R—hwy 25—West Liquors.* (Mark died from liver disease. Our motel was in a dry county.) Then, in my mother's handwriting, shaky, sideways, all over the page: *open@8 critically ill 12:45 2:30 rushed to the hospital Anteus unit manager visit w/him?*

Another preserved sheet carries only my mother's handwriting—a white, lined scrap ripped from her notebook. Standing at the pay phone in the Waffle House in Lexington, my mother had called the hospital and asked questions. She scribbled the answers: *massive bleeding from the esophagus . . . esophageal varices . . . Multiple endoscopic procedures . . . Time bomb waiting to go off . . . Procedures not adequate . . . in and out of consciousness . . . Probably no pain . . . Vomited and passed out.*

Somehow, we can stand to look at both these gruesome reminders.

The note we can't stand is one from Mark, written a few days before his death—instructions for our visit: *Get there early to get the pizzas—the round ones, not the triangle ones. We'll save the biscuits and gravy for Saturday morning.*

~

"The end of an era," my mother said. She said it in the room at the Days Inn, she said it as we pulled away from the prison with the three cardboard boxes in the trunk of the rental, she said it in the family restaurant where she drank black coffee and I pierced my yolk and watched it bleed into corn grits that I would never eat, and I'm sure she said it again when we made for the airport, Mark in a box on her lap.

"The end of an era."

~

My mother: *After Ian got burned, I was in shock for quite a while. I remember drinking a lot of tea with milk, and I don't remember anybody helping, really. All my friends had moved away, everybody was working. I remember being very alone at that time, but maybe nobody realized how bad it was. I don't know. I knew I would leave if he died. And I do remember one event. Ann Hutchinson from RISD came to visit—do you remember Ann? She had Ethan and Sarah? Ann came to visit in Providence with Ethan and it was hard to see a mother with a child—he was outside in the yard, and he was playing, and he was whole. Even after you were born, I never took for granted that you guys would be alive the next day—Ian's burning changed my worldview, that's for sure. I realized that things don't just go along like in a book—terrible things happen and they can happen to you—and it's not the things you worry about that happen. You'd be totally neurotic if you tried to keep every accident from happening. You have to have an acceptance of fate, in a way. There's somebody in control and it's not us.*

～

In the boxes from the prison I find a stack of yellow receipts from the FMC Lexington commissary—they're in chronological order and held together with a pink paperclip. The final invoice is dated July 28, 1997. At 1:58 P.M. on that day Mark made the following purchases: one twelve-inch fan, a ten-dollar vending machine credit, one "cookie cream" (at $2.75, I hope it was a whole box), and a single pack of Marlboros. I notice this final item because Mark didn't smoke Marlboros—I confirm his regular brand by flipping back through the flimsy yellow sheets: Camel filters. Why would he buy Marlboros? Because they were out of Camels? Or maybe he needed them for some sort of trade?

～

All visits will begin and end in the visiting room. Kissing, embracing, and handshaking are allowed only on arrival and departure. (FMC Lexington *Admission and Orientation Handbook*)

～ That Place I've Been Looking For

Is that the image you want to be left with? This is the question when you're trying to decide whether to look at a dead body or not. A funeral director posed Mark for this picture. Of course he was not moving—this was not cinema mimicking real life, this was a still. Still image. Still as death. Not still Mark, but still his flesh. Still the frame, but with Mark torn out of the middle. This image stayed with me for about a month, overtaking all other images of Mark—those I'd memorized from photos, those I had from life, those I'd created into life from photographs. Not this time. The image I'd taken in from the still Mark, snapped with the shutter of my eyes, developed with the fluids of my brain, was not of the whole body. I remember his whole body, but in soft focus, and vaguely—just enough to make a description: the skin on his face looked taut and polished, without expression, lips closed, eyes closed. Neither peaceful nor agonized. He was a glossy print of his living self. I didn't stay with his face because I began to think about the wires holding together this nothingness that surely wanted to gape. No pennies on the eyes. Gray hair combed, coifed, glistening—like the prepared face. I focused on his forearms and his hands, resting on the smooth fabric of a white hospital gown that looked soft and comfortable. How strange it would have been to see Mark in a suit! The hands held on to each other, fingers alternating hand to hand, right thumb on top. Here, we can identify the position as Not Mark. Mark, in life, would not lace his fingers. But here also was what I needed to see. On the inside of his right wrist, still clinging to the flesh: a black peace sign the size of a nickel. Here was Mark. I don't remember Mark without this tattoo, so I'm guessing he got it before I was born. I have searched through all the pictures in all the albums, and there is no record of this peace sign—always, his right wrist is turned down, away from the camera. I am relieved. This is something, then, that I remember unprompted. On the left forearm is another tattoo, more elaborate, visible in many of the photographs

227

taken of Mark in the prison, so I can't say whether I remember this image, or whether I've had it planted. *Photographs promote forgetting.* This tattoo appeared during Mark's time in the Sheridan FCI, and we were surprised by it on a visit. Covering the whole of his left forearm was a kind of jungle scene, not particularly well-rendered: a wolf, an eagle, and a bear surrounding a big-breasted nude woman. I wanted to hear about how tattoos were done in prison, how it was that he'd been spared time in the hole when I knew that tattoos were against prison regulations—this was something the guards had failed to notice? Mark had no comment about process or procedure, and he didn't seem thrilled by the results, but he did say, by way of summary and conclusion: *All of my favorite animals.*

～

I don't have a photograph of Mark's body laid out in the coffin in that Kentucky funeral home. I don't need one. And this is one of the arguments that goes on after death, in those families not dictated by some version of formal mourning ritual: Should we look?

The hope: to see him one more time, perhaps to discover that he isn't really dead; if not, to see that he is, to accept death.

The fear: this will be your image of him.

Dead.

～

Mark was transferred to the prison hospital in Kentucky to have his right knee replaced with an artificial one. He could have used a new liver, too, and perhaps they could have rebuilt him, abused body part by abused body part, until nothing of the original remained, but he knew it was too late for his liver. A transplant would have failed because as soon as his hepatitis-infected blood ran through it, the disease cycle would have begun all over again. I used to wonder about the logic of the plastic knee.

So, apparently, did the Bureau of Prisons. Two years after his death I've seen more paperwork—though I daresay, not all of it—and I now know that the prison never had any plans for a plastic knee. None at all. They'd tested Mark's liver, and they knew how bad it was. When surgery was performed in Kentucky, it was to band the vessels in his throat. As far as any of us can tell, they brought Mark to Kentucky to die. And when he showed signs of doing just that, they left him alone to fill three bed pans with vomited blood before they loaded him into the ambulance. I'm not saying this was a conspiracy to kill Mark—not yet, anyway—but I am saying that they took the path of least resistance and let him die.

> Bah bah, black sheep,
> Have you any wool?
> Yes, sir, yes, sir, three bags full.
> One for the master,
> one for the dame,
> one for the little boy who lives down the lane.

He filled three pans with blood before they took him to the hospital. Three pans full.

~

Since Mark's death I have learned some salient facts about cirrhosis of the liver in general, and esophageal varices in particular. In a healthy body, the portal vein conducts spent blood from organs like the spleen and the large intestine through the liver and back to the heart for reoxygenation. As the liver hardens, however, it becomes increasingly difficult, and eventually impossible, for the blood to pass through—but this isn't the end of the story. The body adapts, and collateral veins take over to bypass the jammed liver. The body carves new channels, like a river branching out around a beaver dam. But this rerouting is only a stopgap measure. Eventually the collaterals can't transport the blood quickly enough, the blood backs up, and the veins engorge and rupture, draining blood into the stomach, where it accumulates for the short time it takes for the stomach to take notice and reject it. An R.N. friend tells me that this stomach blood looks different from regular bleeding—dark, gelatinous, and grainy—like grape jelly with coffee grounds stirred in. Once you see this thick blood, he says, you need to work fast, and even with decent medical care, the vomiting person only has a 50 percent chance of survival.

I listen to my friend, and I do the math. The average, largish adult male has about six liters of blood. Most bedpans have a one-liter capacity. If Mark filled three bedpans before he was transported to the hospital, then he'd already vomited half his body's blood. He didn't have a chance.

~

The best understanding of alcoholism I have does not come from my experience with my own bottle of Absolut Citron in the freezer— even at my worst, when I was drinking vodka straight at three o'clock in the afternoon, there was still some pleasure there. The *ahh* of the first swallow. The tingling of the second and third. Then the heat, the buzzing, the numbness, and finally, grief mitigated. Moderated. Controlled. And in that control, again, there was some pleasure. No, the only good understanding, gut understanding, that I have of alcoholism, my closest link to Uncle Mark, came through my bulimia. In the beginning, there was pleasure. If my bulimia evolved into a desire for mummification—not death but a drying out, a cleaning up and out of all the wet and sloppy, a preservation—I sit here and wonder, my uncle two years dead, then what was *his* desire? What was his alcoholism a wish for? Not numbness. Numbness is never enough.

~

Mark pled guilty to the manufacture of one thousand plants; between one thousand and three thousand mature marijuana plants equals ten years, and that's that. He saw murderers and rapists come and go. To my knowledge, Mark never hurt another human being. His greatest crimes were all perpetrated against himself.

~

A corpse has a presence of its own. It resembles the dead person, yet it is not that person. (Ruth Richardson, *Death, Dissection and the Destitute*)

A corpse is like a photograph. A photograph is like a corpse.

~

Think about the dead bodies you have seen. How much is this thought like a photograph? I have seen only two dead bodies in my life. I watched my grandmother take in her last breath. I watched that breath leak from her body. I watched her go from being my grandmother to being a dead body, and when I pushed up her chin to close her gaping mouth, gravity pulled her lips back open.

~

In prison Mark made me a wallet from three colors of leather: deep brown, tan, and red. He made the wallet to my specifications, so that it would have all the spaces that I needed, so that I would really and always use the wallet. I still do. There is a place for my checkbook with its carbon copy pages—I remember that Mark was frustrated because the FCI wouldn't let him have the hard plastic interior wallet that slides into the leather slot. He needed to insert that trifolded piece of plastic that would prevent me from writing through to the next check, writing over, but they wouldn't let him have it. The wallet came with a note of explanation tucked where the plastic would be; I finished the wallet right away and wrote to let him know that the work had been done. The wallet was perfect. So I am puzzled by the hard piece of plastic that covers the slot for my driver's license. I put my license into this place, but I have never removed the cardboard piece that filled the slot when I received the wallet in the mail. The card is white and has been traced around the outside, just a trace, to achieve the effect of burning. With the point of a sharp, black pen Mark drew a cat-o'-nine-tails emerging from a written message: I [heart] YOU. The heart is filled in with hundreds of tiny dots, most of them black, but some of them red. Using dots, he created the shadow and light. One portion in the upper left of the heart is white, like the reflective space on the balloons I drew on my notebooks when I was a kid. I've had the wallet for more than five years now, and I see this card every time a cashier wants to record my driver's license number or a bouncer wants to check my age. Only sometimes does it catch me: *I love you.*

~

Real life, real time, and I'm out at an Italian restaurant in Tuscaloosa, Alabama. My dinner companions—let's call them Woman Friend and Man Friend—actually feel more displaced here in this Italian restaurant in the middle of Alabama than I do. Each is possessed of a zealous northeastern metabolism, and they are engaged to be married to each other in the spring. They are, they say regularly, prepared to be together for *a very long time.* Not forever. *A very long time.* Our conversation digs right in—psychological imbalance, psychosomatic drugs, major life traumas—and the pepperoncini that I pluck from our shared Greek salad takes a nip from the warm Merlot that coats my tongue and skips drunkenly down my esophagus, where all the chewed bits make up a festive party. My stomach lining serves as the hors d'oeuvre table. I am trying not to play Crazy Girl here, but somehow I'm telling them the whole story: the eating disorder, remembering, Colin's accident, the end of the bulimia, the coming back.

Woman Friend tears a piece of bread from the round loaf and dips it in the olive oil glistening in the dish at the center of our table. The bread is spongy, aggressively absorbing the oil in a way that reminds me of the time-lapsed migration of the blue liquid from the beaker onto "Pad A" in a Playtex commercial. Impressed, I watch the oil draw up in the bread's pores.

There is a sound reel. Woman Friend tells me, "You know that I consider you to be a model of resiliency. How wonderful to be able to point to one event in childhood as the root of all your personality problems."

This makes me laugh. "Well, it's not like it puts me in the mood to go out blithely and get raped every day or anything, but somehow those things—excuse the therapyspeak—integrate. You adapt, get used to it. You can pretty much get used to anything, right? There are worse things. Like Colin. I never got over that. I don't know how you get used to people dying. You must. People in war-torn countries *must*, right? What do they do? Imagine losing everyone in your family. I can't. I can't even imagine that."

"Still, you seem so normal. Happy. Are you happy?"

"Yeah, right. I guess I am. For the most part."

"Nothing really bad has ever happened to me, and I'm miserable. I always feel like I'm going to die. No, I know that I'll be dead. Impermanence. I have this refrain that runs through my head: What does it matter? I'll be dead anyway. Whatever. I'll be dead. What did you do?"

"Nothing. Colin died. I don't see how it could be so simple, and I don't recommend it as a therapeutic practice, but Colin was my miracle. He came into my life, he pulled me up, and he left so that I would live my life. He is my angel."

Woman Friend is crying. Her bread is on her plate, leeching oil into her salad, and she is crying. "Is that in there?"

"In where?"

"In your book. Do you write that Colin was your miracle?"

⁓

Colin's death cured my bulimia. I stopped puking. Death is amazing in its capacity to rearrange perspective. If he hadn't died, I might never have learned how to take care of myself by myself. I didn't ask for this, but I can see the miracle.

⁓

Any number of deaths could have served as the occasion for writing this book. My grandfather died of a heart attack when I was sixteen years old, and after I heard how my Uncle Mark had found him dead on the toilet, I vomited into the trash can of my dorm room at Pacific Lutheran University until the Summer Scholars folks packed me up and put me on a plane. My boyfriend picked me up at the airport in Spokane, and halfway home he pulled down a dirt road. He said he couldn't wait, so we climbed out of his Jeep to do it in the dusty sage brush, and he came too fast, but I was glad because the brush was tearing holes in my skin, and I was sure my dead grandfather, who had spent the last sixteen years teaching me Shake-speare and Longfellow, could see me and finally knew what kind of girl I was. *Poor Jill, the grass is on her grave, has forty years been growing.* That was thirteen years ago. At twenty, the occasion came around again when Colin was killed. That was nine years ago. Such a long short time. Maybe that could have been the occasion, but I was exhausted. Grief can be so tiring, and telling takes so much energy. When I was twenty-five, my grandmother died of an intestinal blockage. It was my cooking. I'd made her a grilled cheese sandwich the night before, and I could have played this up, pretended that she wasn't going to die anyway, imagined greater agency in that grilled sharp cheddar on white bread than I could have ever melted into it, but by then I was entering a writing program. By then I was learning that the dying grandmother story was beyond uncool. Everybody's grandmother dies. Big whoop, says the writing workshop. Give me another epiphany. That was four years ago. Then, just last year, my Uncle Mark, son of my dead grandfather, son of my dead grand-mother, beloved brother to my still-living mother, bled to death in federal prison. Here was something that demanded telling, right? Here was the occasion for the telling of our family's story. Because, really, who really cares? We've got families, or we don't, but eventu-ally everybody dies. It's no great thing. It happens. And it's sad. And then it happens again. But when Mark died, I felt a tugging in my gut, and the story began to emerge from my throat like a magician's handkerchief, knot by knot—red, purple, blue, green, yellow—and with every knot I gag.

Mark was bled out. Made empty. Mummified. I wonder: is this what he wanted?

~

3/14/94

Dear Mom,

Just a quick note to say hi. The weather has been absolutely gorgeous, too nice. The robins are sucking down worms and the buds are a poppin'. . . . Thank you for my card and the encyclopedia. It hasn't arrived yet but the thought is already there. They may end up scratching their heads for some time, staring at it wondering "What evil lurks?" It's a nice feeling having 3 faithful fans out there who at least pretend that I can do no wrong. Thanks. . . .

love, Mark

~

Mark's final work assignment at Kentucky FMI was the flower garden in the courtyard. When my mother and I were there to pick up his three cardboard boxes on the day after he died, one of the counselors pointed it out to us: *That's Mark's garden. He did a nice job, didn't he?* And my mother was mad, because she was sure that they were never as nice to Mark when he was alive and in there as they were being to us on this day when he was dead and gone. But all I could think of was the letter Mark had written just weeks before. Mark had told us that he missed pissing outside, and so we knew what he meant when he wrote, *You know that place I've been looking for? I found it.*

Mark was cremated on a weekend, so the funeral home was closed, and we waited in the parking lot for the director to come back from the crematorium with the ashes. On a strip of grass between the funeral home and an apartment building, sheltered by bushes, I unzipped my pants, took them down to just above my knees, squatted, and peed. This time the stream of my urine was celebratory, absorbed into a bed of cool pine needles before I could see yellow, but I knew it was there because I could feel the steam on my bared skin.

⌇ *Is This the Image You Want to Be Left With?*

Writing this book has altered the course of family history. Before I started asking questions, my brother, the burned red baby on the green sheets, didn't know that his father had gone off to graduate school while the burned baby was still in the hospital. We can think of reasons the burned baby's father might have wanted to leave— mainly, that he was only twenty-three years old and freaked out at the prospect of being the father of a dying baby—but we have to agree that it was a pretty shitty thing to do. My mother sold her diamond wedding band to make the first payment on Ian's hospital bills. When my father's aunt heard that she was planning to sell it, she bought it herself, to keep the ring in the family. "I don't know why Grammy and Grandfather didn't give me any money," my mother says. "Maybe I didn't want it. I don't know." Always anxious to level the playing field, she adds, "It seems like your father traded some sculptures for part of the bill, too. The doctors were very nice." My mother sold her ring to my father's family. My father traded sculptures. Together, with the doctors, they saved Ian's skin.

⌇

Ian: "My first memory is actually a memory of a dream. I think it's a dream that I actually had as a baby, but maybe I was a little older, dreaming I was a baby. In the dream, I'm in my crib at the hospital, and the bars, and the shadows of the bars, make it seem like a prison. That part's obvious. I'm a baby and I'm burned, so I can't sit up or even move really. I'm stuck. Then these animal paws start reaching up through the bars. Just the paws. I can't see the whole animals, but the paws are coming up to get me, and I scooch a little to one side to get away from them, but then the paws come up on the other side. I can't get away from them."

⌇

I have a recurring dream in which I'm naked and there's somebody trying to get me. I never know who it is, but he is always sneering and laughing. Instead of rolling away from the animal paws, I have to escape the line of my attacker's vision. I snake-crawl across the floor to pull the drapes so he can't see me through the windows, press myself to the back of the closet to sweat behind coats and sweaters and hanging umbrellas. Hiding, pursued, naked. But I am too big to hide. He sees me. Protruding flesh gives me away. I squeeze under the couch, but the whole couch rises like a dinghy lifted from the ocean's surface by the massive back of a blue whale. I am the whale. Then I am the boatful of tiny people screaming and falling falling falling overboard.

My brother is the red baby on the green sheets, rolling away from the claws.

⌒

If any pictures were ever taken while Ian was the red baby lying on the green medicated sheets, nobody ever saw fit to put them in an album and save them. We have to trust my mother's memory: *He didn't even look human.* We hear about the red against the green. We hear about the grotesque swelling and the daily scrubbing of Ian's scalp to remove the rising layers of dead flesh. *The nurses made me do it. They said that if they did it, he would never forgive them, never let them hold him, or bathe him, or feed him. He'd forgive me, no matter what I did. The scrubbing was the hardest thing I've ever done. Imagine hurting your own baby like that. I scrubbed and he screamed. Every day. I dreaded it. Sometimes, afterwards, I'd have to go away, into the hall or somewhere, and just cry.*

Sometimes, my mother tells me, *babies are easy.* Does she forget?

⌒

When Mark was in prison, he and my mother kept up a relay of collages. The collage became the way my mother could use pictures to transform our image of Mark's world: Mark in the American Flag vest that he chose from a catalog, or Mark relaxing in a dreamlike

solarium with a couple of dancing fairy folk. Mark pushed harder and made us wince: my mother with the body of a dog (*my* dog), my mother and me being held up by Mark in his khaki uniform (our truncated legs dangling shortly), my grandmother posing with a handsome young Marlon Brando, who is leering at her generous bosom (with Mark's caption, "Scrutiny on the Bounty").

My mother defines collage as a combination of things unexpected. The artist can *choose things that appeal to her visually, and put them together psychologically.* Thus, she took photos of her beloved brother, cut out from the context of prison, and let him *romp with the fairies.* Or: *a window in a tree. . . . flowers growing in unlikely places, the way you might wish they would. In collage, you can put whatever you want anywhere. You make your own order out of the real stuff you are given to work with.* My mother told me this, and then she called a few days later to amend her original statement. *Mark's collages weren't like mine,* she said. *I choose disparate elements and see how they fit together, what they might make. Mark decided what he wanted to make and then chose the pieces specifically to make that preconceived picture.*

What if I took the picturebooks that my grandmother made and snapped open the rings in every binder, let the plastic pages spill out onto the floor, and then attacked them with my scissors?

Those books, pasted together by my grandmother, year after year, replaced the cognitive exercise of memory for me. Sitting on a section of wall-to-wall carpeting, drinking the bubbling red birch beer from a tinted brown glass, I reestablished my relationships with the members of my family. This is where I put it all together and perpetuated the lies. Not malicious lies, but lies with so many years to develop that we forgot the truth because nobody rehearsed it. When Mark was sentenced to sixty days in a twelve-step rehab program in 1991, he wrote an inventory of his experiences with drugs and alcohol that filled a whole notebook, and then he gave it to us to read. It was in those pages that I learned he had once tapped the powder out of horse tranquilizer capsules, melted it down, and shot it into his veins for a high that lasted fourteen days. My God, I thought. Oh my God. This is Mark's story? Okay, now put the cooked-down, shot-up horse tranquilizer against the pictures in the album. What do you get? Collage. Dry made wet and introduced to the body. Cut cut cut. It's not so radical.

"It was radical to breast-feed!" my mother cries. She will never forgive herself for not being conscious when we were being born. Born in the passive voice.

～

My mother has never kept a photo album the way that her mother did, or the way that her daughter does. She loves photographs, but she keeps them all in an old, faded lavender Harry and David's fruit box. They're all in there—*way back to when you kids were little*— but they're in no particular order. This disorganization, my mother claims, is exactly what makes going through the pictures interesting: *You never know who's going to pop up next. Through the years, they've gotten more and more shuffled, so what I end up seeing, as the pics get more mixed, are surprise combinations, juxtapositions, of you guys, as babies or now, and people we have known in our lives who would never have showed up on the same page. They get scrambled, and the non-order is what makes it interesting. It's an alternative to the photo album. My box of pictures takes on a different arrangement. I mean, it's a horrible mess. Some of them stay together with rubber bands, some of them don't. The confusion that comes from being a disorganized person. Or the child of a disorganized person.* She laughs. *It's just a hodgepodge.*

~

Family photo albums may sometimes be revised—someone goes back and pulls out an unfaithful husband or perhaps some people that nobody is alive to remember anymore. Perhaps something more violent—perhaps pictures are removed from their protective covers, mutilated with knives and scissors, leaving only the photographic subjects still in good favor, and then the altered photos are replaced, maimed, between the plastic pages. But our albums were never vandalized. They were never revised. Almost thirty years after the picture of the giant bubble was pasted into the pages of Picturebook Number Three, no picture has been removed or changed. The picturebooks are still telling the same story, and here I am, trying to tell that story in words, and in the three years that I have been working on this text, everything has changed. The story has been revised. For example, I began the chapter on Mark in the present tense, when he was still calling me collect from prison. Now he is dead. I initially wrote the section on Ian's burning without ever having spoken to my father about that day in 1966—and he was the only other person, besides Ian himself, who was there in the apartment for the burning. Then, *because* of the book, I had to muster the guts to write to a father with whom I rarely speak, and say, *Dad, I'm writing a book. It begins with Ian's burning. If you want to, I'd like to hear from you what happened.* (This is the question I asked, but of course, I was terrified to ask, and so this single question—*What happened to Ian?*—was pillowed deep in a typed letter that went on with five pages of explanation. Artist to artist.) And he responded. Multiple times. He responded after all these years, and I wondered if it wasn't too late. And, again, the story needs to be revised, is *under revision* as I type these words. The only way to write an autobiography, I suppose, is to keep writing indefinitely. As soon as your fingers stop moving, this act—your fingers stalling on the keyboard—changes the story. There. I can't keep up. And this idea that it should all be working toward something, that the autobiographical subject in the present tense should be working through the biggest puzzle of her life and arriving somehow at . . . something. Something big. At what? Happiness? Understanding? Forgiveness? A baby? A book?

I have not arrived.

~

I love the sound of a train in the distance, especially after dark. Flying through the night, going, going, whistle echoing through the city, nudging sound through the fog. The echo of its whistle overlaps with each new pull of the horn, coming in Doppler waves of sound that is and sound that was—comfort and danger in one long sound. If you're close enough, you can hear the rhythm holding up the whistle—the clacking of metal on metal as the train moves along on its double track. The only sound that I like to be wakened by in the night is the sound of a train whistle. I can't stand the phone, and I startle at the bark of a dog, but if I hear a train, and I'm sleeping with someone, I kiss a warm shoulder beneath the blankets. I make love to the sound of the train. All at once I feel safe, as though I'm going somewhere, coming toward something.

When Grammy was dying, blocked off by the sandwich and drowning in her own fluids, she had waking morphine dreams in which she told me that she was listening for the sound of the train. She told me that she needed to be awake when the train came by so that she could catch it and fix the problem. She didn't tell me that she would be leaving on the train. That last afternoon she must have heard the train coming, because I heard her hum, "Mmm. Finally." The wait had been long, and my grandmother was ready for the ride.

When I was two, we went to the Miami Zoo and rode the train through the African Jungle exhibit. My grandmother sat stoutly on the bench beside me as we chugged along, and when she opened her pocketbook, I smelled leather and Juicy Fruit gum. We both chewed contentedly as we moved along, holding hands and wondering where all the animals were hiding. How do I know this if I was only two? I've seen the picture of us at the depot, sitting on the red wooden stairs, and I remember the smell of leather and Juicy Fruit gum.

I have seen the picture, and I know that these might not be my memories.

~

I had friends at the Savannah College of Art and Design who liked to tell this story about the first day in my father's 3-D Design class. He'd made this little book out of clay—textured cover, straight spine (nobody could ever tell me the title of the book or if there was a title), and clay pages. The book was open to the middle, forever open, and the pages, my friends told me, were as paper-thin as clay can be. It must have taken him forever—rolling, slicing, pasting the pages together with slurry, crimping in the permanent wrinkles of a well-thumbed text. He passed his clay book around the room and let everybody touch it. The whole class oohed and ahhed, passing it hand-to-hand, careful not to nick it on the tabletop, and when it got back around the table, my father held the book up in the air with an exhibitor's flair, and then he opened his fingers. He let it drop. The pages of his lovely book smashed into jagged shards that skittered under the feet of the students like cockroaches.

~

They have not considered that memories are like corks left out of bottles. They swell. They no longer fit. (Harriet Doerr, *Stones for Ibarra*)

~

I have had five therapists. *The most important relationship in your life right now is the one you're having right here in this room,* insisted the second-to-last one (and the only man). I get most of my best lines from him—lines that when repeated can foster accusations of "therapist-bashing," and I confess that five years after our final session, I don't regret my time with him, but I do get defensive. I'm only bashing insofar that I'm sharing what went on in that room—as far as I know, the doctor-patient confidentiality agreement goes in only one direction—and I'm picking out the bad stuff, I'm sure, because whatever good stuff there was must have been run-of-the-mill good stuff, and I simply don't remember. Believe me, if you ever see your therapist at a local fair swathed only in silver paint and a loincloth, just a week or so after he admonishes you to recognize the sex in the therapy room, you *will* remember—unless of course you totally forget. It's like those famous lost-in-the-mall studies that are supposed to demonstrate how easily false memories can be planted—the one where the research assistants brought in their younger siblings, and said something like, "Don't you remember the time you were lost in the mall? Remember? It took us half an hour to find you! Remember?" Sure, some of the sibling subjects said, sure we remember. It seems an easy enough thing to forget, doesn't it? Could have happened to anyone. The research assistants don't ask, "Remember that time you got lost in the mall and the naked silver man kidnapped you, smeared body paint on your nose, and then tied you up in the ham and cheese cooler at the front of the gift store and forced you to distribute samples on toothpicks to passersby? Remember? That's why you've always hated ham! Don't you remember?" Well, no. . . . But I digress. My point is that every memory seems possessed of a varying caliber, and a brain is not going to be affected in equal measure by a plastic BB and a bullet from a .45-magnum. The exact impact will vary, of course, but there will always be a difference.

So, between the ages of nineteen and twenty-four, I had five therapists—an average of one for every year. I can't say I ever found my match, and I know I was never a good patient—I have never trusted the process. As a person with self-esteem issues (and what person sitting in a therapy office *doesn't* have self-esteem issues?), the fundamental flaw in the system is the premise that I am *paying* someone to sit and listen to me for an hour. I never got it through my head that I could be participating in something more than a business transaction—that I was, in fact, supposed to be engaging in this thing called a "therapeutic relationship." *It has come to this?* I would think, the self-revulsion rising behind my eyes like seawater in a sinking hull: *I have to* pay *someone to sit and listen to me?* Add to this the relentless pressure of time—one hour per session, one session per week, unless you're in a *bad period* or a *time to push it* period, in which case your one hour per week can be multiplied by a factor of three, but then there's the twenty-session maximum laid down by the insurance company, and the timeframe of your own *healing*, however it's being defined that week; and then there's the possibility that the time you're talking about here is forever because you're being trained to *like* this, this paid-for-through-the-nose attention, and you know people in your life who talk about their therapists the way they would talk about their own mothers, if they talk to their mothers, of course—but I never wanted that. Never. I knew from the first day in Dr. A's office that I didn't want to be there forever. I wanted to get out. I would not make it my life. I will accept the memories—they are mine. But I will not *be* the memories.

These five mental-health professionals did nothing wrong—exempting, perhaps, those unfortunate silvery minutes at the fair with Mr. Second-to-Last—and perhaps they did more good than I recognize. I believe it's possible that I give myself too much credit for my own happiness. But there are worse things than that.

I began my time on the couch at age nineteen with that psychiatrist at the University of Oregon—she knew that you have to use the right tool for every job, so she prescribed the Prozac (for cessation of the vomiting behavior), and six months later she shot me in the ass with the sedatives (for the temporary cessation of grieving behavior), and that was that. But in between the Prozac and the shot in the ass, I lived for three months in Seattle, and since I was loony-bin crazy, I found another psychiatrist, whom I remember only oh-so-vaguely, as it was a confusing time. I remember that she was quite pretty and that her office was bright and pleasant. I remember, too, that she scolded me for going cold turkey on the Prozac—I was vomiting again—asked me many, many questions about my father, and then doubled my Prozac dose. Using her forefinger as chalk, she traced the shape of a square in the air between us and said, "This is your therapy window. This is the space where you can talk." She retraced the shape in the air, so that I would remember the size and location of the windowpane. "When you don't have enough medication, you fall down." Her hand clenched into a fist and fell toward the floor like a rock. "You fall down." The hand unclenched and tried to finger-walk back up to the imaginary frame, but it was no use. The finger-legs stumbled, curled, tumbled down again. Her whole hand flailed helplessly in the air. "You fall down," she repeated, "and you can't see through the window. You fall out of your frame."

I remember this session specifically because when I left, I fought the downtown lunchtime traffic to the closest drugstore and tried to fill my Prozac prescription, but they wouldn't accept my out-of-state Oregon checks, and I didn't have any cash. "You don't understand," I cried. "I *need* these pills. I've fallen down! I can't talk!"

They didn't care—they had a *policy*—and I completely and totally lost it. I was half an hour away from the apartment, and now there was no way that I was going to make it back: I couldn't drive. I couldn't get the Prozac. I remember thinking—and I know this is ridiculous—but I remember thinking that if I could only get that prescription, I could pop a couple of those pills and I would have my fix. I would take a deep breath, fill myself with air, and rise like a balloon up to that window. Then, with my clear view of the world, I would climb into the car and drive happily south on I-99.

Instead, I found a gas station with a pay phone, and I called Colin. He got a friend from work to drive him up to get me and the car out of the wet drugstore parking lot. "Bring cash," I said. "I need my pills."

"What *window?*" Colin asked, and again I traced that box in the air with my finger, ducked down below it, to show him how I'd fallen underneath and got stuck down there, under the frame, stuck, and that's why I was pathetic and had to make him come all that way when he should have been sleeping. "Oh, honey, you'll be okay. We got the pills. Come on. Come on, get in the car."

I called the woman in Seattle a few days after Colin died: "Colin's dead. *Now* what do I do?" I believed that she would do something for me, but of course, I was back in Eugene, and she was still in Seattle, and there was nothing to do—she knew it, and she said so. She was sorry, she said, maybe she could ask around for a referral in Eugene for me. But I hung up. What did I think she was going to do? Drive down and pull Colin out of that pile on the ground and back up into his therapy window? When grief is fresh, you look for miracles in the strangest places. I bought a plane ticket for San Jose, Costa Rica.

When I returned to Eugene, I found a therapist who was *plugged into the universal healing power of the universe*. She was a Reiki master who seemed to expect much more from the universe than she did from me, and at first, that was good. Once a week I'd go into her office—a shed in her backyard that had been suited up with lights and pillows and a massage table. I'd lie down on the table, she'd hold her hands over different parts of my body—my eyes, my heart, my right shoulder—and I would cry.

We didn't talk much. "This is your grief," she would say. "Let it out."

When I couldn't cry anymore, we said an amicable good-bye, and I lived therapist-free for two years until, in the midst of relationship turmoil with my free-spirited, river-running, pot-throwing, trail-blazing boyfriend, I was struck by a bolt of insanity and had this thought: *If my problems are with men—in trusting men and communicating with men—then what better way to work through them than with a male therapist?*

Enter Silver Man. You've heard how he liked to analyze my dreams and point out the apparent electric sex that buzzed all around us. After nine months of therapy, we ended badly one afternoon at an arts and music festival.

On that afternoon, a man walked toward me through the crowd. He was wearing only a loincloth and a pair of mirrored sunglasses, but all exposed hair and flesh (and there was plenty of that) had been laminated in silver. He moved through the crowd, laughing, and leaving silver smudges on the noses of those he passed by. He was coming toward me fast on the crowded, dusty path when I confirmed that this nearly naked man was my therapist.

I stood still. Here was the sex that had been in that room—shining and free. Maybe I should have tried to hide in the crowd, but I didn't. I just stood there, and he came closer, and I hoped that the scrap of cloth between his legs wouldn't catch a breeze, blow to the side, expose a silver-dipped dick looking like a Christmas tree ornament from an adult gift shop. What was it with this guy and his dick? *This* is what I was supposed to learn how to deal with by working with a male therapist?

When he was close enough, he reached his hand up to touch my face. I turned my face away abruptly—I didn't want him touching me—and his painted finger left a wet smear across my nose and cheek. I glared, and at that moment he recognized me. Perhaps it was something in my eyes—but wait, I wasn't wearing any costume. I was just standing there in a tank top and shorts. Maybe he'd known it was me, but what he recognized now was my easy identification of *him.*

"Uh-oh," he said. "I guess I'd better tell you who I am."

"I know who you are," I said.

"How do you know?" he shouted in my face. Other people in the crowd turned to see why the smiling, naked silver man was shouting.

"I can *see*," I said. Transference and counter-transference had locked hands and tangoed off the dance floor of our therapeutic relationship. I backed into the crowd and ended our final session.

The incident at the fair fucked me up—the metaphor of the silver smudge across the face would not leave me, and when I arrived in the psych lab the next morning for work, the campus paper sported a photo of my now-former therapist on the front page. The caption read, "Precious Metal." I felt hunted. I needed another therapist to recover from the last therapist.

She was a woman of great affirmation. Yes, the silver guy was unethical. No, he should not parade around in silver body paint in the same community where he practices psychotherapy. Yes, the people who told me not to be so uptight didn't understand. Yes, he was a big, silver jerk. Did he really say that about telling you to fuck off? And the sex in the room sign? Yes, yes. Terrible, terrible. Big, unethical, silver asshole. Precious metal, indeed. In only a couple of sessions, I felt much better—phew, I thought, this was an easy one, I must be getting better at this—so I told her about my relationship with my current boyfriend—not the free-spirited one now, but the one who would later go with me to Alabama and leave without me, but at the time of this fifth and final therapist the relationship was fresh, and the sex was frequent and fantastic.

"You have *orgasms?*" she asked, sounding incredulous. She leaned in toward me, elbows on knees, her fingers lacing together like a commitment. Her hands were richly adorned with thick silver rings, and she emitted a sort of lushness—Eastern European accent, flowing scarf, musky amber. I felt proud to be pleasing her.

"Well, yes," I said. "Not always, you know, but usually. I love sex."

At this, she clapped hands together with such delight that it sounded as though she were catching jewels from heaven. How could I help but be happy about that? I mean, how often does someone *clap* for your orgasms? I felt so much better that I stopped therapy that day. It was never my intention to be in this for the long haul.

I lied. Technically, I've had six therapists—but the last one doesn't really count. I went to see her one time, just last spring, and I can't even remember her name. Again, this is not her fault—although I daresay she was no dynamo of psychotherapeutic innovation, but between the heart Reiki and the trick with the silver paint, I guess I'd had enough of that. As usual, I was a wretched, pissy patient. I walked in the office, sat straight up on the couch, and said, *I don't want to talk about my childhood or any traumas. I just want to talk about one thing.* And so I did. And as I talked and talked and talked, I felt as if I floated above myself—dissociation always has been, and continues to be, a métier of mine—and there I was, sitting on the comfortable couch, talking, and there was this stranger, sitting across the room from me, looking at me as though I were some sort of a specimen in a jar. And I cannot remember a word she said—something about love and passion being overrated in a long-term relationship and something else about having babies—but I thought, *I cannot do this. I will not go back on the couch.* So I wrote her a check, thanked her for her time, went home, and made the decision I'd been meaning to make anyway.

So it has been more than ten years since my first appointment with Dr. A, and I am finally finished with the couch. I don't mean that to sound defeatist, or aggressive; I simply mean I don't want to be there anymore. I'm done. I'm all my parts—wet, dripping, dry, flaking, tender, and moist. I can bite, chew, swallow, stomach, and keep it all down.

What's funny is that I have also swallowed the therapeutic model—from Dr. A to Dr. Z—hook, line, and sinker. In critical moments, there are two of me: one asks questions—she isn't always nice—and we talk. I have become my own therapist.

～

"Where are we?"

"In the book? Nearing the end."

"No. In space. Physically, where are we? You never describe the room. Are we in a therapy office? You know, with a potted ficus in the corner? A fake one, of course, so that the leaves won't get brown on the tips and fall off, possibly depressing the already clinically depressed. Maybe there are inspirational posters on the wall: a rainbow-striped hot-air balloon, a clipper ship on sparkling blue waters, a snow-capped mountain. Metaphors of rising, floating, climbing to the top. . . . Or are we in a hospital somewhere? The perfect whiteness broken only by the institutional green of your hospital-issue gown and the mustard brown of the plastic ice pitcher on your rolling side table?"

"Sounds like you've got all the details worked out. Pick whichever one you like. I was thinking we were nowhere. Just words."

"Disembodied voices?"

"Sure."

"Do I have a name?"

"No, and soon you'll just be the ink marks on these pages."

"So will you."

"Yes, I know."

～

My mother chooses passion over security. I have tried this, and down deep I am like her in this way: I follow my gut. I let it hurt. But heart and common sense refuse to reconcile. Take men, for example. My heart wants a man who plunges down waterfalls in a small plastic boat, a mysterious man who whispers dark secrets to me in the night and then says nothing at all for three days, a man who gives up everything for passion, for art, for me. But my mind says, *Nothing lasts forever. Not passion. Certainly not passion.* Choose a man who makes a list before he goes grocery shopping, a man who puts comfort before art, a man who remembers things: the dry cleaning, your anniversary, a hypothetical first-grader standing on the steps of her school waiting for her daddy.

And it is here where my mother and I can become a bit mutually contemptuous.

She says: *You've always liked that in a man.*

I say: *What?*

She says: *Oh, the cooking and the cleaning.*

I say: *And you wouldn't?*

She says: *Well, I've never had that. . . . No. I don't think I would. No. It seems wimpy or something. I have two qualifications for a man. One, that he be able to* do *something, and two, that he be adventurous.*

I say: *Adventurous enough to have a peyote-induced vision and drive away in a school bus bound for South Dakota?*

Or, Adventurous Man's sister conversation:

She says: *Well, if it's a baby you want, have a baby.*

I say: *First, Jill—find a father.*

She says: *That shouldn't be too hard, should it? Babies are easy. They're portable. When you were a baby, I'd just take you to the movies with me, and stick your little chair under the seat. And walking. We went walking all over the place. I'd pop you in the stroller and off we'd go.*

And still I look for fathers.

~

Out of all of it—the abuse, the forgetting, people dying and being killed, the puking, the raping, the loving and the losing—there is only one thing I would change if I could. I can see a pattern in the rest of it—a life being shaped, taking shape, in a way that almost makes sense beneath the fading echoes of the muttered, the screamed, the mantra: *But it isn't fair.* I'm finished expecting life to be fair but for that one injustice. I'm even willing to go as far as to say that I'm a little bit grateful for most of the things—if I took away the pieces of my life that are on-the-surface-not-to-be-mentioned-in-polite-company *bad,* I would break apart and decompose. I would be the photo album cut apart, disassembled, revised. I would be a fiction—and I would not be the author of myself.

But Colin. Colin will stay dead. No amount of coping ever makes that better. Not for me, not for his six brothers and sisters, not for his parents, and certainly not for Colin himself.

Grammy was ready for death. She'd been waiting for that train.

And Mark. So much of Mark's life hurt more than death. Born into the wrong world, at the wrong time, robbed of his freedom, and then his spirit. Bled dry. Mark got out while the getting was good—in fact, he'd probably argue that he didn't get out soon enough.

But Colin. Colin I want to bring back. Not for me anymore—I don't think I'm lying when I say that—he wouldn't even know me, would he? Our lives would not be the lives of two twenty-year-olds in their first Seattle apartment, would they?

But Colin's death was too soon for *him*. I look and I look and I look and I can't find the lesson or the logic in there. Ten years ago, I thought, *How could he leave me? What about our life together? Our wedding? Our house? Our children? What about me? What am I supposed to do now? How could he bring me this far and then leave me?*

I ran a lot in the months after Colin died. Before I ran all the way to Costa Rica, I ran along the quiet roads of Springfield, Oregon, through the suburbs and out into the open, past thin rows of corn and horse farms, past lonely fields where I could sometimes see Colin walking out of the rain and coming toward me. I wore headphones when I ran—snapping that first Indigo Girls cassette onto the gears and turning up the volume; all I knew of the world was the music in my ears—*I am looking for someone who can take as much as I give, / Give back as much as I need, / And still have the will to live*—and the impact of my falling feet on the pavement, pounding hard so that I could feel the solid ground resonating in the fibers of my thighs. I imagined running so hard that I could crush my legs into dust: *I am intense. I am in need. I am in pain. I am in love.* I ran as far as I could run.

I grew up, and Colin didn't. Before he died, I was three years younger than Colin—now I'm seven years older. I passed him. I think about him, and I think: I could help *him* now. I could be the strong one.

◌

My mother suggests that I choose a father who wouldn't fight for custody in a break-up. *Then you can just have the baby.* This makes sense when she says it. Later, I cry for hours. I would choose a father on the basis of his willingness to go away? This is my mother's advice? Later, she reads her own words in these pages and retracts them, takes it all back, tells me that's not what she meant. She just wants me to have what I want in this world, and sometimes you can't wait for everything to be perfect. *Babies are easy. If you wait until everything is perfect, you could wait forever.* My mother is right. Never is everything perfect.

This year I'll be thirty. Thirty is not forever. Forever is not yet.

~

A brand-new Colin dream: he comes back as he has done before, as he did when he came with the rent check from the unknown bank, but this time there's a catch. He isn't dead. He's *been* dead. That much he acknowledges. But he's finished with death, and he's back. One detail that remains consistent is his pragmatism. In this dream Colin is unimpressed by the details of life and death. He died, and now he's back. Get over it.

I ask him what I should tell my boyfriend.

"Whatever," he says. He is smiling. "You'll think of something." He flops down on my bed, long limbs solid and everywhere, and reaches out to pull me down beside him. "Where are all my clothes?" he wants to know. "Do my brothers have them? I'm going to need to get my fucking clothes back."

I am awake before we can make love, but my sense was that we could have if I hadn't opened my eyes. My sense was that the prohibition was over.

~

I was the last one to leave the mound that we had made of Colin's ashes. When everyone else had headed down the hill, turned away from the circle of stones and the pile of ashes—that was their brother, their uncle, their son—and hanging onto each other, moved back down the hill, I was alone with him, and I heard him talking to me: *Go ahead, Jill. Go down the mountain. I'm not staying here. I'll come with you.* I heard his voice in my head saying these words, and this was a comfort to the part of me that could believe; but still there I was on my knees in the breaking pine needles, the November wind blowing on my neck, and Colin's pile, thick grains of ash rolling down, lighter flakes catching on the air, and I wished for rain to soak it all down, hold it in place, hydrate and make a sturdy clay of what was left of him, so the pile, at least, would stay where we had put it. *I'll come with you.* I heard him, but I couldn't trust myself—perhaps these were mere hallucinations, created by my brain to keep me calm. *I'm okay.* I thought he was in there somewhere, in that pile, so I pinched my fingers together, scooped some of him up, and sprinkled him into my palm. I wanted to be looking for the outline of his face in the falling grains, a visitation, but the down-on-my-knees part of me was wondering how well-mixed he was—if the hand grains were with the other hand grains, or if the hands and the hips and the head were blended equally, the way you would sift together the baking soda, salt, and flour before pouring in the wet ingredients. I wished for the rain to come hard, and I held those ashes in my hand, and decided he hadn't been cooked long enough, that perhaps it takes longer to burn the body of such a young man. He wasn't done. Colin's pile was gritty with chunks of bone—like coarse sand, not dust. Not ashes to ashes. I kissed the grains of him that I held in my palm. Kissed him and licked his granules from my lips. Crunched him with my teeth.

I am taking you into me, I told him. I caught up his dryness with my tongue, knowing he would cling to me.